SPORT AND CHRISTIANITY

'*Sport and Christianity* opens up new perspectives on the spiritual dimensions of sports through a winning combination of sophisticated theological reflection and cutting-edge studies of lived religion. Hoven, Parker and Watson have devised an ingenious structure for exploring the intellectual, affective, and ethical facets of sports from a Christian standpoint. In assembling a collection that is interdisciplinary, ecumenical, historically well-informed, attentive to practice, and duly attentive to the darker aspects of sports, they have covered all of the bases and produced a comprehensive textbook. With its special focus on the theology of play and the role of sports in spiritual formation, the book is a boon for scholars, practitioners, and students alike.'

—William A. Barbieri Jr, The Catholic University of America, USA

SPORT AND CHRISTIANITY

Practices for the Twenty-First Century

Edited by
Matt Hoven, Andrew Parker, and Nick J. Watson

LONDON · NEW YORK · OXFORD · NEW DELHI · SYDNEY

T&T CLARK
Bloomsbury Publishing Plc
50 Bedford Square, London, WC1B 3DP, UK
1385 Broadway, New York, NY 10018, USA
29 Earlsfort Terrace, Dublin 2, Ireland

BLOOMSBURY, T&T CLARK and the T&T Clark logo are trademarks
of Bloomsbury Publishing Plc

First published in Great Britain 2020
This paperback edition published in 2021

Cover design by Toby Way
Cover image © Jonathan Knowles/Getty Images

A catalogue record for this book is available from the British Library.

A catalog record for this book is available from the Library of Congress.

ISBN: HB: 978-0-5676-7860-7
         PB: 978-0-5676-9888-9
       ePDF: 978-0-5676-7861-4
       ePUB: 978-0-5676-7862-1

Typeset by Integra Software Services Pvt. Ltd.

To find out more about our authors and books visit www.bloomsbury.com
and sign up for our newsletters.

Matt: For Crystal and my grandmother. To Andrew and Nick:
thanks for your encouragement.

Andy: For Don Jenkin—without whom none of this would have been possible.

Nick: To those who offered me grace: Kate, Charles and Cath Walters,
David and Geraldine Caswell, Chris and Vivienne Bell,
Jo and Anthony Stones, John and Hilary Hield, Andrew Parker, and
Nathan and Ruth Venables.

CONTENTS

Part III
SPORT AND CHRISTIANITY:
PRACTICES FOR THE MORAL LIFE

CONTRIBUTORS

Brian R. Bolt is Professor of Kinesiology and men's golf coach at Calvin College in Grand Rapids, Michigan. Bolt's academic work focuses on philosophy, psychology, and skill acquisition in kinesiology and sport. He serves as an academic mentor for students in sport management, physical education teaching, and coaching. On the golf course, his teams have won multiple conference titles and earned trips to the NCAA Division III championship tournament. Bolt's research and leadership connecting sport and Christianity have made him a sought-after voice locally, nationally, and internationally. Bolt serves as the codirector of the Sport and Christianity Group, which produced *A Declaration on Sport and the Christian Life* (https://sportandchristianity.com/declaration/), and he recently authored the book *Sport. Faith. Life.* (Calvin College Press, 2018).

Chad Carlson is Associate Professor of Kinesiology and Director of General Education at Hope College in Holland, Michigan, where he formerly served as an assistant men's basketball coach. He was also the codirector of the Second Global Congress on Sport and Christianity held at Calvin College in Grand Rapids, Michigan, in 2019. With a PhD from Penn State University in the History and Philosophy of Sport, his research focuses on the nature and value of games and play, and the history of college basketball. He is the author of *Making March Madness: The Early Years and Origins of the NCAA, NIT, and College Basketball Championships, 1922–1951*, and numerous academic journal articles and book chapters.

Trevor J. Egli is Associate Professor and Director of the Sport and Fitness Leadership major at Johnson University in Knoxville, Tennessee. He earned his doctorate in Sport Psychology and Motor Learning from the University of Tennessee and is also a certified mental performance consultant (CMPC) through the Association for Applied Sport Psychology. His research interests include spirituality and sport, the use of spirituality and religion in applied sport psychology, prayer in sport, and the health and wellness of college students. His previous publications have appeared in a range of outlets, including *The Sport Psychologist*, the *Journal of Christianity and Psychology*, *Journal for the Christian Society for Kinesiology*, *Leisure*, and *Sport Studies*, and the *Journal of American College Health*.

Robert Ellis is Principal of Regent's Park College Oxford and a member of the Faculty of Theology and Religion at the University of Oxford. His research interests include systematic theology and faith and culture, particularly theology and film, and theology and sport. A lifelong sports fan, much of his recent work concentrates on theological reflection on sport, working from both theoretical perspectives and empirical data. As well as several articles, his book *The Games People Play: Theology, Religion and Sport* (Wipf and Stock, 2014) is one of the first full-length theological treatments of the subject. He is a member of the Advisory Committee for the Vatican's new initiative, "Sport at the Service of Humanity," which held its first global conference in October 2016.

Mark Hamilton has been Professor of Philosophy at Ashland University, in Ashland, Ohio, since 1981 and their NCAA Faculty Athletics representative since 1998. He has taught many different philosophy courses—including applied ethics courses with a focus on sports ethics and bioethics—and a course on C.S. Lewis. Hamilton has published articles on Christian sports ethics and is the author of *A Primer on Biblical Ethics*. He also serves on the editorial board of the *Journal of Philosophy of Sport*. He coached college baseball for eight years and is an elder at Providence Church. He is married to Pat with two daughters, two sons-in-law, and two grandchildren.

Ed Hastings, PhD, received his doctorate from Duquesne University in Pittsburgh and wrote his dissertation on "A Spirituality of Competition." He also holds a master's degree in systematic theology from the Washington Theological Union. He played basketball at Villanova University in Philadelphia, making it to the national title game in 1971, and was a cocaptain in his senior year. He was a graduate assistant at Villanova under coach Rollie Massimino the year after he graduated. Previously Hastings taught at the Neumann University Institute for Sport, Spirituality and Character Development and now teaches theology and spirituality at Villanova, including a course entitled "Sports and Spirituality."

Doug Hochstetler is Interim Director of Academic Affairs and Professor of Kinesiology at Penn State University, Lehigh Valley. He holds a BA in physical education from Northwestern College (IA), an MS in physical education from West Chester University (PA), and a PhD from Penn State in Kinesiology (sport philosophy emphasis). His research interests focus on the philosophy of sport, in particular on areas such as American philosophy in relation to endurance sport, sport ethics, and the relationship between religion and sport. He is the current editor of *Quest*, the official journal of the National Association for Kinesiology in Higher Education, and has published in journals such as the *Journal of the Philosophy of Sport* and *Kinesiology Review*.

Matt Hoven is the Peter and Doris Kule Lecturer in Catholic religious education and Associate Professor at St. Joseph's College, University of Alberta, in Edmonton, Canada. He earned his doctorate in religious education at the Catholic University of America in Washington, DC, and now focuses his research on sports and religious education: youth, educator-coaches, spiritual practices in sports, Catholic education, philosophy, theology, and history. His published articles have appeared in *Sport in Society, Practical Theology, International Journal of Children's Spirituality,*

Religious Education, and *Journal of Religious Education*. He presents about sport and education to practitioners, along with writing sport and spirituality modules for local Catholic high schools. Matt is married with three children and enjoys biking and playing squash.

Robert K. Johnston is Professor of Theology and Culture at Fuller Theological Seminary, Pasadena, California, where he teaches students how to engage both biblically and theologically with movies, popular culture, and contemporary fiction. A codirector of Fuller's Reel Spirituality Institute and a past president of the American Theological Society, his fifteen books include: *God in the Movies* (Brazos, 2017, with Catherine Barsotti), *God's Wider Presence* (Baker, 2014); *Don't Stop Believin': Pop Culture and Religion from Ben-Hur to Zombies* (Westminster John Knox, 2012); *Useless Beauty: Ecclesiastes through the Lens of Contemporary Film* (Wipf and Stock, 2004); *Life Is Not Work/Work Is Not Life* (Wildcat Canyon, 2001); and *The Christian at Play* (Wipf and Stock, 1983, 1997). He is a former provost, both at North Park University in Chicago and at Fuller Seminary, and still enjoys body surfing.

Patrick Kelly, SJ, is Associate Professor of Theology and Religious Studies at Seattle University, where he teaches courses such as "Sport and Spirituality" and "Religion and Sport in a Global Context." Fr. Kelly has lectured internationally about the history and theology of sport and sport as it relates to human development and spirituality. A former captain of his college football team, he is the author of *Catholic Perspectives on Sports: From Medieval to Modern Times* (Paulist Press, 2012), the editor of *Youth Sport and Spirituality: Catholic Perspectives* (University of Notre Dame Press, 2015), and has participated in and contributed to Vatican events and initiatives dealing with sport.

Scott Kretchmar is Professor Emeritus of Exercise and Sport Science at Penn State University. He is a founding member of the International Association for the Philosophy of Sport and served as its President. He has been editor of the *Journal of the Philosophy of Sport*, is a Fellow in the National American Academy of Kinesiology and Physical Education, and has published over eighty refereed articles and more than thirty-five book chapters on such topics as ethics, the nature of sport, and the operation of human intelligence in physical activity. He has received many scholarly awards, including more recently the Charles H. McCloy Research Lecturer by the NASPE Research Consortium in 2012. He was the founding editor of the *Journal of Intercollegiate Sport* and served four years as Chairman of the Board for the NCAA Scholarly Colloquium.

Andrew R. Meyer is Associate Professor in Sport Foundations at Baylor University, Texas, teaching in the Department of Health, Human Performance and Recreation, and earned his doctorate from the University of Illinois Urbana-Champaign in 2010. His research examines the interplay between athletes, contemporary American sport culture and religion, and, more specifically, how historical muscular Christian values and themes persist in contemporary American sport. His research interests include sport ideology in the contemporary social context, muscular Judaism, Radical Orthodoxy, sport media, disability and health in religious contexts, and meaning creation at "for-cause" athletic events. His previous publications have appeared in the *International Journal of Sport and Society*, the *International Review for the Sociology of Sport, Journal of Religion and Popular Culture*, and *Practical Theology*, as well as book chapters in sport history and sport policy compilations.

Andrew Parker is Professor of Sport and Christian Outreach and codirector of the Centre for Sport, Spirituality and Religion (CSSR) in the School of Sport and Exercise at the University of Gloucestershire, UK. He is a former high school physical education teacher and teacher-educator and has experience of working across a range of educational settings. Andrew's research interests include sport and spirituality, sport and social identity, and sport and marginalized youth. He has served on the editorial boards of the *Sociology of Sport Journal* (2005–2008) (Human Kinetics), *Qualitative Research* (2001–present) (Sage), and is a former coeditor of the *International Journal of Religion and Sport* (2010–2012).

F. Clark Power is Professor of Psychology and Education in the Program of Liberal Studies at the University of Notre Dame. He is the founder and Director of "Play Like a Champion Today," a coach and parent education program. He is a past president of the Association for Moral Education, a recipient of the Kuhmerker Award for his contributions to the field of moral education, the Ganey Award for Community-based Research, and the Reinhold Niebuhr Award for his contributions to social justice. His publications focus on moral development and education, faith development, civic engagement, and children's rights.

Lillie K. Rodgers is a 2007 graduate of Princeton University with a BA in Religion and Elementary Education where she played varsity basketball and was the student director of Athletes in Action. She received her Master of Divinity from the University of Notre Dame (South Bend, Indiana, United States) in 2016. Lillie worked as a high school youth minister for four years and is currently serving as the Director of Campus Ministry at the University of Wyoming. Lillie is an avid runner and triathlete, including completing the Madison Ironman in 2014.

Don Vinson, PhD, is Principal Lecturer in Sports Coaching Science at the University of Worcester, UK, and Senior Fellow of the UK Higher Education Academy. Don's interests surround sports pedagogy, coaching, leadership, performance analysis, and research methods. Don is an active coach currently operating within the England Hockey National Age Group Girls' U16 program and was a Head Coach for several years in the England Hockey League Women's Premier Division. He is also an enthusiastic coach-educator for England Hockey across a wide range of its provision. Don is passionate about most sports and, in addition to hockey, can also be regularly found playing squash, badminton, and golf.

Nick J. Watson is Chief Operating Officer at The Archbishop of York Youth Trust, York, UK. Formerly, he was Associate Professor of Sport and Social Justice, York St. John University, UK. His research and practice are interdisciplinary and focus on the relationship between sport and Christianity. Nick's most recent research interests examine fatherlessness, faith and mentoring in and through sports, chaplaincy in sport, and sport-dementia initiatives. Nick's publications reflect these research interests and he actively collaborates with churches, charities, and practitioner organizations, for example, the Sport and Church Office of the Vatican, Sports Chaplaincy, UK, and the public theology think-tank Theos. Nick is married with two daughters and enjoys golf, running and hiking.

FOREWORD

Tony Campolo

Professor Emeritus, Eastern University

Religion and sports have always been intertwined. In ancient Greece, as the Harvard scholar Henry Cox pointed out in his best-selling book, *The Secular City*, the connections were overt. In Hellenistic society, athletic events were made into religious rituals. In today's world, however, the religious roles sports play in society are what we might call "latent functions." The "manifest functions" of sports are claimed to include such things as providing entertainment, building comradeship, and teaching character. There are coaches on the public speaker's circuit who are known to claim that they are teaching their players some basic lessons for life.

In some societies, sports can, on the other hand, actually replace religion. In many instances, they have become the primary Sunday activity for families rather than worship at church. From the time that children are old enough to carry a bat or kick a soccer ball, Sunday mornings often are dedicated to "little league" games. These games not only involve children but also keep parents, who car pool, coach, or just serve as cheering spectators, away from church. We've come a long way from the thinking of the runner Eric Liddell who would not compete in the 100-meter race for his country in the 1924 Olympics, because the event was held on Sunday.

When children reach their teen years, high school sports can and do become community rituals. In many small towns in the United States, people so identify with the success and failures of their high school football team that what happens on "Friday nights under the lights" crowds out all other concerns and activities. Once, when I was conducting a week of evangelistic services in a small town in Indiana, I was told that there could be no service on Friday evening because most people in the community would be at the high school watching a football game. There was no doubt in my mind that for this particular town the weekly football game had become what the distinguished French sociologist Émile Durkheim would have called a "collective ritual" with religious overtones. Given what Durkheim wrote in his book *The Elementary Forms of the Religious Life*, such sporting events have a solidifying effect on communities bringing people together via a real sense of group identity. There is an underlying quasi-religious quality to such community gatherings as the participants, following the prompting of cheerleaders, experience what Durkheim would call a "collective effervescence." At times, fans are lifted out of the mundane and transported into a mindset wherein their shared communal ecstasy creates what another sociologist has called "communion." Many a Catholic priest or Protestant minister could only wish that such spiritual enthusiasm might emerge *sui generis* during their congregations' times of worship.

In his popular book, *Rumors of Angels*, the American sociologist Peter Berger contends that both players and spectators can, on certain occasions, experience a kind of transcendence as they are transported out of linear time. Consider, he asks, a basketball game in which one team has a four-point lead and is trying to hold off a rally by the opposing team during the closing two minutes of the game. For the team that is leading, those two minutes can seem unimaginatively long, while for the team that is behind, those same closing minutes of the game seem all too short. For the team that's ahead time seems to stand still; for the rallying team it seems to be rushing forward inordinately. For both teams, normative time is suspended temporarily. Berger argues that if religion transports people out of the normative time-space continuum then something that is very close to a religious experience is taking place—that a sense of "transcendence" is being experienced. Berger even suggests that something sacramental may be happening.

When it comes to a manifest function of sports, there is little doubt that religious leaders use outstanding athletes to endorse religious commitments. As a young person, I attended many youth gatherings at which there was sometimes a testimony from a sports celebrity. And it isn't only young people who can be enamored by sporting superstars; even adults can be awed when a champion takes the stage to speak.

It is common to use sports personalities to endorse religion. When Muhammed Ali won the world heavyweight boxing championship, his testimony for Islam, which was broadcast worldwide, gave great recognition to his new religion and bestowed upon it special credibility in the black community. All of us have seen on television many players who, after scoring touchdowns or goals, point upward, seemingly glorifying God for their achievements.

Such gestures have their effects. I remember how proud I was to be a Christian when the great track star Gil Dodds, who held the indoor record for the mile for years, competed and won the featured event at the annual Penn Relay at Franklin Field in Philadelphia. I know my non-Christian friends who were with me certainly were impressed by his testimony.

There is something that does bother me, however, about Christian athletes who credit their winning to Jesus. I understand that while athletes might want to thank God for the physical gifts that they enjoy and which help them succeed, I wish they would take the advice of Jesus who warned about making a public show of prayer "that they might be seen of men" (Matt. 6:5–6).

When I was a teenager, strange as it may seem these days, religious lectures by the Roman Catholic bishop Fulton Sheen were prime time features on one of the only three television stations available in most homes. I remember that in one interview with a sportscaster, Bishop Sheen was asked about the then heavyweight boxing champion of the world, "When Rocky Marciano crosses himself before each round, does that make him a winner?" Bishop Sheen wisely answered, "Yes … if Rocky is the better boxer." What a good answer! Not many would argue against the claim that praying helps an athlete to get focused and to mentally prepare herself or himself for an upcoming contest, but asking God to take sides in a boxing match generates some questionable theology.

As you read through this book you may likely ask yourself whether contemporary theologians have given the attention they should to the development of a theology of play. They certainly have had no trouble developing a theology of work. Sociologists, especially since Max Weber's and R.H. Tawney's writings on the role of religious thought in the development of capitalism, have been aware of how much attention religious thinkers have given to developing a theology of work. Indeed, the theologies of the Puritans, as some sociologists have pointed out, may have contributed to nurturing many of us into being workaholics. This book may be one of the few works that focuses on a Christian understanding of play. Perhaps, for those of us living with the leisure brought about by the modern technology so carefully defined by Jacques Ellul, there is now an urgency to develop a more profound theology of play. Consider those who ask what they should do with all the time on their hands.

With many people in modern societies living longer than ever before imagined, and with retirement occurring when so many people are still physically strong and mentally alert, the question of what they should do with themselves once their working days are over is a question that has the ring of urgency. So many senior citizens don't know how to play. Having been raised to believe that playing is poor stewardship of the time that God has given them, men and women actually may feel guilt if they spend time playing. Fortunately, in the retirement housing community where I live, many elderly men and women have found joy by avidly playing golf.

Then, there is the question of play in the afterlife. As an old man pushing eighty-four years of age, with death creeping up on me, I am thinking these days about what life might be like in Heaven. Will it be a place beyond time and space where we will enjoy playing? I well remember the preacher in my boyhood church telling the congregation that in Heaven God has a lot of work for us to do. I hope there will be a place for play in the afterlife. The famous American theologian Reinhold Niebuhr once said, "I know almost nothing about Heaven, but I am hoping that there will be a lot of playing there and then."

In this book authors write about what some great Christian thinkers like C.S. Lewis and George McDonald had to say about the joys of playing. Sports, which are a major form of playing, are examined through their eyes. Their thinking, along with insights of other theologians, raises questions about the nature of God, such as whether or not we have a playful God and to what extent creation itself might be a manifestation of God's playfulness.

Ed Hastings, who is also a former basketball star on one of America's great collegiate teams, writes an interesting chapter, in which he expresses the hope that there will be basketball games for him in the afterlife. It might be hard for him to imagine Heaven without basketball. If you think that to imagine such things is ludicrous then ask yourself whether or not any, if not all, of our imaginative visions of Heaven are ludicrous.

This book about sport and Christianity will not only be groundbreaking for the thinking of both athletes and theologians, but will also address a variety of philosophical and theological issues for Christian sociologists such as:

1. What does Christianity have to say about intense competition?
2. When do sports become idolatry?
3. How should Christians respond to the violence, sexism, racism, and the exercising of pride and power so often present in sports?
4. Are there spiritual experiences that can be had while playing sporting events?
5. How are dedicated fans affected spiritually by the winning and losing of their favorite teams?
6. Is there a need for value clarification when sports are compared with religion?
7. How does God regard play?

Sociologists like Robert Merton would posit that one of the "manifest functions" of sports is to provide recreation, but this onetime Dean of American sociology undoubtedly would add that its "latent functions" are so much more, and that among them, he might agree, there are religious functions. As you read about many of those latent functions, I hope that this book provides the latent function of being fun for you!

INTRODUCTION

Matt Hoven, Andrew Parker, and Nick J. Watson

For many the combination of sport and Christianity sounds novel, if not strange, yet the connection between these two entities increasingly attracts attention across the globe. Indeed, as Watson (2018) has noted, interest in the multifaceted relationship between sport and Christianity from academic scholars, faith representatives, and sports-practitioners is growing rapidly. For example, in 2016, the Inaugural Global Congress on Sports and Christianity, hosted by York St. John University (UK), drew nearly 200 delegates from twenty-four countries and from across Christian traditions. In recent years the Vatican has also hosted several international conferences related to sport, most recently an event entitled "Sport at the Service of Humanity," in 2016, which brought together civic, religious, and business leaders; elite athletes; and media representatives for the purposes of discussing how sport might serve as a mechanism for social improvement, that is, as a vehicle for social justice.

Of course, such impetus has not gone unnoticed in terms of academic commentary with multiple publications appearing within theology and across a number of wider sub/disciplines comprising the social-scientific study of sport.[1] Concurrently, a number of university research centers have emerged (e.g., at the University of Gloucestershire [UK], University of Tennessee [US], and Neumann University [US]), all of which seek to promote further investigations into the sport/Christianity dyad. Watson (2018: 4) notes that "the exponential increase in publications within the sport-theology field" has been paralleled by three trends among sporting and religious practitioners:

(i) a significant increase in the engagement of the major institutional churches within the sports realm; (ii) increased understanding and collaboration between practitioners – clergy, academics, politicians, athletes, sport chaplains and sports ministry personnel; and (iii) the continued growth and development of para-church sports ministry organizations (since the 1950s) alongside more recent engagement by the institutional churches.

Examples of these trends, as outlined by Watson, include (i) the London-based *John Paul II Foundation for Sport* (2004–), which offers theological reflection and educational programs for church-based schools, and (ii) *The Declaration on Sport and Christian Life* (2014), an accessible list of statements on the sport–faith nexus that is underpinned by academic research, and which was published by the Sports and Christianity Group, comprising practitioners, social scientists, clergy, and theologians. Worth acknowledging also is the increase in sport-based initiatives delivered by the main institutional churches (who often work collaboratively) at the Olympic and Paralympic Games, and other sporting mega events. Similarly, over the last seventy years a number of sport chaplaincy and sport ministry organizations have emerged, who work with professional, amateur, and collegiate athletes, for example: Athletes in Action, Sports Chaplaincy UK, Baseball Chapel (US), Christians in Sport (UK), Catholic Athletes for Christ (US), and the Fellowship of Christian Athletes (US).

The various themes addressed in this book are situated at the intersection of researcher and practitioner concerns over the sport–Christianity interface. To this end, it aims to expand this particular field of study by taking seriously the experiences of Christian sportspeople and, moreover, to examine how people of faith might utilize theological tradition to rethink and reshape their sporting endeavors. The intention of contributors is to explain and contextualize some of the complex nuances that arise in sport around faith-based practices. For instance, how might we better understand, critique, and challenge athletes who pray on the side-lines or publicly demonstrate faith-based practices and/or allegiances.

To enable the examination of these experiences, this book is interdisciplinary in nature, drawing on fields of inquiry, such as philosophy, sociology, psychology, theology, anthropology, and history. Chapter contributors are engaged in different Christian traditions at colleges and universities in the United States, UK, and Canada, which further enriches their diversity of ideas.

As editors, we believe that by exploring the day-to-day scenarios that characterize sport, there is an opportunity for participants (i.e., athletes, practitioners) to more clearly understand the spiritual meaning of the activities which they passionately engage in. Interrogating Christian thought and practice can also assist with addressing the many ethical and moral questions that arise in the sports domain.

Traditionally, Christianity has sponsored and endorsed a number of physical practices: for instance, sacraments as mediating signs of Christ's grace, hospitality as an imitation of God's generosity, pilgrimage as a religious quest to a holy site, or scripture reading as spiritual nourishment taken from the Word of God. This book focuses on practices that can benefit people of faith in and through sport. What we mean by practices is important, as it should not simply be equated with practical things. Following McIntyre (1981), we are thinking here of actions performed that engage the intellectual, social, affective, and moral dimensions and that ultimately lead to human flourishing in sport. Practices are not superstitiously completed for success, or merely undertaken to learn how to do something. Instead we are thinking here of practices that can lead to moral and spiritual growth and development.

In their work on practical theology, Swinton and Mowat (2006) stipulate that Christian practices are not the design of individuals but that they require persons to faithfully participate in God's action today—which includes critical reflection in different situations. In reflecting on sporting situations, a community grapples with what the gospel means to a particular context. The contributors featured in this collection consider religious and spiritual traditions as a means by which to mediate Christianity in sport today. Following Swinton and Mowat's argument, it is important not to assume that practices in sport are contradictory to those modeled and advocated by Jesus himself. For instance, the love shown among teammates in sporting competition can reflect much of Christ's sacrificial love but may fall short in terms of its depth toward opponents. Engaging sport and Christian traditions together establishes an opportunity for people of faith (and those not religiously affiliated) to (re)examine their thoughts and attitudes in sporting contexts.

The book is structured around practices that connect to notions of heart, soul, and mind. In Matthew's Gospel, a lawyer asks Jesus to name the most important commandment in the Law of Moses. Jesus responds, "You shall love the Lord your God with all your heart, and with all your soul, and with all your mind … [and] you shall love your neighbor as yourself" (Mt. 22:37–39). This central commandment asks for a comprehensive loving response for everyday living (including in and through sport) that engages the whole person instead of ignoring intellectual, affective, and moral dimensions of faith. Our reading of this tripartite understanding of the human person, and holistic approach to loving others, has led us to organize the book into three thematic sections.

The first section is based upon the commandment to love God with one's mind and examines the intellectual considerations around the reshaping of sport. This allows us to reconfigure how Christians think about sport: investigating, for example, the meaning of play and competition, and how dialogue through sport can enliven a state of play informed by interdisciplinary study. The first two chapters examine a theology of play and its implications for sporting endeavors. In Chapter 1 Robert K. Johnston presents the shortcomings of the contemporary "cult of work" in Western industrialized society that has instigated a "death of play" in wider culture and in sports. His analysis of the foundations of play offers practical suggestions for the resuscitation of play in modern sports at all competitive levels. In Chapter 2 Scott Kretchmar and Nick Watson outline Catholic writer G.K. Chesterton's theology of work and play and illuminate Chesterton's insistence that part of the brilliance of Christian orthodoxy lies in its ability to "combine furious opposites … and keep them both furious." Their analysis concludes that paradoxicality in athletic experience and understanding is necessary in order to see sport as both radically in need of repair, and indescribably lovely.

Taking discussion of play one step further in Chapter 3, Robert Ellis challenges us to rethink sport in terms of its theology of play and its capacity to highlight participants' God-given gifts. He argues that the element of competition is frequently seen as problematic in Christian accounts of sport and discussed in terms of sin and the fall. He seeks to resolve this issue by incorporating elements of the doctrine of creation with ideas on redemption so that competition can be held as a divine gift for human flourishing. In Chapter 4 Father Patrick Kelly examines the spiritual side of sport that bears remarkable similarities across religious traditions. Based upon a phenomenology of sporting participation, Kelly brings aspects of Christian, Zen, Confucian, and Taoist spiritual traditions into dialogue with flow theory and one another. Similar to Ellis, Kelly builds upon the play dynamic in sport and enriches it through theological and experiential dialogue. In drawing to a close our considerations on this particular topic, in Chapter 5 Andrew Meyer offers an overview of the historical relationship between sport and Christianity and, in particular, the varied historical responses to sport by the Christian community, that is, St. Paul's use of sporting imagery in the New Testament, the creation of medieval games by the Christian upper classes, the Puritanical rejection of Sunday sporting events, and the rise of muscular Christianity in the nineteenth century. Examining the relationship between sport and Christianity within these historical periods raises numerous critical questions for anyone seeking to embody Christian practices within modern-day sport.

The second section of the book examines faith practices in sport that represent loving God with one's "heart and soul" as drawn from Christian worship and prayer. Here contributors discuss sport as a possible means of affective formation in the Christian faith, where one is shaped through desire more than the intellect and consider the significance of prayer, ritual, and Christian spirituality in sport. Opening our discussions in this area, Matt Hoven presents a sociological framework for understanding sportspeople's spiritual practices: as explicitly expressed toward God, toward creation, through embodiment, and as ethical action. Organized according to these categories, Hoven draws from examples of elite sport to highlight the diversity of Christian practices, their importance to participants, and how religious traditions may act like spiritual storehouses within this context.

The remaining three chapters of this section examine affective practices in different sports settings. In Chapter 7 Douglas Hochstetler presents an examination of running as a contemplative practice. Instead of understanding conscious breathing techniques solely as a means toward improved performance goals, Hochstetler encourages us to see breathing in running as a spiritual discipline intimately connected to both the activity itself and our spiritual nature as humans, leading to better focused breathing habits and spiritual growth. In Chapter 8 Lillie Rodgers and Clark Power draw from a biblical tradition of play and wisdom to reshape contemporary experiences of play: an activity of the embodied spirit which discloses God's abiding presence to and delight in human movement. They argue that this Christian practice can embody a human response of worship, where one's body and entire self make a sacrificial offering to the Creator God. Offering insight into how the Christian tradition might inform the integration of faith in the lives of athletes and coaches, in Chapter 9 Trevor Egli and Matt Hoven explore the contribution of sport psychology to debates surrounding sport and Christianity. They suggest that while this disciplinary field typically seeks to enhance athlete performance through psychological skills training, it might also present opportunities for growth in self-awareness as a more holistic experience that transcends sport through actions like prayer, study, and practicing the presence of God.

The final section of the book investigates Jesus' commandment to love one's neighbor as one's self and, in particular, the morality of sport through this lens, that is, how can people of faith participate wholeheartedly in sporting culture while maintaining their integrity? The chapters within this section raise a series of ethical questions about the overall complexion of modern-day sport and offer suggestions as to how faith practices might provide insight and critique within this context. In Chapter 10 Don Vinson and Andrew Parker consider the lives of Christian sports coaches examining how individuals in this role align their coaching practices with their faith and how they reconcile potential contradictions in coaching with competitive sport. In an environment where a "win at all costs" attitude can be damaging and detrimental, they provide a number of pointers about the relationship between sports coaching and Servant Leadership and the potential that this concept has for the reconfiguration of coach–athlete relations. Furthering analyses of the vices of sports practice, in Chapter 11 Brian Bolt and Chad Carlson examine envy in sport. As a competitive endeavor, sport necessarily sets participants against each other, and the need for excellence in performance often results in dissatisfaction, resentment, and rivalry. Appropriating the work of Comenius and René Girard, Bolt and Carlson question the fundamental ethics of sports participation, identifying particular practices that people of faith might use to combat envy in sporting environments.

Reflecting one step further upon how sportspeople might view others, in Chapter 12 Mark Hamilton discusses the offerings of fifth-century saint Augustine of Hippo, and the concept of *ordo amoris*—the proper ordering of one's affections— as essential to living the good life. Understanding the proper value of the objects loved, including sports, raises further questions about one's adoration of sports and its effects on human relationships and priorities. In closing, Ed Hastings looks interiorly at sports participants to build practices for living with others. Exploring self-knowledge as a spiritual practice in athletics, Hastings reviews the writings of some major Christian authors, such as St. Augustine of Hippo, St. Theresa of Avila, and Thomas Merton, along with reflection of his own collegiate basketball career, to highlight how self-knowledge may open a way to know God and observe Jesus' commandment of love. Hastings concludes by naming practical ways that sportspeople might come to a greater awareness of themselves and, in turn, move closer to God through self-examination. The book concludes with a brief analysis of the major themes and insights stemming from the preceding chapters.

In sum, the contributions contained within this volume reveal a shared ecumenical effort by scholars (mostly, who also play, watch, and/or coach sport) of different Christian traditions. As editors we have intentionally avoided a formal ecumenical dialogue between these traditions, instead encouraging theological diversity and richness in order to make a positive and critical insight. This openness among contributors echoes the tone of ecumenical friendship in much of the sport-Christianity field, where common interest and shared beliefs and practices allow for collaborations around a united purpose. In this spirit, it is hoped that readers will gain encouragement and insight and consider incorporating practices of the mind, heart, and soul in and through their sporting journeys.

Note

1   For example, see: Adogame, Watson and Parker (2018); Ellis (2017, 2014); Evans and Herzog (2002); Harvey (2014); Hoffman (2010); Kelly (2012); Lixey, Hübenthal, Mieth and Müller (2012); Parker, Watson and White (2016); Watson (2018); Watson, Hargaden and Brock (2018); Watson and Parker (2015).

Part I

SPORT AND CHRISTIANITY:
PRACTICES FOR THE MIND

Chapter 1

HOW MIGHT THEOLOGY OF PLAY INFORM THEOLOGY OF SPORT?

Robert K. Johnston

Why should we care about our sports?

As a theologian of culture, I have spent a significant part of my career reflecting on the Christian value of play, particularly the experiences of reading a novel or watching a movie. My doctoral dissertation was on a constructive theology of play (later published as *The Christian at Play*, 1983). This study has served me well. Throughout my career I have put various play experiences into dialogue with Christian theology, and I have done so as someone who enjoys play activities, himself, both as a participant and as a fan. With regard to sports, I enjoy bodysurfing in the Pacific Ocean near where I live. And with Michael Novak, I have also asked myself, how I can be 40, then 50, then 60, and now 70, and still care what happens to the Los Angeles Dodgers (Novak 1976: xi). I also have inherited the cherished rights to my father's seats for the University of Southern California (USC) football games, something I have attended for over 60 years with quasi-religious devotion. Why is it that I am slightly depressed for an entire weekend when the Trojans lose? After all, isn't it just a game? With Michael Novak, this question, in fact, might be the focus of my reflection in this chapter. Why should we care about our sports?

Learning from a theology of play

So though my focus for the last three decades has been on how one's play experiences at the movies, or while reading a novel, might be theologically important for the Christian, I would like to take those insights and ask, "How might a theology of play inform a theology of sport?" For don't playing a game of basketball, watching a movie, listening to Mozart, going to a U2 concert, binge watching a TV show like "Breaking Bad," hiking in the mountains, bodysurfing, getting caught up in a football game, and playing hide-and-go-seek as children all share something in common? And if they do, what is it? And what results from it?

In *The Christian at Play*, I opened my book with two epigraphs. I have already mentioned the one from Michael Novak about being immersed in watching a baseball game such that it carries back into one's ongoing life. The other is from the theologian Dietrich Bonhoeffer. In a letter that he wrote from prison to his friend Eberhard Bethge months before he was executed for his part in a plot to assassinate Hitler, Bonhoeffer asked:

> I wonder whether it is possible (it almost seems so today) to regain the idea of the Church as providing an understanding of the area of freedom (art, education, friendship, play), so that Kierkegaard's "aesthetic existence" would not be banished from the Church's sphere, but would be reestablished within it? … Who is there, for instance, in our times, who can devote himself with an easy mind to music, friendship, games, or happiness? Surely not the "ethical" [person], but only the Christian. (Bonhoeffer 1971: 198)

For Bonhoeffer, play was understood as part of that area of freedom, along with the arts and friendship that could be associated with aesthetics. And even the extreme situation of Nazi German in 1944 could not cancel out its value and possibility for the Christian. We are to work for justice, but we are also meant to enjoy music and friendship and play, for this is God's world.

Given life's injustices, given the need to right life's wrongs, which are "oft so strong" (How can we help the millions of immigrants from the Middle East who are seeking new lives anywhere that will have them? What should be our response to those in Kabul who are burying their dead, the funerals for the five Dallas policemen who were assassinated in cold blood by a sniper, or the innocent black man in Minneapolis who was stopped in his car for a broken tail light and tragically killed by the quick trigger of a policeman? And what of the protests in the United States in support of "Black Lives Matter" that are being held on campuses and in cities across the United States, including at Fuller Seminary where I teach?), who is it that can play? Bonhoeffer's suggestion is a surprising one: it is particularly the Christian. Do we agree?

Given the growing racial and religious intolerance across the globe, who is it that can afford to pause and appreciate the beauty of a curving penalty kick by Lionel Messi that finds the upper corner of the goal, or a forty-foot shot by Stephen Curry of the Golden State Warriors? Can one really afford such aesthetic moments? How can one devote himself or herself in our troubled times to music or games or movies? Surely not the "ethical" person—the person whose very humanity is defined by acts of justice, but only the Christian, whose humanity is defined not by what we do, but by who we are, children of God. For Christians believe that play, as an event of the inventive human spirit, finds ongoing validation as an expression of humankind's God-given nature alongside our actions on behalf of others in the world. Though the wrong, which is "oft so strong" must be addressed, the life of God's creation and creatures also deserves celebration.

Two core questions

There are two core questions a Christian theologian might ask of culture—two questions that will define one's understanding of a theology of sport as well: "What the hell are they doing?" is the first and perhaps the most common. This is the question which lies behind Andy Crouch's 2016 editorial in *Christianity Today* where he challenges what he believes is the myth of engaging the culture, arguing that we should resist being bound and tempted by the culture around us—that is, we should resist being "conformed to this world" (Romans 12:2) and instead should "learn to care for what is lasting and valuable in our particular time and place, and begin to create alternatives to things that are inadequate and broken" (Crouch 2016: 33–34). Here is Kierkegaard's "ethical" individual. It is consistent with Eugene Peterson's paraphrase of Romans 12:2 in his *The Message*, where he includes in Paul's warning concerning not becoming too well adjusted to our culture the phrase—"always dragging us down to its level of immaturity"—even though this is not in the biblical text. Peterson's addition is a conclusion of those asking the question, "What the hell are they doing?" Certainly this was one question central to Bonhoeffer's last five years of his life, when the wrong threatened to overpower everything else. In our context today, the question might be phrased— given Donald Trump, or Paris, or the poverty of Rio, should we even be thinking about, let alone participating in something as unimportant in the larger scheme of things as sports? Surely that could have been Bonhoeffer's question too, as he sat in Hitler's jail cell in a world hell bent on destruction. But surprisingly, it was not.

When applied to our reflection on play, "What the hell are they doing?" raises the tragic reality of a fallen world—a world of competition, violence, consumerism, power, sexism, racism, idolatry—a world of which sport is a part and which cries out for righteousness and justice, a world in need of redemption. As one surveys current studies in a theology of sport, much of the literature focuses here. As Robert Ellis rightly summarizes our contemporary situation, "There is this sinful sporting world" (Ellis 2014: 81). Shirl Hoffman's wonderful study *Good Game: Christianity and the Culture of Sports* might also be mentioned in this regard (Hoffman 2010). The book seeks those "good" games, while offering a cautionary look at competitive sports today and noting much that is bad. For Hoffman, too, "the wrong seems oft so strong." And he is no doubt correct. Professionalism in sport with its "win at any cost" attitude threatened even the Rio Olympics, as the drug scandals involving the Russian team, as well as other athletes, repeatedly revealed.

But there is also a second fundamental question central to the Christian theologian of culture, one that also pertains to the world of sport. That is, "What in heaven's name is going on?" And which question one chooses to focus upon will, of course, shape one's understanding of and response to the culture we live in— including our theology of sport. To ask, "What in heaven's name is going on?" is to focus on play's aesthetics, not its ethics. Rather than a hermeneutic of suspicion and separation consider Peter Leithart's review of Robert Ellis's *The Games People Play* in which he concludes, "Ellis's tempered Victorianism might best be tempered further with a strong dose of Pauline and patristic and Puritan skepticism"

(Leithart 2014). The question, "What in heaven's name is going on?" invites a hermeneutic of engagement and appreciation. What is the compelling power of our play, including sport? For Ellis, as Leithart rightly notes, every "human activity [including our sport] *can* be done in union with Christ and in the power of the Spirit." Rather than focus on the question of sin, this alternate question centers on play's ability "to make us more fully human, more fully in the image of the playful, powerful, Creator." When we are truly at play, we participate in God's creative life; it is a foretaste of heaven.

The one question a theologian of culture asks, "What the hell are they doing?" looks at much in the sports' world today and with Karl Barth cries, "Nein"— "No." The other question we ask of culture, "What in heaven's name is going on?" discovers in sport, what Friedrich Schleiermacher recognized as the sense and taste of the Infinite in the finite. With Paul Tillich it seeks to illuminate the spiritual lines that, otherwise, too often remain hidden within our human activity. There is, surely, Christian truth to be discovered in both perennial lines of questioning. The one focuses on how evil might be overcome—on redemption; the other recognizes in creation and creature that this is "my Father's world." The one filters its theological observations through Christology; the other, through creation, recognizing the Spirit's presence not only as the *paraclete*, the Comforter, whom Christ has sent, but also as the Spirit of Life, sent from God the Creator to give breath, sustenance, and verve to his creation.

Perhaps a well-known example from the world of play can illumine this second option. C.S. Lewis, in his autobiography, *Surprised by Joy*, highlights a number of play experiences that were formative—even transformative, in his life: listening to his mother read to him from Beatrice Potter's *Squirrel Nutkin*, playing with a toy garden he made in a biscuit tin, hearing Wagner's music, reading Longfellow's *Saga of King Olaf* or later in university, the Greek play *Hippolytus*. Lewis had a number of these sporadic play experiences that each seemed to him more real than ordinary life. He said these events produced in him stabs of "Joy." When they first occurred, Lewis believed the "Joy" he experienced to be what he really desired. But as he grew up, he realized that his joy was actually only the by-product of something or someone more fundamental—"a pointer to something other and outer." It was only when Lewis gave his full attention to his experience of play, and not to what it produced in him, that paradoxically play opened him outward to something external to the play experience—to the Transcendent. It was when Lewis became a player that such surprises of joy sometimes came, causing him to ask, "What in heaven's name is going on" (Lewis 1955: 72, 168, 170).

This joy—"this pointer to something other and outer" as he described it—was only a distant longing until he read George MacDonald's *Phantastes, A Faerie Romance*. As he read this book, he recounted that he was simply changed:

> It was as though the voice which had called to me from the world's end were now speaking at my side. It was with me in the room, or in my body, or behind me. If it had once eluded me by its distance, it now eluded me by proximity— something too near to see, to plain to be understood, on this side of knowledge.

Lewis went on to clarify that reading this fiction had been the occasion for him of a Divine encounter. He wrote: "That night my imagination was, in a certain sense, baptized; the rest of me [for Lewis this meant his intellect and will], not unnaturally took longer. I had not the faintest notion what I had let myself in for by buying *Phantastes*" (Lewis 1955: 238, 180–81).

Like all true players, Lewis had simply immersed himself fully in the play experience of reading MacDonald's science fiction. He had no larger or ulterior motive. Rather in play's parenthesis to life, entering fully into the story's new space and time, freely accepting its "rules" as the operating procedures and caring about those in its world, he nonetheless found himself ushered into the Presence of that which was and is basic to all life, his own included. As Paul Tillich wrote of a similar play experience he had, when after being on the front lines in the First World War he stood in a Berlin museum before a Botticelli painting titled *Madonna and Child with Singing Angels*, "A level of reality was opened to me which had been covered up to this moment, although I had some feeling before of its existence." Tillich, not unlike Lewis, understood himself to have had "an encounter with the Power of Being itself" (Tillich 1966: 27–28; cf. Tillich 1987: 12). What became crucial for both theologians in their lives and thought were these foundational encounters with the Divine that occurred not within the church or with explicit reference to Jesus Christ, but while at play.

But lest we get too far afield from our focus on a theology of sport, though the connection should be clear to most of you, let me give a final example from the world of sport of how we might consider play from the standpoint of "heaven," not "hell." It comes from an essay in the *New Yorker* by the American novelist John Updike. He wrote:

> There is a goodness [he might also have said "a beauty"] in the experience of golf that may well be … a place where something breaks into our workaday world and bothers us forevermore with the hints it gives. (Updike 1972: 76–78)

Those familiar with Updike's novels will immediately recall the conversation in *Rabbit, Run* between Harry, or Rabbit, and Eccles, the humanitarian minister with little, if any, faith in God who is cynically questioning Rabbit as to why he is so restless in life: "What is it? What is it [that you want]? Is it hard or soft? Harry. Is it blue? Is it red? Does it have polka dots?" Eccles is belittling Rabbit's quest for transcendence amid the traumas of life, and Rabbit has no answer—that is, until he steps up to the tee and for the first time hits a perfect drive. "'That's it!' Rabbit cries, and turning to Eccles with a smile of aggrandizement repeats, 'That's it'" (Updike 1960: 112–113).

Two potential criticisms

Play's and, thus, sport's fundamental anchorage in the Transcendent has, of course, not been without its critics. Theological arguments within the Christian community against this axiological orientation have usually taken one of two trajectories: (1) some have thought that such a claim reduces play to a "means to an end," effectively aborting the play experience, and (2) others have claimed that play cannot have such restorative possibilities, for redemption is only in Christ Jesus and sin has blurred beyond recognition any revelatory possibility for the play experience. Let us look at each challenge in turn:

Does play become instrumental?

Although play has proven notoriously difficult to define, descriptors are more easily come by. Johan Huizinga's description of play's characteristics in his classic *Homo Ludens* (1938; EV 1955) remains the gold standard. He wrote:

> Summing up the formal characteristics of play we might call it a free activity standing quite consciously outside "ordinary" life as being "not serious," but at the same time absorbing the player intensely and utterly. It is an activity connected with no material interest, and no profit can be gained by it. It proceeds within its own proper boundaries of time and space according to fixed rules and in an orderly manner. It promotes formation of social groupings which tend to surround themselves with secrecy and to stress their difference from the common world by disguises and other means. (Huizinga 1955: 13)

Central to Huizinga's description is the recognition that play is an activity that is freely entered into, complete in itself and outside "ordinary life." Play is, in this sense, the complement of work. As such it is disinterested, though as a complement to work it adorns life and amplifies it. Put most simply, the whole point of play is playing. Most theologians of sport have stressed this point, noting play's autotelic nature. As Lincoln Harvey observes, for example, "We should simply accept that play is what it is: it is radically unnecessary but internally meaningful. It is genuinely free from the serious business of life" (Harvey 2014: 69). But we also know the issue is more complex than this, for someone might play a game in order to work out, or to make a business contact, for a paycheck or an Olympic medal, but yet once in the game be captured by it, so that the sport activity becomes what it is, actual play.

But while Huizinga's description is helpful, it is also limited, for play is also more than this. Written during the Nazi buildup when play was being manipulated for political purposes, *Homo Ludens* mistakenly sought to divorce play from the larger world. For though radically unnecessary, play's meaning, nonetheless, extends beyond the playtime back into the everyday world (that is why Novak and I both remain sad when our sport's teams lose). Theologians of play and sport have struggled to describe this paradox. I have described play as "non-instrumental, yet productive." For this reason, I critiqued Jurgen Moltmann's understanding of play which was printed in English as *Theology of Play* for instrumentalizing play. I wrote:

Moltmann's hermeneutical predilections for promise over fulfillment, for ethics over aesthetics, and for mission over rest … cause him to ignore play's self-contained meaning and instead to explore the *function* of play in contemporary society. (Johnston 1983: 70)

In Moltmann's schema, play as the way of the clown negates the negative; it keeps the revolution human by thrusting us into life's incongruities; and it anticipates our future with God, functioning as foreplay. The risk in saying this is, of course, that play's autotelic center is forgotten and the play experience as a result is aborted.

Ironically, Lincoln Harvey suggests that the same criticism can and should be offered concerning my own position. Unintentionally, he says, I have also aborted the play activity by suggesting that while it is non-instrumental, it is nonetheless productive. In particular, he takes exception to my suggestion that the play experience can open one out to communion with others and the Other/the divine Spirit of Life. He writes:

Almost without noticing it, Johnston himself falls into the instrumentalist trap. He first recognizes what is at stake here, arguing that "play must be entered into without outside purpose … [and] be connected with [no] material interest or ulterior motive." But having established this vital point, Johnston recognizes that play has a number of outside consequences, one of which – he argues – is a "presentiment of the sacred." (Harvey 2014: 91)

It could well be that I am guilty as charged. Work is needful; play is needless. To instrumentalize play is to abort it. Yet even Harvey, while criticizing me for turning play into a means to an end, similarly concludes that play is "unnecessary-but-meaningful" (Harvey 2014: 93). "Non-instrumental, but productive," "unnecessary-but-meaningful"—it is this paradoxical reality that is at the heart of sport. Harvey seeks to protect play's uselessness by saying there is only an internal meaningfulness. That is, it has no meaning beyond the game. But surely this is not the case, for our larger world is transformed by our experiences of play. Just ask C.S. Lewis, or any of the soccer/football fans in Brazil after the Olympic finals in 2016, or the Swedish female soccer player at the same Olympics who accidentally kicked the ball into her own goal, providing Germany its winning margin.

For Harvey, play should have no connection with larger life. This causes him to make the questionable theological conclusion that in all of life, only the sports experience is unconnected with our chief end which is to glorify God. Only sport is truly secular. Everything else in life—including other kinds of play experiences it would seem—is meant to glorify God. Besides wondering how this jibes with the whole of the Old Testament which takes as an axiological assumption that God is everywhere present in our lives, even in our sin (cf., David taking a sinful census because God incited him, 2 Samuel 24), the social meaningfulness of play in sport seems indisputable. Gordon Preece, for example, recalls that Michael Novak in his landmark book, *The Joy of Sports*, argues that while play is an end, with a purpose in itself, "The virtues generated from sports should 'inform one's family life, civic life, political life, work life." For Novak, in short, sports civilize life (Preece 2009: 30). Preece goes on to comment appreciatively that Novak rightly both defends sport as an end in itself and affirms the virtues of sport. Preece himself agrees with Huizinga that "play can have no ulterior or material interest" and compares it to worship. Yet, he says, "it does often have important secondary or indirect consequences such as reinforcing relationships with ourselves, others, the earth; emancipating and expressing our spirits; reconnecting to the wholeness of life; experiencing long-lasting joy" (Preece 2009: 31–32). And to the list I would add, "experiencing the sacred." Surely this is the witness of countless participants of sport.

One example will need to suffice. At the 2016 Sundance Film Festival in Park City, Utah, I saw a screening of the documentary film *I Am Yup'ik* (d. Anastasion and Golon 2016). It is about a basketball tournament in Alaska for Yup'ik youth, where teenagers from small towns in rural Alaska either fly or drive snowmobiles to a host village for competition between the towns. It is the Yup'ik "Super Bowl." The movie is uplifting, showing the social importance of a sport's tournament that brings together a wider community, providing hope and purpose for teenagers throughout their nation who are struggling. The teenage star of the team, Byron Nicholi, was present for the Q&A after the screening, as was the movie's director, Nathan Golon. Nicholi said he and his friends play basketball, because they are doing what they love and they are doing it together. With suicide a major problem in the villages, and many homes fatherless, life is confusing for many of the teens. However, Nicholi said, "When I'm playing, I forget about all the problems I'm having. It makes me feel alive." The movie's director added, "Basketball is a way into other issues of cultural identity; basketball for the Yup'iks is more than just a sport."

Here again is the paradox: Only when one is freely participating for the love of the game does it become actual play. But at the same time, these Yup'ik basketball games have meaning far beyond the play court and game time. They reinforce relationships between the players, with their tribe, and with their surroundings; they revitalize the spirits of fans and players alike, who for the duration of the game, experience something of the wholeness of life; and they produce long-lasting joy. There is, in Novak's words, a value beyond the basketball court—sport has meaning "for family life, civic life, political life, work life" (and I might add, "spiritual life").

Does sin block out the divine presence?

But this brings us to the second critique concerning play's potential for ushering one into a sacred space. The critique, this time, comes not so much from the side of sports per se, but from an increasingly disputed theological judgment, that men and women in their sinful state are unable to receive anything meaningful from God's general revelation in life. The claim is that humankind's sin blocks out any meaningful sense of the divine presence and for this reason humanity stands isolated from God without the further work of Christ in accomplishing our salvation. Romans 1 is usually referenced in support of this position. So even if it is true that play can usher us into the presence of others, it would be wrong, so the critique goes, to suggest that God could meet us in our sport activity, that is, outside the church and without direct relationship with Christ. Here has been the standard Reformed position in Protestantism with regard to general revelation. It is the position of those wanting to know of play and sport, "What the hell is going on?" Here is the operative understanding in much of the church, despite countless personal testimonies to the contrary.

In my book *God's Wider Presence* (2014), I have attempted to rethink the "rumors of angels" (to use Peter Berger's provocative term), which come in and through our play experiences (Johnston 2014; see Berger 1970). A majority of individuals both within and outside the church can recall a play event or time when through either creation or human creativity including the arts and our sports, we encountered God's Presence. Such occasional experiences are not self-produced or even planned for; they come when they are not sought. But they are remembered years later and are often foundational for people's lives as they move forward.

Having taught classes in theology and film for close to two decades, I have read literally hundreds of testimonials where students recount such numinous occasions when they were watching a movie. Like all play, watching movies is non-instrumental, yet at the same time productive. Entered into freely, the world of the film's story has its own rules, and its own play space and time. Moviegoers lose themselves in the movie's story, as the film provides a timeout from life. Yet, this film watching, at least at times, is anything but frivolous. My students sometimes describe how they met God at the Cineplex, and these sacred moments invariably produce humility and awe, give direction, calm anxiety, instill hope, clarify vocation, and fill the moviegoers with joy.

The claim that there are divine encounters that happen outside the church and without direct reference to God's saving acts should not come as a surprise to Christians, for Scripture records several such examples of God speaking outside Israel's religious institutions and within everyday life. Abimelech heard God in a dream (Genesis 20); Elijah heard the "sound of sheer silence" in the stillness immediately following a storm (1 Kings 19); Balaam heard God through and within his own religious practices (Numbers 22–25). We are not sure how Melchizedek, the priest of Salem (Genesis 14) or Pharoah Neco (2 Chronicles 35), heard God speak to them, but Scripture is clear in saying that God revealed himself to them outside any Jewish/Christian setting. And Paul compliments the Athenians for experiencing their world as spiritually charged, even if they were wrong in then building idols to worship these unknown gods (Acts 17) (cf., Johnston 2014: 69–119).

God's Spirit is present in life and reveals God's presence to us. Here was C.S. Lewis's experience which baptized his imagination and sent him on an intellectual search to find out more about the God he had encountered in his playtimes. Here was Paul Tillich's experience looking at a painting by Botticelli. Here perhaps was even Karl Barth's experience as he listened to Mozart, though he was leery of any hint that humankind by its own efforts could "produce" God's presence. But again, this is exactly what play suggests. The experience of the sacred through play is not something we work at (in German, *aufgabe*); rather, it is a pure gift (*gabe*). It is not a sacrament; but it can be sacramental.

Play as an occasion for God's in-breaking presence

But though the gift of divine in-breaking within the play of Christians and non-Christians alike is experienced as foundational and deeply spiritual, we have as a church largely ignored the importance of such experiences theologically. This is particularly true of sports. While we have been open perhaps for play to be character-building, or play as providing an arena for evangelism, we have been leery to allow our sports participation, whether as athletes or as spectators, to be the occasion for God's in-breaking presence. Peak experiences, states of flow, moments of deep play, sporting mysticism—these need not, as Nick Watson and Andrew Parker argue, require a supernatural, religious source (Watson and Parker 2015: 260–281). The psyche can produce these. True, but some of these experiences might have as their source God, the Giver of Life. Denying such occasions as legitimately Transcendent, Watson and Parker argue instead that there is a "yawning abyss" between "the experiences of religious pilgrims and modern sporting mystics." Such experiences, they suggest, are simply not the equivalent to those of Paul, Jonathan Edwards, or John of the Cross (Watson and Parker 2015: 263, 271, 273). Again, while this might be true, it is hard to know with any certainty and, truth be told, few of us have spiritual experiences to match John of the Cross, or St. Paul!

But is there not a middle ground between Paul's Damascus road experience and experiences that are purely psychological? If not, most of the Christian community would have no theological explanation for their experiences with God. Could it not also be the case that experiences like Rabbit's perfect drive in golf, or a long-distance runner's "flow," might be the occasion for the gift of the divine Spirit's surprising presence? Such experiences need not be considered salvific, though they might set persons on such a trajectory. But they might still be revelatory. And though they might stop short of Paul being struck blind, they might nonetheless be spiritually illumining and even life transforming.

Do we need to categorically rule out the Spiritual/Numinous from our sporting activity and instead posit with Watson and Parker the spiritual to be only the psychological flourishing of the human spirit? Or with Harvey, must we call all sport purely "secular"? Both conclusions seem supported neither by biblical teaching nor by the experience of countless players. It is my suggestion that if we are open to the reality that God meets humanity not only in the sanctuary and in Scripture, but also in the midst of our everyday lives, not only in creation, but also in experiences of human creativity, we then can be open theologically to God meeting us also on the playfield. Too narrow a theology of general revelation has, in my opinion, caused many in the field of Christianity and sport to minimize sport's peak experiences, claiming they are at best but traces or echoes of God's historical play in creation and of little, if any, theological significance. We need, instead, to listen to the growing testimony of individuals in our post-secular, neo-romantic, postmodern age, who testify to the spiritual importance of events in our everyday lives, including in their sports.

Conclusion

In considering a theology of sport, we can either ask, "What the hell is going on?" or we can ask, "What in heaven's name is going on?" Much of the theological discussion of sport at present has centered on the first question, as we ask, what are we to make of sport's violence, consumerism, sexism, racism, and the like? Hasn't sport become idolatrous? Such theological probing assumes sport to be defective in our modern age; it assumes God's absence from our sporting life.

I would suggest that more attention needs to be given to the alternate theological question, "What in heaven's name might be going on?" Here is the question concerning sport's possibilities—possibilities to express our full humanity, to meet with others, and to be met by the Other. If, as John Drane suggests, "one of the most remarkable and unexpected features of life in the twenty-first century is what has been referred to as 'the desecularization of the world'" and with it the concomitant "emerging sacramentality of popular culture," and I believe it is, then participation in sport, like all play experience, can become the occasion for "the rediscovery of … [a] creation-centered spirituality" (Drane 2004: 37, 39).

Study Guide

The author asks, "Why should we care about our sports?" Turning to a theology of play for possible answers, he argues that play (and sport) is paradoxically both non-instrumental (an end in itself) and productive (our larger world can be transformed by our experiences of play). To lose this tension is to lose the play experience. Students might be interested in discussing this topic of sport's meaning and purpose by exploring the strengths and weaknesses of framing the question as either "What the hell are we doing?" or "What in heaven's name is going on?" If the latter, has play (or sport) ever been the occasion of experiencing the Spirit's Presence for you?

Study Questions

1. The words of a hymn from the beginning of the twentieth century begin, "Be strong! We are not here to play, to dream, to drift; we have hard work to do, and loads to lift" (Maltbie Babcock 1901). How does this legacy that play is a distraction from life's important activity still influence a theology of sport today?

2. Can sport become work and not play? How? Are some professional athletes still "playing" while others are working? Can you give examples?
3. What is there in modern sports that often aborts its "play" possibilities?
4. Why are you sad when you lose a game or match? Isn't it only a game?
5. Have you ever had a transcendent experience while playing, when you felt the Spirit's Presence? When you were opened up to what C.S. Lewis calls "Joy"?

Further Reading

Johnston, R. K. (1983), *The Christian at Play*, Grand Rapids: Eerdmans.
Johnston, R. K. (2014), *God's Wider Presence: Reconsidering General Revelation*, Grand Rapids: Baker Academic.
Lewis, C. S. (1955), *Surprised by Joy*, New York: Harcourt, Brace & World, Harvest Books.

Chapter 2

THE PARADOXICAL ATHLETE:
CHESTERTON ON PLAY AND WORK

Scott Kretchmar and Nick J. Watson

Introduction

The great Catholic writer and apologist G.K. Chesterton was a fan of paradox. He loved to show how seemingly incompatible elements were not only compatible but keys, as he put it, to the truth about things. Among those things was Christian orthodoxy. We will employ a similar strategy in investigating another one of Chesterton's favorite topics—namely play—and see how play, work, and orthodoxy are related.

Much of Chesterton's brilliance can be traced to his unique epistemology—his theory of knowledge; how we know what we know. His approach revealed strong tendencies toward realism and holism. His philosophic realism was based on his faith in reason and drove him to strongly criticize materialists, relativists, and skeptics of various stripes. His holistic tendencies required that reason venture into new and sometimes uncomfortable places. Where many thinkers like Aristotle championed the logic of the excluded middle and saw A and not-A as mutually exclusive options, Chesterton often saw them as part of a difficult-to-comprehend whole. Much like Dewey, Chesterton never met a dualism that he liked. Yet his holism was not one that focused on the ambiguous middle as some American pragmatists, and later, Merleau-Ponty, were inclined to do. Rather he focused on the colorful extremes and the exciting tensions that existed between them.

While Chesterton wrote about play (more about that later), it is useful to note that his play commitments included his penchant for conducting his own inquiries playfully. In addition to his masterful use of language that teased, surprised, challenged, entertained, and enlightened, he loved to take the slower, circuitous—but arguably more enjoyable—route to the truth. The patient unraveling of a paradox was one of his favorite intellectual ploys.

Chesterton would often begin his analyses by rehearsing the "truths" of others and concluding that they seemed reasonable enough. But then he would challenge us with the paradox. How could something that seemed to be so patently true not be true at all? And conversely, how could claims that often bordered on the outrageous actually be right? Chesterton, in short, engaged Christian theology as if it were a giant puzzle, one that was irresistibly and enjoyably challenging. What fun, he seemed to be saying, to enter such a labyrinth! What fun to find one's way, amid many false starts, to the distant and difficult-to-reach exit that revealed the truth!

Chesterton's epistemological commitment to realism and holism is perhaps most clearly reflected in his well-known volume, *Orthodoxy*, in particular Chapter VI, The Paradoxes of Christianity. He begins with a review of several charges leveled by certain skeptics or agnostics against orthodox Christianity. These charges portrayed Christianity as "oddly shaped" and inconsistent, if not utterly incoherent. Chesterton was quick to reply, "Whenever we feel that there is something odd in Christian theology," he wrote, "we shall generally find that there is something odd in the truth" (1908: 88).

Chesterton provided examples. Some critics described Christianity as unduly optimistic, others as fatally pessimistic; some regarded Christianity as a progenitor of haughtiness, others as cause for extreme humility. Some, citing historical events as evidence, described Christians as overly aggressive and hostile; others claimed they were long-suffering, enduring, and naively passive.

Rather than fall into the dualistic trap of deciding which of these As and not-As was true and which was false, Chesterton argued that there is truth in both extremes. That is, as hard as it might be to comprehend, both conclusions could be true at the same time. Once again, such paradoxes were not to be solved by locating the average of the two or some other middle position. The truth, in other words, did not lie at the mean. It could be grasped only by embracing the extremes in their gloriously contrasting colors, even by exaggerating them. Christianity got over the problem of contradiction, Chesterton wrote, by "combining furious opposites, by keeping them both, and keeping them both furious" (101). Chesterton resolved the paradox by suggesting that the truth of the extremes is the product of the stance or perspective one takes on Christianity.

> [From one perspective, the Christian] ... was to be haughtier than he had ever been before; in another way he was to be humbler than he had ever been before. Insofar as I am Man I am the chief of creatures. Insofar as I am *a* man I am the chief of sinners ... The Church was positive on both points. One can hardly think too little of oneself. One can hardly think too much of one's soul. (italics in original: 100–101)

Interestingly, this is the same kind of answer provided in a different domain by quantum physics. Scientists had puzzled for centuries over whether the ultimate stuff of the universe is a wave or a particle. Quantum, paradoxically, said it was both—at the same time. Measured one way, its particle qualities are evident. Measured another way, its wave-like features are visible. It is the perspective employed, in other words, that accounts for the different ways in which matter reveals itself. So too, the tenets of Christianity and certain aspects of Christian behavior reveal themselves in radically different ways depending on the perspective employed to view them.

Furious opposites and play

Play is often depicted as a paradoxical phenomenon. It seems to be horribly important in one sense but utterly insignificant in another. It is said to create its own time and space but everyone knows that play occurs in the real world of minutes and hours, mornings and afternoons, nearby playfields and distant mountains. It is a domain of frivolity, of dancing around the Maypole, but also one that can demand complete concentration and warrant an attitude of utter seriousness. Play, according to some, is of lesser importance than work and should take place, at least among mature adults, after work is completed. But some individuals recommend play before working, while working, and instead of working. More than a few poets, philosophers, and theologians have argued that play is the proper end of life. Chesterton (1908/2006: 40) himself was among them.

> It is not only possible to say a great deal in praise of play; it is really possible to say the highest things in praise of it. It might reasonably be maintained that the true object of all human life is play. Earth is a task garden; heaven is a playground.

However, as we will see, Chesterton was also a strong advocate for reformation, even revolution, and the intense work that goes into making our "task garden" a better place in which to live. It would seem that Chesterton might once again be hinting that his formula of retaining furious opposites would get at the truth about the place and value of work and play for Christians. Be that as it may, we will attempt to flesh out the characteristics of play using Chesterton's holistic, oppositional strategy—that is, by "retaining the furious opposites and by keeping them both furious."

The nature of play

Huizinga argued that play is freely chosen. In other words, it has nothing to do with necessity, compulsion, moral duty, or any other kind of extrinsic motivation. As Huizinga (1950) put it succinctly, "play interrupts the appetitive process." We play, in short, because we want to play. Play is autotelic. The doing is its own reward. When at play we can do anything we want, whenever we want, for as long as we want to do it. Players are motivated intrinsically, not extrinsically.

However, the opposite may also be true. When we are under the spell of play, or at least when we are under the influence of what some have called deep play (e.g., Ackerman 1999), we are decidedly unfree. In fact, when in the grip of a powerful play experience, we may well lose our very ability to make rational decisions. A Bacchanalian-like spell is cast over us. We forget what time it is. We take risks we would not normally take. We dance to the point of exhaustion—and then dance some more. We neglect family and friends to play yet another few holes of golf before the sun sets. We, like Nero, get caught wiling away our time at play when propriety or duty say we should be doing other things.

We may see part way through this paradox if we separate two moments in many play experiences. Choosing to play seems to emphasize our freedom. Being chosen by play, being captivated by play experiences emphasizes the forfeiture of our freedom. We choose to play while, at the same time, expecting that play will return the favor and choose us.

By choosing to play, we encounter ourselves as fully in control, as masters of our play fate. We select tennis, not baseball. We expect to play for forty-five minutes during our lunch break and return to the office for a one o' clock meeting. However, in being chosen by play, we risk forfeiting that control. We lose ourselves, as we say, in our playground. We get carried away on the wings of delight. We fall under the spell of the ritual, the celebration, the game, the contest. We capitulate and then rationalize that very surrender. We say to ourselves that we can make up the missed work later, trying desperately to make sense of our commitment to this silly interlude, perhaps also trying to convince ourselves that we were in control all the time when quite the opposite was the case.

Thus, one paradox of play could be this: We use our freedom in order to lose it. We hold off necessity in order to experience an even stronger sense of compulsion. We honor certain playgrounds by choosing them over others only to have the playground surprise us by carrying us away to unexpected places of delight. Play, in other words, seems to involve a reciprocal experience of giving and taking, of choosing and being chosen—an experience similar to what Buber (1958) found in the I-Thou interactions of "will" and "grace."

"Will" speaks to human agency and capability, to putting oneself in a position to receive, to laying the groundwork, as it were, for the possible relationship. It may require relinquishing one's agendas, being still, listening carefully. "Grace," on the other hand, speaks to human passivity and incapability, to receiving the gift, the blessing, the unmerited confirmation by the other—whether that be a lover, a friend, or a playground. When both "will" and "grace" do their appointed work, we lose ourselves in play—and we are grateful.

On some occasions, play falls flat. We may be preoccupied by issues at work and the quality of our "will" was not what it needed to be. On other occasions, "will" is up to the task, but it is a one-way relationship. "Grace" does not make an appearance. We are not carried away by the play experience. Once again we tend to rationalize in order to locate some value in the still-born play experience. "At least we got in some exercise," we may say to ourselves. But in our hearts we know that nothing special happened. We never really fell under the spell of play. We had to settle for increased heart rates and the expenditure of a few extra calories when we were hoping for something more. The freedom showed up. The un-freedom did not.

Two other contraries have been used to describe play. Play is said to be useful and useless. Evolutionary theory would suggest that it has to be useful. This is so because any physical traits or behavioral tendencies (what anthropologists call phenotypes) that are maladaptive would have extinguished themselves across generations. In other words, if play reduced the likelihood that players would reach reproductive maturity and thus lessened opportunities for passing on one's genes, the play tendency would slowly be lost to the human genome. Those who embodied a stronger sense of prudence and duty and thus, were less likely to be distracted by play would survive and pass on their work-a-day genes to the next generation. Under this scenario, the population would shift in the direction of prudentially prone individuals. However, because play tendencies have been preserved across the animal kingdom, it would seem that play is adaptive and thus useful, albeit in some hard-to-determine way.

It is hard to determine for at least two reasons. First, energy is a scarce commodity, particularly in times of need. Because play expends this precious energy, it leaves less for more important ends. Second, play is, or at least can be, dangerous. This fact was immortalized in Aesop's Fables in the characters of the ant and the grasshopper. The ants were the sensible creatures, those who stored up food and prepared for the coming winter. They refused to waste their precious time on play. On the other hand, the profligate grasshopper could not resist the play impulse. He played foolishly and paid a dear price for it when winter finally arrived.

While this fable was more about ethics than evolution and was intended to celebrate the virtues of prudence and planning over self-indulgence and spontaneity, the point remains that play can be found across the much of the animal kingdom. Perhaps then it is both dangerous and useful, a potential cause of our demise and a resource for human flourishing. On the plus side, some anthropologists have argued that play prepares children and adults to meet future challenges by presenting them with novel circumstances that require new skills. Play is also said to recharge our batteries. Most of us have experienced the refreshment that comes with play, a kind of revitalizing force that counteracts the grinding routine of work. At the end of a long week in the office we realize that we need to relax; we need to play. If asked if play served a useful purpose in our lives, we would have to respond affirmatively.

Still, play *is* silly and useless. It is doing something for "no good reason," just because we want to do it. It is a serendipity, an oasis, a break in the action, a time to "go offline," a diversion. It carries us away from the grind of duty, work, and worries about survival. That is its nature; that accounts for much of its charm; that lies at the heart of its distinctiveness as play. Play is fundamentally useless!

We know how the play experience can be lost when the activity becomes too useful. A young boy or girl learns to play tennis, falls in love with it, and develops a good degree of skill in playing. But then pressures are added by cheering crowds, meddling parents, offers of scholarships, win-at-all-cost coaches, and excessive practice regimens. Sadly, the original joy in playing fades away. The once delightful playground recedes to the background. In some cases, it is lost forever. A number of college athletes have reported that, once their last game is over, they will never return to what were previously their beloved childhood playgrounds. In a word, play became too useful, too much like work. In point of fact, it was no longer play.

Conclusions about play

As we have seen, two sets of contraries have been attributed to play. First, play can be understood to require maximal freedom as well as result in utter captivation. We freely choose to play; and play, in turn, "chooses us" and puts us under its intoxicating spell. In one sense, play is an aspect of life that requires full control and agency, but it is also a place of full surrender. Second, play is useful from one perspective, but from another point of view it is, and must be, utterly useless. In some ways it contributes to our fitness, our humanity, of love of life. But in other ways it contributes absolutely nothing of consequence. To play is to enjoy the experience, not to bargain for a future payoff. As Novak (1976) put it, it is to participate in the Kingdom of Ends, not the Kingdom of Means.

If Chesterton is right about the retention of "furious opposites" as a key to understanding the truth about some things, and if play is one of those things, we should be able to resolve these twin paradoxes. We should be able to see that there is a sense in which play required maximal freedom, the kind of freedom we see in children who have no cares in the world, who give themselves to their playgrounds, who are utterly free to accept play invitations. This is unfettered agency. But at the same time, we can acknowledge the other extreme, the grip that play can have on us, a grip that is even stronger on occasion than the moral force of duty and work requirements for survival and well-being. Aesop's grasshopper who plays to his own demise symbolizes the absolutely powerful and delightful foolishness of play.

We should also be able to unravel the second paradox about the utility and uselessness of play. It could be the case that play is maximally useful, when (and only when) it is experienced as maximally useless. In other words, play may adorn life best when no thought of adornment is given to it by the players. Play may also carry the most fitness benefit when no thought of survival or Darwinian fitness enters the play landscape.

In play then we are freely captivated, in charge of our own surrender, at once the chooser and the chosen. In play we find the greatest utility in the most thoroughly useless activities. We care most about things that hardly matter at all. In play, we seem to be most passionate about projects that produce nothing important. By retaining furious opposites and by keeping them both furious, we may have captured a little more of what Chesterton kept finding in Christian orthodoxy— namely, an oddly shaped truth.

Play, work, and Christian theology

Given Chesterton's musings on the existence of paradox and the need to retain furious opposites furiously within the Christian life, a brief reflection on the main theological positions with regard to play and work is warranted. In our age, philosophers and theologians have lamented the loss of playfulness (and festivity and joy) in industrialized Western civilization. Sport is perhaps the cultural artefact that best demonstrates what the historian of sport Allen Guttman (1978/2004) describes as an aggressive "ludic diffusion." Writing in the middle of the twentieth century, nearly fifty years after the publication of Chesterton's *Orthodoxy*, the German Lutheran theologian Dietrich Bonhoeffer asks:

> I wonder whether it is possible (it almost seems so today) to regain the idea of the Church as providing an understanding of the area of freedom (art, education, friendship, play), so that Kierkegaard's "aesthetic existence" would not be banished from the Church's sphere, but would be reestablished within it? (1944, cited in Johnston 1983, in front matter)

Arguably, Bonhoeffer taps into the narrative of paradox that characterizes Chesterton's work, as this is something we all may experience in creating/ observing art, playing and loving others in human relationships and learning via diverse pedagogies/epistemologies. In turn, Bonhoeffer identifies how the Church, especially the American Protestant evangelical institutions over the last 200 years, has often dichotomized theological reflection and praxis. The widespread influence of the dualistic Greek philosophy of Plato (the mind–body split) on Christian doctrine in the early centuries of the Church, especially in the writings of Church Father, Origen (*c*. 182–251), appears to be the root cause for this. As the Hebrew-Christian scholar Marvin Wilson (1989: 131) suggests, "the American Church has struggled vainly to support itself by a variety of artificial roots. Consequently, its growth has been stunted, its fruitfulness impaired," mainly because it has been "severed from its biblical Hebraic roots." And so, historically, the importance of the body in Christian theology and life has been sidelined, as has knowledge of the sacred dimension of play. However, this is something clearly alluded to in Huizinga's seminal work on play in 1950 (cited in Mathisen 2005: 281):

> We may well call play a "totality" in the modern sense of the word ... In all its higher forms [play] at any rate belongs to the sphere of festival and ritual—the sacred sphere ... The Platonic identification of play and holiness does not defile the latter by calling it play, rather it exalts the concept of play to the highest regions of the spirit ... In play we move below the level of the serious, as the child does; but we can also move above it—in the realm of the beautiful and sacred.

Following Huizinga's seminal work on play, in which he argues that play is imbued with a sacred and spiritual dimension, a number of Christian theologians have taken up the Bonhoeffer challenge. Hugo Rahner, a theologian and Church historian within the Jesuit tradition, locates God in the role of the creator as the "ultimate player" in his book *Man at Play* (1972). He also emphasizes "the lightness of spirit" and builds bridges to the concept of "grace" that may be attained through humans playing. David Miller (1969, 1971) and Robert Neale (1969) have also contributed notable studies around this time, *Gods and Games: Towards a Theology of Play* and *In Praise of Play: Toward a Psychology of Religion*, respectively. These works both support and challenge Rahner's theology of play on several conceptual and doctrinal points.

However, it was the well-known German Protestant Theologian Jürgen Moltmann (1972), who published the text *Theology of Play*—which was followed by a broader analysis of the Olympic Games—who has perhaps had the most significant impact on the development of theologies of play, work, and sports. Not unlike Chesterton's appeal to maintain a "fierce delight" in our human endeavors and to celebrate furious opposites, Moltmann advocates a whole-hearted passion for those athletes competing in sports events. That said, he also warns of the dangers of an unhealthy obsessive commodified work ethic (a Marxist position) in sporting competition, which, at its worst, ends in an idolatrous quest to find one's worth and significance in the activity—an approach that typically leads to the alienation of the other on a range of fronts. Rahner, Miller, Neale, Moltmann, and in the early 1980s Robert Johnston were all, to varying degrees, influenced by the Protestant liberal theologian Paul Tillich—who pioneered the theological investigations of culture in the twentieth century.

Johnston's book *The Christian at Play* (1983) provides arguably the most in-depth examination of play, drawing on literature from across the Christian traditions. Interestingly here, there is significant discussion in Johnston's work surrounding C.S. Lewis' autobiographical work, *Surprised by Joy*, which, like Chesterton's *Orthodoxy*, champions joy, freedom, and playfulness as bulwarks of the authentic Christian life that are more often than not experienced in paradox. Charting the theological reflection of play from the Church Fathers (e.g., Augustine) through to the modern era, Johnston provides a biblical model of play (and work) that is rooted in Hebraic, Greek, Protestant, and Catholic thought. In particular, Judaic theology and history are important in understanding how Chesterton urges us to retain furious opposites furiously, embrace existential paradox, and be generally playful in life. This is rooted in his Judeo-Christian starting point.

In his treatment of play, Johnston also warns against humanizing or deifying play, that is, conceiving a "theology of play" as another "pop theology" (e.g., the death of God and human potential movements) and therefore erroneously adopting "current opinion" and identifying it with the religion of Christianity *per se*. That said, Johnston is very positive about the necessity and worth of play but acknowledges, as did Bonhoeffer, the Church's historical suspicious (e.g., Augustine and the Puritans) and ambivalent (and at times avowedly negative) approach to pleasure, play, and sport. However, given that the Catholic tradition has generally been more consistent in advocating the positive dimensions of play, sports, and pleasure (as evidenced in the writings of Chesterton, Novak, Pieper, and Rahner), Johnston identifies an important caveat in the historical development of theologies of play: "evangelical Christians are so prone to 'instrumentalize everything'" (ix), including play and sport.

Since the late 1960s this claim that has been leveled at the Protestant community has been a central point of scholarly debate, in particular in North America. Catholic voices, such as Michael Novak, in his seminal text, *The Joy of Sports* (1976), contend that the Protestant work ethic (rooted in individualistic Calvinistic doctrine) and the philosophy of Marxism are the major forces in initiating the secularization of sporting experience and the subsequent loss of playfulness, creativity, freedom, and joy. In agreement with Novak, Huizinga states that "we have an activity nominally known as play but raised to such a pitch of technical organization and scientific thoroughness that the real play-spirit is threatened with extinction" (1950: 199). The "sweet tension" (not unlike Chesterton's "fierce delight") that Kretchmar suggests exists in healthy sporting competition is then lost in a quest to dominate at all costs, to win-at-all-costs—dichotomies then prevail in the sporting encounter and Chesterton's holistic oppositional strategy is trumped! Play and sport have become work.

Building on devastating Marxist critiques of the modern sporting institution, by Bero Rigauer (1981) and Jean-Marie Brohm (1978), which contend that sacred play moments in sports have been lost through the aggressive forces of industrial capitalism, scholars such as Allen Guttman and Steve Overmann (2011)—building on Weberian theory—have persuasively argued that "sport is now work." This model of professional sport is characterized by quantification, commercialism, and dry rationality, which is a seed-bed for the multitude of ethical and moral problems that exist in modern sports. This is the very antithesis of what has been called *The Riddle of Joy* (1989) that permeates Chesterton's and C.S. Lewis' writings on play and work. Chesterton's personal and scholarly journey into the riddle of joy is based on an anthropological and rational holism that rejects the sea of dualisms that have polluted Christian theology and practice in the modern era, and in particular American religious institutions (Wilson 1989).

In examining theories of embodiment and theological and philosophical dichotomies (an insufficient epistemology that underplays the complexity of things—Chesterton's main point), a growing number of scholars have suggested the need for a holistic Judea-Christian and Pauline theological paradigm when examining play, work, and sport (e.g., Kretchmar 2011). The writings of Thomist philosopher Joseph Pieper have informed this work and are again demonstrative of the generally more balanced epistemological stance of Catholic scholars over time. Drawing mainly on Aquinas (c. 1225–1274) and thus Aristotle, Pieper champions the worth and necessity of both leisure and play and bemoans the "cult of work" that is now embedded in our culture. His holistic anthropology and theory of embodiment closely mirror—if presented in a very different style—Chesterton's views on play and work articulated in *Orthodoxy*. Both Pieper and Chesterton, alongside Rahner, Novak, Moltmann, Johnston, and others, have helped to counter the epistemological and theological error of dualism and its manifestation in theology and modern-day sports.

Chesterton's view of play and work

Christianity, according to Chesterton, extends two invitations at the same time—namely, to become radically sober *and* experience full intoxication. Chesterton called life on earth, as we noted, "a task garden," a world in which we must acknowledge "danger and honour and intellectual responsibility." We are not permitted, he argued, "to [simply] enjoy the pleasures and deny the perils." He (1908/2006) argued that Christians should experience a "fiercer discontent" than others with the sorry status of the world and the suffering it includes.

In Chesterton's view, discontent should lead to work—specifically to reformation. Chesterton contrasted reformation with two other ways of dealing with the broken world. The first is evolution, a coping with the inevitable, a far too passive reaction to a negative turn of events. The second is a rigid sense of progress which can lead to movement in the wrong direction. Chesterton suggests a third option. He is an epistemological realist who believes that we have the God-given power to discern better destinations from those that are less desirable.

Chesterton wrote, "Reform is a metaphor for reasonable and determined men: it means that we will see a certain thing out of shape and mean to put it into shape. And we know what shape" (1908: 112). He expressed his confidence in the powers of reformation. He wrote that we have been and are "slow but sure in bringing justice and mercy among men" (112). Christians, in short, have serious work responsibilities guided by a "vision fixed on Eden" (117). Paradoxically, then, one of the fruits of the spirit is a "furious discontent."

On this analysis, Christians should be, in one sense, angrier than non-believers with legal injustices, suffering, economic discrimination, racism, cheating, and all other harms that we find in the world. Christian athletes and others who love sports should be less patient with the economic exploitation of athletics, distortions of games for nationalistic purposes, selfish mining of sport for personal gain, instrumental ethical attitudes that pay little heed to the quality of games, cheating, and any number of other problems that are seen regularly in our sporting venues. There is work to do. There is no time to waste.

This speaks to the importance of what might be called a Christian ethics of athletic stewardship. But whether this stewardship is grounded in Christian faith or secular ethics, it would involve an unwavering commitment to preserving what is best about sport, improving sport, making sure that sport is a cultural jewel that can be enjoyed by generations to come. In short, we will see sport as "a certain thing out of shape and mean to put it into shape. And we know what shape." While no sporting Eden is likely to be reached, it is nevertheless important to keep the goal in mind and pursue it—with fervor!

This, however, is not the whole of the story for Chesterton. As noted, he argues that Christians also have cause to exhibit a "fiercer delight" as a foundation for celebration and other forms of play. He argues that there is no better cause for dance and celebration than the "good news." The Christ figure then is both the Lord of Reformation and, as the popular hymn puts it, "Lord of the Dance." Faith inspires the greatest obligations known to humankind and the most joyous celebrations; once again, at the same time. Christianity solved the work–play problem, at least on Chesterton's terms, by keeping them both and retaining them in their brightest colors.

Chesterton rails against the times in which we put up with a mixture of good and evil with a "decent satisfaction and a decent endurance" (1908: 77). He writes:

> I know this feeling fills our epoch, and I think it freezes our epoch. For our Titanic purposes of faith and revolution, what we need is not the cold acceptance of the world as a compromise, but some way in which we can heartily hate and heartily love it. We do not want joy and anger to neutralize each other and produce a

surly contentment ... We have to feel the universe at once as an ogre's castle, to be stormed, and yet as our own cottage, to which we can return at evening. (77)

The paradox, however, is still troubling. How can one be sober and intoxicated, driven by need and captured by serendipity at the same time? As always, Chesterton has an answer. He argues that both are based on an inherent loyalty, love, commitment—the subject of fairy tales. He sees both delight and discontent being grounded in "a primal loyalty to life" (75).

Chesterton continues to unravel the paradox by railing against suicide as "the ultimate and absolute evil, the refusal to take an interest in existence; the refusal to take the oath of loyalty to life ... The suicide insults everything on earth." He insults work, hope for improvement, goals, and duties. But he also insults play by "defiling every flower and refusing to live for its sake" (78).

The commitment to life can provoke us to hate enough to work and love enough to play. The martyr, who risks her life for a cause, and in stark contrast to the suicide, lives closer to the truth than the Stoic who merely endures and misses the vibrant colors at life's work and play extremes. Chesterton argues that the ethical strictures of Christianity produce a place in which it is safe to play. Once again Chesterton uses paradox to instruct us.

Catholic doctrine and discipline may be walls; but they are the walls of a playground. Christianity is the only frame which has preserved the pleasure of Paganism. We might fancy some children playing on the flat grassy top of some tall island in the sea. So long as there was a wall round the cliff's edge they could fling themselves into every frantic game and make the place the noisiest of nurseries. (152)

Sport, work, and playgrounds

Christian traditions, as we have seen, have been ambivalent regarding the value of play. Some have argued that play is inappropriate, at least for adults. Reformations should trump celebrations. Restrained gratitude should trump any tendencies to sing, dance, and drink. Discipleship is full-time work.

However, if Chesterton is onto something, a Christian theology, and, perhaps by extension, *any* theology should pay more heed to delightful physical activity. If the ultimate purpose of a theology is to make sense of a commitment to life, to live life as if it really mattered, a story that accommodates and celebrates the most extreme forms of love and duty, sufficiency and need, the desired and the distasteful might be very compelling.

To be sure, it is a weird world in which the ultimate stuff of the universe is both a wave and a particle at the same time. And it is a weird world that pulls us humans in two opposite directions at once, toward freedom and dependency, toward love and reformation, toward celebration and duty. It is a good world, one that allows us to play sport as among the most and least important things we do. In honor of Chesterton, we might call this the orthodoxy of the spiritual athlete.

Study Guide

The concept of play has always been a central element of sports through history. However, in recent times as sports have become more professional and commercialized, there has been a loss of the playful dimension of sport. This is, in part, due to the many external rewards on offer to sports people, which often leads to a "win-at-all-costs" culture. This chapter uses the ideas of the Catholic scholar and social commentator G.K. Chesterton to explore the dynamic between play, work, and sport from a religious standpoint and will stimulate you to consider "why" we "love" to play and watch sports.

Study Questions

1. How did playfulness influence you, if at all, in starting to play, and/or watch sport, as a child?
2. What are the differences and/or similarities between play, sport, and work?
3. Discuss examples of sporting experience, observed or your own, in which "deep play" was encountered. What characterized this experience and was it linked to peak performance?
4. In what way does Chesterton's views on play, work, and "furious opposites" inform your understanding of competitive sports?
5. Modern competitive sports, especially professional sports, have largely lost the play ethic and are more like work. Discuss.

Further Reading

Ackerman, D. (1999), *Deep Play*, New York: Vintage Books.

Chesterton, G. K. (1908), *Orthodoxy*, San Francisco: Ignatius Press/John Lane Company.

Kretchmar, R. S. (2011), "Why Dichotomies Make It Difficult to See Games as Gifts of God," in *Theology, Ethics and Transcendence in Sports*, ed. by S. J. Parry, M. S. Nesti, & N. J. Watson, 185–200, London, UK: Routledge.

Acknowledgment

This chapter first appeared in 2018 in *Sport, Ethics and Philosophy*, 12 (1): 70–80, and the entire issue was later converted to an anthology: Kretchmar, R. and Watson, N. (2019), "Chesterton on Play, Work, Paradox, and Christian Orthodoxy," in *Sport and Spirituality*, ed. by S. Kretchmar and J. White, 70–80, London, UK: Routledge. https://doi.org/10.1080/17511321.2017.1291713.

Chapter 3

CREATION, SALVATION, COMPETITION: ELEMENTS IN A CHRISTIAN DOCTRINE OF SPORT

Robert Ellis

Introduction

At first sight, theology and sport may not seem a promising combination. Theology is often understood to treat matters generally considered of considerable weight; sport, on the other hand, seems trivial and ephemeral, a cultural phenomenon that sometimes competes with religion for our attention. However, sport has become an important part of our contemporary world. For some it has become a matter of importance in their lives, while for others it is a source of great pleasure and a sphere in which they report experiencing growth, joy, and deep satisfaction; governments and third-sector organizations deploy sport in projects to improve quality of life and make or mend social and community relationships. If sport is truly trivial and ephemeral, this is a matter of some concern and requires some explanation. How could such activity be considered in any way important, how can it legitimately give pleasure, and why would it be used in community projects if it is merely a diversion or distraction?

Within the Christian tradition some critiques have been offered of sport that continue to demand a hearing—and it is no part of the argument that follows to suggest that sport is always unproblematic and that it cannot be a site of what Christians call "sin." I will argue, though, that to dismiss sport because of its problems is to miss its true theological significance. Every aspect of our world, and certainly all human activity within it, is properly the subject of *theological* enquiry. Theology is concerned to investigate human life in the world—Christian theology believes that every life is "life lived before God" and that therefore every aspect of such lives is open to theological investigation. For instance, we ought properly to ask how any given activity takes its place in God's purposes for humanity as shown in Jesus Christ: do such activities lead to human flourishing, or to a stunting of human life? Are such activities just a distraction, or are they something more sinister?

A further assumption in this chapter is that every human activity and practice already assumes a (usually) implicit theology, that is, a web of beliefs about what it is to be human, the purpose and destiny of human life, and those values and practices which are most important to us. It was the twentieth-century theologian Paul Tillich (1968: 1, 45) who spoke of the need to discover the "theology behind all cultural expressions." Tillich had high culture in mind when he spoke in this way, but his argument works very well for sport, too. Tillich spoke of God as that to which we give our "ultimate concern." It is a commonplace to say that, therefore, everyone has a "god," something to which they give ultimate concern—and many a Christian preacher has labored the point that it is often an idolatrous or false "ultimate." To the extent that we might make sport our "god," then that would indeed be idolatry. But Tillich's argument was very subtle. He understood that very often when we encountered a penultimate concern it might somehow point beyond itself. He spoke of the way in which the "dimension of depth" in our lives might open up through our experience of the penultimate, and that through these experiences we might be brought to an awareness or experience of the ultimate. Tillich had in mind music, poetry, fine art, philosophy, and science, but we might make a similar case for our reading of the Scriptures and for our sharing of the bread and wine at the Eucharist: through these experiences of the penultimate we come to know the ultimate. Can the same be said of sport, at least some of the time?

Common Christian critiques of sport

What we know as our modern sports are, for the most part, comparatively recent developments and are generally the result of a period of refinement and development lasting generations and coming to something approximating their contemporary form during the nineteenth century. Within the space of a few decades a range of traditional games and pastimes became codified into regulated sporting activities. A key engine in this development was the elite school system in England, and within these establishments another decisive change was nurtured: the church gradually came to form a more positive view of sports and embraced them as a medium for developing Christian virtues.

In truth, the church has been historically ambivalent about games and pastimes. The apostle Paul appears to have been relaxed: his use of athletic metaphors probably suggests familiarity with a form of sporting contest that still owes a great deal to the noble Greek tradition—and he may well have practiced his tent-making to support himself during the Isthmian Games in Corinth. However, the Roman games were much more bloody and barbaric and the early church fathers, like Tertullian (*c.* 155–240) and Augustine (354–430), were very critical of Christians who went to the games of their day—effectively trying to forbid attendance. They noticed with disapproval not only what happened on the floor of the arena, where the gory fight for survival brought out the worst in the most noble gladiator, but also how the crowd was transmuted into a mob, beside themselves with a kind of mass hysteria. Eventually the Roman games ceased—though whether because the Christian leadership of the empire saw them as inherently sinful, or because the economic infrastructure that supported the cycle collapsed, is not entirely clear.

Through the middle ages all kinds of games and pastimes were practiced— some clearly military, such as jousting or archery; some appearing to have their roots in ancient fertility rites, such as some traditional forms of football like the Haxey Hood game still re-enacted each year in Lincolnshire, England; others were variations on races and ball games that appear to have been mostly a happy diversion from the seriousness of hard toil and mere survival for the participants. Local churches often sponsored these events, and there is some evidence that sometimes these games were given some quasi-sacred status, as with a French church who incorporated a ball game into its Easter liturgy, or Gloucester Cathedral which has medieval stained glass appearing to show a golfer or hockey player.

After the Reformation the Puritans saw these games as problematic. Their complaints tended to fall into three categories. The first category related to when the games were played and concerned questions of time. Believing that Sundays should be days dedicated to worship, prayer, and other spiritually edifying activities, they felt that participating in games on Sundays was a distraction from more important matters. Alongside this were two closely related concerns. First, *whenever* they were played, such activities tended to distract and divert their players from more productive and proper pursuits. Games sapped energy and attention from the kinds of activities that would feed one's family or save one's soul. Second, apart from Sundays, the main opportunities for such pastimes were the numerous saints' days. For the Puritans these were popish occasions and sullied the games by association.

The second and third categories of Puritan complaints about sports were similar to the criticisms made by the early church fathers. One related to the way playing competitive games impacted upon the players themselves: playing such games had a tendency to bring out the worst in its players. The football of their day, for instance, was described by English Puritan Phillip Stubbes (1555–1610) as "a freendly kind of fight ... a bloody and murthering practice" (Stubbes 1573: no page numbers). There was perhaps a less clear distinction in the sixteenth century between players and spectators in these games and pastimes, but the Puritans also noted the way in which these games had a kind of intoxicating effect. The other kind of complaint noted that "sporting activities" tended to attract and even nurture other, less wholesome, activities as a concomitant. In Rome, the brothels and bars had been close by the stadia, and a millennium and a half later alcohol could still be a problem even at church-sponsored events, and Stubbes and his peers condemned what they saw as lascivious behavior as men and women competed together in some games.

It is tempting to dismiss the Puritan critique of games and pastimes as old-fashioned and narrow. However, it is perhaps also necessary to notice how contemporary these critiques can sound: sports continue to distract us from other matters, to eat up our time and resources; playing or watching sport can make us into unpleasant people if we become obsessed with winning or "our" team;

and one has only to think of some of the problems associated with gambling and match fixing, and unhealthy "macho" behavior on and off the field of play, to see that sports often spawn and nourish bad and harmful behaviors. Even as we try to make a positive case for sport we must take seriously the problems associated with it. To the ones we have noted above we could add several more, no doubt: the way in which modern sports have become a site for consumerism, or the ways in which many of the complex problems of ethnicity and gender in our society are reflected and sometimes exacerbated in sport. How, then, might a positive case for sport be made? We must turn to Christian doctrine, to doctrines of creation and salvation in particular, as we seek to understand the place of sport in God's world and in human living.

Sport and God's created order

Sport is a subset of play. This means that most things that we want to say about play we may also say about sport; it also means that we will want to say extra, more particular, things about sport that may not apply to play in general.

We begin with the creation stories found in Genesis. There is no mention of play or sport here, of course—though perhaps there are clues about human beings (and even about God) as players. Genesis tells us that God created human beings in the "image of God." The Latin term used to translate Genesis 1:27 and deployed in theological discourse ever since is *imago dei*. Theologians and expositors have debated what this term means for centuries, and there remains no unanimity. Interpretations focus on: human rationality or its linked characteristic of language; freedom; openness to God or relationality in general; a reference to the statue of an ancient ruler that would be placed in a colony as symbolic representation of the ruler's power there; a sign of human creativity—in the Genesis narrative, after all, the distinctive activity of God is creating, so that to be made in God's image may involve creating, too.

The correct interpretation may well include several of these dimensions, which are often not mutually exclusive. In particular, notions of rationality, relationality, language, openness, and creativity appear to tessellate with one another, though we may seek a more inclusive concept that gathers all these overlapping notions together. If we consider the experience of play, for example, we can see how all are involved in a distinctive way: playing *creates* "new worlds" (where rules or conventions redefine time and space—as on a football pitch, or even a scrabble board), and this creativity is harnessed by rational engagement and usually relational—while we can play alone, playing is frequently a social and relational experience. Our experience of play is akin to stepping into a kind of parallel created order where other rules and a different sense of time apply. This "parallel world" is one that we have created in play.

Perhaps for this reason sociologist Peter Berger (1971: 70) is able to suggest that play is a "signal of transcendence." By this he means that it is an ordinary, everyday activity (he calls it a "prototypical human gesture") that is not quite fully explained in our ordinary and everyday terms: somehow it points beyond itself to what we might call another dimension of reality. Berger refers in his argument to the work of Dutch cultural historian Johann Huizinga (1920–2008), who had argued that play was the basic formative element in all human culture: play is the way we are. The arguments of Berger and Huizinga, coming as they do from different disciplines, offer an interesting commentary upon, and perhaps confirmation of, the suggestion that play is somehow understood to be part of what it means for human persons to be in the *imago dei*. Shirl Hoffman (2010: 274) thus remarks that "all forms of play are expressions of the same characteristic human response to the world, a response so universal – evident in animals as well as humans – that it is difficult not to believe that it is part of God's design."

Huizinga refers to human beings as *homo ludens*, the hominid who plays. But if the distinctive form of human playing is part of our being made in the *imago dei* we might expect something similar could also be said of God. Here we might consider Proverbs 8:22–31, where the personification of Divine Wisdom appears alongside the Lord at the creation. Translation of the passage is not straightforward, and there are a number of uncertainties. However, a credible translation runs:

> [22]The Lord begot me, the beginning of his works,
> the forerunner of his deeds of long ago;
> When he fixed the foundations of earth …
> [30] … I was his delight day by day,
> playing before him all the while,
> [31]Playing over the whole of his earth,
> having my delight with human beings.
> (New American Bible, Revised Edition)

Here is a Scripture that suggests that creation is made in play, playfully made.

Christian theology has always held that God did not need to create; rather, God did so from an act of gracious gift-like love. That there is something rather than nothing is because God has willed that it be so and made space for creation as his world. Speaking of the world as "God's creation" is usually meant to imply this theological sense in which the world is "unnecessary," and creation in turn is understood as an expression of God's good pleasure and purpose. As Jürgen Moltmann (1926–) suggests, "creation is God's play, a play of groundless and inscrutable wisdom. It is the realm in which God displays his glory." Commenting on this passage in Proverbs, Moltmann (1973: 41) says that "creation has the character of play, which gives God delight and human beings joy."

Moltmann even suggests that human persons may understand their relationship with God through the metaphor of play, and twentieth century scientist-turned-theologian Arthur Peacocke (1979: 111) also suggested that we understand creation as the play of God, with chance being understood as a sign of "the overflow of the divine generosity … displaying the delight and sheer exuberance of play in the unceasing act of creation." Lest all this sound too new-fangled, early church fathers

Gregory Nazianzus (*c.* 329–390) and Maximus the Confessor (*c.* 580–662) also spoke in similar ways of the Divine Logos at play in creation, cajoling and teasing the world into being.

We could look elsewhere in the Scriptures for help in assembling resources for a well-rounded theology of sport, but our prime purpose here is to establish that men and women are, as it were, born players, and that this playing is part of what it means to be created in the *imago dei*. Furthermore, God the Creator too is a player—*homo ludens* is created by and for *Deus ludens*. Our playing seems to be not only a reflection of God's "playing" but could even be considered to be a kind of "connecting" to God, of sharing God's life.

We have so far spoken only about play, and not about sport. It is true that we might have considered some of the apostle Paul's sporting references—they probably constitute the only sporting material in the Bible. While these passages have their theological uses in relation to sport, they do not help us much further in locating sport within the doctrine of creation. This is primarily achieved through thinking of play, of which sport is a subset.

Creation and "fall"

The Western theological tradition has, crudely, considered that God made the world perfect and that it has become broken. The language frequently used is that of a "fall," though with fewer theologians now believing in an historic or literal Adam and Eve such language requires some careful restating. The Genesis account of creation is usually retold as creation-in-perfection followed by a fall from grace into sin and imperfection. The most trenchant critic of sport may believe that sport's very existence is a product and sign of this fall; for others, sport's actuality in our world is "fallen" and problematic, but perhaps no more so than other activities.

Speaking of a "fall" has involved Christian theologians in further debate about the *imago dei*. If human persons are fallen from grace and into sin, is the image of God in human persons damaged, or even destroyed, in them? The tradition has usually opted for a variation on the former: the *imago dei* in human persons is damaged but not destroyed, and human persons remain—at least to a degree—rational, relational, creative, open to God and others, and so on.

Something of a "minority report" in the tradition was put forward by Irenaeus (*c.* 130–202), and his ideas may also help us to consider an alternative perspective on creation and fall. Irenaeus suggested that the "fall" of the Genesis story was more a lapse of immaturity on the part of newly created Adam and Eve, rather than the moral failure of perfect beings. He understood the command of God to Adam and Eve not to eat from the tree of the knowledge of good and evil was given not so much to place a ceiling on human aspiration, but in order to prevent them from attaining to a knowledge for which they were not yet fully prepared. This disobedience described by Irenaeus is the lapse of the immature rather than the overweening pride of the fully formed person. For Irenaeus, to be made in the *imago dei* was not to be made perfect, fully formed, but to be created in potential and incomplete—with room and need to grow. This growth would entail a move toward flourishing—or indeed away from it, into degradation. For Irenaeus, then, the creation narrative suggests not that human persons are made perfect and fall away from that, but that human persons are created in potential and grow toward or away from their calling as God's creatures made in the *imago dei*. Here we might find the more inclusive notion that binds together these various elements of the *imago dei* we have been considering.

The *imago dei* is understood here as the potentiality of maturity and flourishing; of growing, and growing into a relationship with God—or falling away from it. Indeed, in the Eastern tradition, in which readings of the "creation and fall" narrative like the one we find in Irenaeus are more common, salvation is often understood in such terms. Whereas Western thought often conceptualizes salvation in terms of forgiveness or reconciliation, and often uses forensic language to explain its mechanism, Eastern thinkers often speak of salvation as attaining unity with God, or even as "deification." Thus the early Christian writer Theophilus of Antioch (1970, ii/24) claimed that "God gave man an opportunity for progress, so that by growing and becoming mature and furthermore having been declared a god, he might also ascend into heaven." A modern writer summarizes this idea of divinization as follows: "God's aim [for humanity] is to participate in God's life. The earthly life is for growth and development for this eternal communion" (Karkkainen 2004: 21). (This echoes the way some Scripture passages such as 2 Cor 3:18, 1 John 3:2, and 2 Peter 1:4, speak of growth in Christ.)

What have these reflections to do with sport, or play? Whereas the Western tradition emphasizes brokenness through the fall of the perfect human persons, Adam and Eve, the alternative perspective sees this brokenness as the result of human immaturity. Our actions and dispositions can lead either to a deepening of our relationship with God or to a diminishing of it. Either way, the world we live in is substantially broken. The reality of creation's brokenness affects every part of God's world, and every human endeavor and aspiration, every relationship and all human structures. It is impossible that we should consider play and sport to be immune from this. However, we have also suggested that the image of God in human persons is not completely destroyed in creation's brokenness. Human persons remain rational, relational, creative, open to God, and playful. Play and sport need not be wholly degraded or without hope—any more than other dimensions of human life and culture. In fact, we also suggested that it is not necessary to think of the Genesis narrative as depicting a once-for-all fall into the enslavement of sin, but that it could be understood as a failure to grow toward God that need not be endlessly repeated. (This can be tied to a distinctively Christian understanding of the *imago dei*, which reads the Genesis narrative along with New Testament texts such as Philippians 2:6, 2 Corinthians 4:4, and Colossians 1:15, in which Jesus Christ is understood to be the *imago dei*. In a Christological understanding of these texts, the imperfect and immature response to God by Adam is recovered and perfected by Christ.) The bad is here a distortion of the good, and our very openness to God is a sign of the possibility of growth and flourishing and moving (or being moved) toward God—of salvation. The capacity and desire to "surpass" our current state is sometimes called human transcendence, and it is part of who we are as God's creatures.

Sport, competition, salvation

I indicated earlier that sport should be understood as a subset of play. It is different from play in a number of respects, even while it retains its "playful" character—indeed, once it loses this altogether, it ceases not only to be play but also sport, which can only exist as a form of play. Play creates its own world with its own sense of time and place, and in which we are fully absorbed and engaged. Sport adds some other distinctive elements to what we already know as play. Sport bureaucratizes its rules, so that the rules of football (for instance) are the same wherever we play it; sport invariably, in contrast to play, is marked by significant elements of skill that can be refined by practice (it is not all luck!); sport is an embodied activity that involves us in physical and mental exertion—after playing our sport we can feel exhausted through concentration or exercise; finally, and most important for our current purpose, sport is always a contest, it always involves trying to "win"— though sometimes the opponent we are trying to beat is really ourselves, or our best previous performance.

This sense of sport as a contest is important because it gives sport one of its most distinctive playful characteristics—competition. We know that playing a sport without trying to win, or indeed without any chance of winning, can soon become dull. When we feel that we cannot challenge ourselves, or our team cannot challenge their opponents, we lose a lot of the point of playing sport. There are, it is true, many reasons why we play sports. These may include a desire to be fit, to socialize, or to escape from other mundane or pressured activities into the "new world" of playful sport. But most players admit that without competition *in some sense*, sport loses its meaning quickly. Even when competition isn't the main reason why an individual plays soccer or golf, without any sense of competition the activity soon pales.

As will be recalled, competition has also been seen as a problem for many Christian observers of sport. As the church fathers and the Puritans knew, competition can sometimes make us unpleasant people; competition can bring out the worst in us. We can easily think of the most egregious examples: drug cheats, foul tacklers, and more. This has meant that when Christians have thought about sports in general, and competition in particular, they have often done so very negatively. They have understood it in terms of an exploration of sin, rather than as in any way concerned with salvation.

The bad is a distortion of the good, and because competition can sometimes have a harmful impact this does not mean it is always necessarily bad—instead we want to assert that competition is bad only when it becomes a distortion of the good. Competition is, as we have established, an important part of our enjoyment of the games we play. But it is more than mere enjoyment. We can argue that competition makes us and our opponents better players—and that this, in turn, enhances our enjoyment of the games we play. As Stuart Weir (2008: 113) suggests, by tackling our opponent fairly but as hard as we can, we make our opponent the best soccer player they can be. Similarly, when a reporter sympathized with Wimbledon tennis champion Andy Murray for playing in the era of Djokovic, Federer, and Nadal, rather than at another time when he might have won more trophies, Murray retorted that while he might have won more trophies in another era he would not have been such a good player: playing against these great players has made him as good as he is. As is often remarked, the very word "competition" derives from the Latin *com* and *petere,* and so it has the root meaning of "striving together." Competition is, we are perhaps surprised to realize, a fundamentally relational thing (Ellis 2014: 205–206).

Players competing, striving together, against opponents and against themselves constantly strive for better—and even, for the best they can be. This perpetual sporting "reaching out" is a form of the human desire for transcendence, for reaching beyond ourselves. The motto of the modern Olympic movement is another clue here: *citius, altius, fortius* means faster, higher, stronger. The connection between this continual movement toward self-transcendence and the *imago dei* comes into focus here: human beings are made to be creative and relational, to grow in potential and maturity, to reach out to God. Christian theology affirms that God first reaches out to us, and in creating human persons in *imago dei* God makes us to reach out to him, to seek to transcend our current selves. The Christian gospel further affirms that in Jesus Christ we see most clearly how God makes that reaching out possible and effective. Human persons made in the *imago dei* are dynamic creatures of potential, reaching beyond themselves to God. In sport we locate one of the most vivid instances of this creaturely longing. The movement toward self-transcendence seems to be hard-wired into all serious sport: players train hard to enable it; those in the stands wait eagerly for it and then celebrate it.

Two theologians help us to think about this, to conceptualize it more sharply. John Macquarrie (1919–2007) contrasts human persons with other creatures, who have their natures "given" to them, whereas human nature is not a "ready made" and complete thing or collection of characteristics. Instead it is a "potentiality that has to be responsibly actualized, man [*sic*] can either attain to authentic selfhood or miss it, and so fall below the kind of being that can properly be called 'existence' in the fullest sense." This, then, is how human persons are to be distinguished from other creatures—the *imago dei* difference, as it were. Macquarrie (1977: 61–62) says: it is our "very nature to be always transcending or passing beyond any given stage of [our] condition."

The Roman Catholic theologian Karl Rahner (1904–1984) offers an account of humanity that is marked by a similar sense of restless desire seeking self-transcendence. Rahner (2010: 34) roots it in human consciousness, which is marked by questioning and enquiry, and which always points out beyond itself.

Man [*sic*] ... is always still on the way. Every goal that he can point to in knowledge and in action is always relativized, is always a provisional step. Every answer is always just the beginning of a new question. Man experiences himself as infinite possibility because in practice and in theory he necessarily places every sought-after result in question.

Rahner has primarily in mind the human capacity and propensity for self-reflection, for curiosity in the face of reality. But his description seems to cover rather well the core of sporting endeavor with its continual refusal to rest rather than press on to new self-transcendence. Rahner describes this restless desire as a quest to answer the question that our very existence poses to us, a question that only God can answer. Therefore in each restless striving, in the raising of a question in the face of the latest answer, he suggests we are reaching out for God. The answer always lies beyond our reach, but human transcendence, says Rahner, strictly speaking, has God alone as its reference point. It "knows only *God* and nothing else" (2010: 58, italics his) and in turn is enabled by God's reaching down to us in creation (*imago dei*) and redemption (Jesus Christ).

Christian thinkers have often portrayed this human reaching out as a form of sin. However, while we must admit that the good is often distorted into the unhealthy and destructive, it need not be. Indeed, our understanding of what it means to be created in *imago dei* already contains this movement of self-transcendence as a distinctive part of what it means to be a human person living before God. The line between sin and salvation is a narrow one, but sporting competition (which now appears integrally related to what it means to be playful, creative, relational, self-transcending persons in *imago dei*) can be a means toward human flourishing and attaining of potential, not just another way in which we manage to show our darker side.

In speaking in this way we have implicitly raised a question about what we understand salvation to be. It will not be possible to give an exhaustive answer here, but we must give some kind of indication of what we might mean by the term. Christians have often spoken about salvation in an individualistic and other-worldly way: salvation understood to be disembodied, a matter of the soul, and often projected into some future disembodied state post-mortem—described as in heaven, or with God. It is not my purposes to suggest that such language is wrong, but only that it is far too narrow an understanding of salvation.

A doctrine of salvation arising from the good news of Jesus Christ will be richer than either a personal life after death, or a social gospel that focuses entirely upon material circumstances. The Greek word *sozo* found in the Gospels and usually translated "I save" has a very rich range of meanings. As well as "save" (and so, salvation) it can mean "making safe from danger, heal, deliver from evil," and more. Jesus' own ministry includes teaching and actions that convey forgiveness and welcome (Luke 6:37), acts of healing (Matt 12:13), and demonstrations of God's deliverance from evil (Mark 1:25). Jesus' teaching affirms those on the margins (Luke 10:36; 14:21) and calls men and women to live without revenge (Matt 5:39, 41). He has various sorts of contact (Mark 2:15) with those whom others take pains to avoid (Mark 1:41). When Zaccheus responds to Jesus' visit and puts right his own misdeeds, Jesus declares that "*today* salvation has come to this house" (Luke 19:9). Whatever salvation is, it is a far richer reality than we usually suggest, and it certainly cannot be reduced to one's individual spiritual welfare, in this life or after it, however important a part of it that may be. Salvation involves justice, health, right relationships, and freedom from evil forces—it involves human flourishing in many of its guises. In the gospels, salvation often appears embodied. Sport can be a site of human flourishing, through which we continually seek to transcend ourselves. In sport we are, ultimately, reaching out to God—who, as Rahner reminds us, is the ultimate answer to every question, every goal, every reaching beyond ourselves.

Conclusion

We began by asking whether it should concern us that sport, ubiquitous as it is in our contemporary culture, gives so many people great satisfaction, and is widely used as an agent of positive change. If sport is trivial, ephemeral, and essentially flawed as its harshest critics allege, how can this be? Our reflections suggest that there is good reason why sport is both satisfying for participants and a powerful agent for change in places of difficulty and despair. Seen as part of human persons' playful creativity and openness to God and others, to play sport is to do what we are made to do, to be who we are meant to be. Made in the image of God, we are *homo ludens*. Playing, we even suggested, brings us close to the very being of God, who is *Deus ludens*.

We conceded that sport can be, and often is, a site of sin. There is a sense in which all the world is broken, and sport is no exception. But we have also argued that the competitive "reaching out" at the heart of sport should be understood as an instantiation of a God-given desire for self-transcendence. When we strive in sport we are being the persons God made us to be, and ultimately all our striving, all our reaching beyond ourselves for and to be better is a reaching for God.

Sport can be a site of sin but also a site of salvation, then. Salvation has too often been construed in a very narrow way. It should be thought of as something much "larger" and multifaceted—embodied as well as spiritual, encompassing all of that human flourishing that allows us to enrich our lives before God. In salvation we speak of God saving us from brokenness and mending our lives, drawing us into God's presence. In our reaching out in sport, though we may not know it, we are reaching out for this same God who made us in *imago dei*.

Sport is not, and should never be, an ultimate in human life. But (following Tillich) there appear to be good reasons for thinking of it as one of those penultimate concerns that opens up the dimension of depth in our lives, pointing us to the ultimate, to God. The theology behind this cultural expression, behind sport, has been hitherto ignored or misconstrued. But seeing sport in terms of the doctrine of salvation as well as creation begins to set this right.

Study Guide

This chapter invites readers to consider where sports should appear on the map of Christian doctrines. Historically, and often today too, the answer has been to locate sport with the doctrine of sin. Instead, this chapter challenges its readers to consider that an understanding of the Christian belief that human persons are made in the image of God allows us to think of sport as located in the doctrine of creation. Linking competition to the image of God also allows a further step—so that we can think of sport also as being part of the doctrine of salvation. Sport can be sinful; but it need not be, and should not be.

Study Questions

1. Do you agree that sports are an activity in which "the dimension of depth" in our lives can open up and through which we might experience God? Can you think of other such "secular" activities where the same might be said?
2. Are there particular types of "sinful" behavior to which sports players and/or spectators are especially vulnerable?
3. The Puritans were down on sport. Were they right?
4. Do you find the portrayal of human beings as being made for and in play persuasive?
5. Is the connection the writer makes between *imago dei*, sport, and transcendence a fruitful one?
6. Could the human flourishing found in sport be a part of what we mean by salvation?

Further Reading

Ellis, R. (2014), *The Games People Play: Theology, Religion, and Sport*, Eugene, OR: Wipf & Stock.
Hoffman, S. J. (2010), *Good Game: Christianity and the Culture of Sports*, Waco, TX: Baylor University.
Johnston, R. K. (183), *The Christian at Play*, Grand Rapids MI: Eerdmans.

Chapter 4

FLOW, SPORT, AND SPIRITUAL TRADITIONS

Patrick Kelly, SJ

Introduction

I grew up playing sports on Catholic grade school and high school teams and then played American football at a state university. I thoroughly enjoyed playing sports in school and it was in this context that I had some of the most rewarding experiences of my young life. This was also the context in which I made friendships that have lasted up to this day. On the other hand, I also had several negative experiences and disappointments along the way, including injuries at crucial moments.

When I was in college I began to take my Catholic faith seriously in a new way and became very interested in growing in my faith. After I had finished college I had a tendency to think that I should put sport behind me and focus on my "spiritual life." Now that I had become a man I thought I should "put aside childish things" (1 Cor. 13:11), as St. Paul says. I discovered over time that this did not work, however. I think now that this is because I was too profoundly formed as a young person by my participation in sport, both for good and for ill. And the human formation that took place in the context of sport was influencing my attempts to live the Christian life.

I eventually began to reflect on my experiences in sports and consider in what ways they were life-giving and had led to my growth as a person and possibly even had spiritual significance. On the other hand, I also began to consider in what ways my experiences had led to personal diminishment and to modes of thinking and being that impeded my attempts to live out my Christian faith. Eventually, I began to consider these questions more broadly in an academic way, with the help especially of the discipline of psychology.

The flow theory of psychologist Mihaly Csikszentmihalyi (1975a, b, 1988, 1990) is one of the most important resources I have come across for considering these questions. This theory provides a persuasive account of why sports are enjoyable and how they can lead to human well-being and growth. Additionally, the way that people describe the dynamics of the flow experience is analogous to the way that many spiritual writers have described the dynamics of the spiritual life over the centuries. For some years now, I have been teaching and writing about experiences of flow in sports and their significance from the point of view of Christian spirituality. More recently, my teaching and research interests have broadened to include other religious traditions. In this chapter, I bring the experiences of flow into dialogue with experiences and insights from Christian, Confucian, Taoist, and Zen Buddhist traditions.

While there might be different terminology (or even understandings of terms when the same terms are used), there is agreement across these religious traditions that what persons experience bodily impacts them at the level of consciousness and spirit. Christians have traditionally insisted on the unity of the person—body, soul, and spirit—and the importance of the body in spiritual practices, against groups such as the Gnostics, Manicheans, Cathars, and others (Kelly 2012). Persons in Confucian, Taoist, and Zen Buddhist traditions have historically understood body and mind as inseparable and viewed embodied practices as related to transformation of consciousness and spiritual growth (Yasuo 1987; Slingerland 2014). In emphasizing the unity of the person, these traditions provide an alternative way of understanding the human person from the dualism that Rene Descartes bequeathed to the modern West. This dualism not only separated body and soul (which Descartes tended to equate with mind) but also omitted entirely the "spirit" as a dimension of the human person.

Flow theory

There are many reasons to use flow theory for the purposes of this discussion. For one thing, Csikszentmihalyi's initial research (1975a, b) was about play, and he considered sport under this heading. Indeed, the study of people's experiences participating in different sports was crucial in the development of the flow theory itself. In addition, flow theory provides us with a way of understanding human experience that is situated in what we know to be true about the world more generally in our contemporary context. Most important in this respect is that the flow theory is situated in an evolutionary understanding of the world. Flow theory is also helpful because it is based on research that has been carried out in many different cultural and religious contexts. Finally, as I mentioned earlier, the way people describe the dynamics of the flow experience is analogous to the way spiritual writers have described the dynamics of the spiritual life. Csikszentmihalyi (1975b: 37) recognized these similarities early in his research, as he wrote in his first book:

> Besides play and creativity, experiences analogous to flow have been reported in contexts usually called "transcendental" or "religious." Maslow's peak experiences and De Charm's "origin" states share many distinctive features with the flow process. The same is true of accounts of collective ritual; of the practice of Zen, Yoga, and other forms of meditation; or of practically any other form of religious experience.

In the late 1960s, Csikszentmihalyi wrote his doctoral dissertation at the University of Chicago about the creative process in artists. For his research he studied painters who had immersed themselves in their craft over many years, and yet who had little expectation that their paintings would bring them much money or recognition. He was intrigued by the fact that these painters were completely absorbed in what they were doing and enjoyed discussing its subtleties and nuances even though they were not likely to become rich or famous as a result of it. According to Csikszentmihalyi (1975b: 7–10), the mainstream psychological approaches of the time such as behaviorism or psychoanalysis did not have a way to adequately explain the experiences he was observing in the painters.

He came to the conclusion that mainstream psychology did not have a way to understand *enjoyment*. To better understand this phenomenon, Csikszentmihalyi and his researchers studied people who were involved in autotelic activities. The word "autotelic" comes from the two Greek words *auto* = self and *telos* = goal, indicating that an activity has its purpose within itself. In terms of motivation, people participate in such activities for their own sake rather than for extrinsic rewards. One composer whom Csikszentmihalyi (1975a: 54–55) interviewed expressed this autotelic mentality as follows:

> One doesn't do it for the money … This is what I tell my students. Don't expect to make money, don't expect fame or a pat on the back, don't expect a damn thing. Do it because you love it.

Based on the way that people he interviewed described their experiences, Csikszentmihalyi made a distinction between pleasure and enjoyment. For him, pleasure is an important part of the quality of life, but by itself does not bring happiness. The taste of food when we are hungry is pleasurable because it reduces a physiological imbalance. Resting in the evening after a long day at work by passively watching television with a beer can be pleasantly relaxing. Pleasurable activities such as these do not require much attention or personal investment on our part, however. And they usually would not come to mind if we were asked to name the most rewarding experiences of our lives or times of significant personal growth.

People say they experience enjoyment, on the other hand, when they give their full attention to an activity and go beyond where they were previously in some domain. "Playing a close game of tennis that stretches one's ability is enjoyable," Csikszentmihalyi (1990: 46) writes, "as is reading a book that reveals things in a new light, as is having a conversation that leads us to express ideas we didn't know we had." After such activities, people often find themselves saying: "That was fun," or "That was enjoyable." Such activities are also related to psychological growth as they add complexity to the self.

Because flow experiences are characterized by this kind of forward movement, activities that are conducive to flow are usually challenging activities that require skills. However, there needs to be a balance between the level of challenge and the person's own skill level (or at least their perception of their skill level). If the activity is too challenging, the person will feel overwhelmed and anxious. On the other hand, if the activity is too easy, the person will feel bored and uninterested. Flow is experienced when the challenge is at the growing edge of a person's skill level.

Another characteristic of flow activities is that they have clear goals and provide immediate feedback. The person knows what they are expected to do and because they receive immediate feedback they know if they are achieving what they set out to do or not. Of course, in sports the goals are clearly defined. And coaches often play an important role in providing feedback as individual players and teams develop the skills needed to reach their goals.

Flow is not an absolute good. Just because a person or persons are experiencing flow, this does not tell us everything we need to know about the significance of an activity. It is possible, for example, to experience flow while participating in sports where long-term damage to the health of participants is possible or even likely. A broader ethical analysis is sometimes required, then, to determine whether participation in a given sport leads to the genuine good of participants.

In other cases, a person might spend too much time on an activity during which they experience flow to the neglect of other activities that their situation in life requires they pay attention to. With regard to youth sports, this can be an issue when high school students devote almost all of their attention to sport—usually because they think they have a future in elite-level sport—to the neglect of their academic studies. Since so few young people actually earn a full college scholarship for sports or play at the professional level, this ends up leaving many ill-equipped for the realities of their lives after school.

Elements of the flow experience

Centering of attention

During a flow experience the person centers their attention on a limited stimulus field. They are completely immersed in the activity and not distracted by other concerns. Participation in sports often requires this kind of concentration. As Former San Francisco 49er quarterback John Brodie puts it:

> A player's effectiveness is directly related to his ability to be right there, doing that thing, in the moment ... He can't be worrying about the past or the future or the crowd or some extraneous event. He must be able to respond in the here and now. (Cited in Murphy and White 1995: 22)

Another way to say this is that the person experiences a "merging of action and awareness" (Csikszentmihalyi 1990: 53–54) as what he is doing and what he is thinking about are one and the same thing.

The reader will likely recognize the similarities between this element of flow and what Buddhists call mindfulness. Mindfulness is fostered in Buddhist traditions by meditation practices. But in all religious traditions, meditation helps us to live in the present moment with greater freedom. Regardless of what religious tradition we belong to (or if we are unaffiliated with religion) as we step off the treadmill of daily life and sit in silence, we start to become aware of thoughts and feelings that we may have been unaware of previously. Let us say, for example, that I am meditating in the morning and have a presentation to make later that day. It could be that during the meditation I notice that my mind is racing regarding the presentation. As I sit longer, I become aware that underneath my racing thoughts is the emotion of fear. This may be unsettling initially, but actually it is a positive development, because now that I am aware of my fear I at least have the opportunity to let it go, along with the thoughts it gives rise to. If I am able to let these go, I can more easily be in the present moment and calmly concentrate on preparing and giving the presentation. In this way meditation practices add something distinctive that functions in a complementary way in relation to flow. They help the person to become aware of unconscious factors which might be impeding their ability to concentrate and be in the present moment.

When material rewards and money are attached to success in an endeavor, it can become more difficult to center one's attention. Four centuries before Jesus lived, the Taoist poet Chuang Tzu wrote about this dynamic in his poem "The Archer":

> When an archer is shooting for nothing
> He has all his skill.
> If he shoots for a brass buckle
> He is already nervous.
> If he shoots for a prize of gold
> He goes blind
> Or sees two targets –
> He is out of his mind!
>
> His skill has not changed. But the prize
> Divides him. He cares.
> He thinks more of winning
> Than of shooting –
> And the need to win
> Drains him of power.

(Cited in Merton 1965: 107)

Notice that the problem here is that the archer "sees two targets." When he is shooting for nothing (for its own sake) he has all the skill he needs to hit the target regularly. But once the brass buckle and prize of gold are introduced as rewards, his attention is divided. He cares now and is thinking more of winning than of shooting. Ironically, because he is so focused on winning (outcome), he is pulled out of the very process he needs to be in, in order to shoot well enough to win. The need to win drains him of power.

This dynamic is easy enough to understand from our own experience of playing or watching sports. When a professional football kicker can win a tie game in the final seconds by kicking a medium-range field goal, the opposing team will usually call a time out if they have one available. They do so to give the kicker some time to think about everything that is at stake for him and his teammates with regard to the field goal, especially in terms of money and prestige. They want him to see "two targets." If he begins thinking about such things, they hope he will feel more pressure to make the field goal. Then he will not be able to be in the present moment and do what it is he has the skill to do when he is practicing on his own during the week.

Egolessness

Because all of our attention is focused on what we are doing during a flow experience, we do not have attention available to also be explicitly focused on ourselves. Consider the experience of a high school girl dribbling a basketball up the court in the final seconds of a tie game. She has a lot on her mind. In addition to other things, she has to be aware of the defense the other team is playing, whether her coach has called a particular play, who has been shooting well on her team, and how much time is left on the clock. She also has to be able to adjust to the fast-changing environment on the spot. She will not be able to play well in these crucial closing seconds of the game and at the same time be wondering whether she should be doing things in this way or whether she will be popular if they win. That is, she cannot be thinking explicitly about *herself*.

After the activity is over the person does have attention available to reflect on herself, however. If she has experienced flow, she will have a richer sense of herself than she did before the activity. Often after a flow experience people describe being more aware of their own talents or gifts, and how they are connected to the world around them. According to Csikszentmihalyi, there is a relationship between the self-forgetfulness we experience when deeply immersed in an activity and our growth as persons. As he puts it:

> When not preoccupied with ourselves, we actually have a chance to expand the concept of who we are. Loss of self-consciousness can lead to self-transcendence, to a feeling that the boundaries of our being have been pushed forward. (1990: 64)

I spent my first year after ordination as a Jesuit priest in a parish in Detroit, Michigan. I was thoroughly enjoying being a priest and was experiencing some of the elements of flow I am describing. I enjoyed celebrating the liturgy and preaching, in particular. I enjoyed the challenge of trying to say something meaningful to the community in light of the readings for the week. During my prayer in preparation for the liturgy I would try to let go of any distractions and center my attention on God and what the readings had to say to our community, given its particular consolations and challenges. One Sunday, Ben, my friend and companion from the Jesuit novitiate, came to visit from London and was at the liturgy. I noticed that while I was preaching my focus began to shift so that I was thinking: I wonder what Ben thinks of my homily? Is he impressed with the depth of my theological insights? Readers who have done any public speaking will recognize that this was not a positive development. From the perspective of the flow theory, this is because my attention shifted from God, the community, and the scriptures explicitly to *myself*.

According to Catholic spiritual writer Beatrice Bruteau (2004: 97), when we make our eye "single," attending only to God, self-consciousness lessens. Indeed, when we are experiencing God's grace working through us in the course of our everyday life "we are scarcely aware of ourselves as the ones who are doing." She continues:

> We do not reflect upon ourselves in order to observe that we are leaving ourselves open to God's work and that such and so is taking place through us. We simply open ourselves and let our whole awareness be of God's life in and through us to whatever the work or expression of divine beauty and goodness is ... The more we can make our eye "single" in this way and not let it divide into a double consciousness – partly on God's act of living and working through us, and partly a reflection on how well we're doing – the more our whole being, like the crystal, will be filled with the divine light. In this way we gradually come to renounce our most fundamental habits of self-consciousness.

Union with one's surroundings

Another element of the flow experience is a sense of union with one's surroundings. The way that this is experienced will be different depending on the activity that one is involved in. In some cases, it might be a sense of union with the objects one is using in the activity, such as a golf club, tennis racket, or baseball. If the person is mountain climbing she might report a sense of union with the natural environment. In team sports, the way this is often described is as a sense of union or "bond" with the other members of the team. This kind of union happens in team sports because in order to accomplish their goals, the members of the team have to learn to rely on one another and work together very closely.

According to former NBA basketball coach Phil Jackson (and Delehanty 1995: 51–54), Zen and Christianity intersect with respect to love and compassion. As he matured in his Zen meditation practice, he said that he came to understand that love is the force that ignites the spirit and that the compassion the Chicago Bulls players had for one another was crucial to their success as a team. He tells the story of Chicago Bulls forward Scottie Pippen, whose father had died in the middle of a playoff series. Jackson had the team gather before a game in a circle around Pippen and pray the Our Father together as an expression of their love and compassion for him. Pippen scored 29 points that night. But in the championship series, just before the final game, Pippen came down with migraine headaches that gave him double vision. Some members of the press blamed him for the team's heartbreaking defeat. Jackson said that he was as disappointed by the loss as anyone, but he "defended Scottie because I knew his suffering was real" (Jackson 1995: 54). The players were deeply moved by Jackson's support for Pippen and rallied behind him. According to Jackson, that spirit of compassion was the foundation of the team's ability to play so well together in the future.

In the Christian tradition, we too often forget that God is love and indeed, is triune or a community of persons. In this sense, relationship is central to who God is. If we are made in the image and likeness of God, then we too are made for relationship and union with one another. As Beatrice Bruteau (2004: 115) puts it:

> If the Trinitarian paradigm should be correct, then our own core reality, presently overlaid by the selfishness of superficial consciousness, is already a mutual indwelling in all our neighbors. The mystics of all traditions have always affirmed that in the ultimate view we are all one: somehow each one's reality and highest good are intimately connected to each other one's reality and good.

Effortlessness

Another element of the flow experience is effortlessness. The effortlessness that is experienced during flow is usually preceded by discipline. This makes a lot of sense when it comes to sports. Think of a sixth-grade boy who is right-handed and wants to learn how to shoot a left-handed layup in basketball. He needs to keep thinking about his coach's instructions regarding what foot to jump off of, how to extend his left hand, and other matters. He needs to practice the shot over an extended period of time. At first it probably feels awkward. And it will take some time before he is able to make the shot regularly. When he has developed the skills after much attention and practice, however, he will be able to shoot the left-handed layup in way that is effortless and graceful. It may look as though he has been doing it his whole life. This notion of effortlessness connects with spiritual consolation and wu-wei, to which we now turn.

Flow and the rest of life: Spiritual consolation and Wu-Wei

One of the reasons I was first interested in flow theory was because of analogies I saw between the way people described the flow experience and the way Ignatius of Loyola described spiritual consolation. Ignatius has in mind when he uses the term "spiritual consolation," the experience of a person who is trying to go from "good to better" in the Christian life, that is, someone who wants to grow or make progress. This does not mean that the person is perfect; from a Christian perspective, we are all sinners after all. But the basic orientation of the person's life is toward wanting to follow Christ more closely and to respond generously to God's call. According to Ignatius, it is characteristic for such a person to experience God's presence in the form of spiritual consolation. Of course, consolation itself needs to be discerned, as there can be "false consolation" as well. But that is a topic for another time. In this section I am referring to genuine spiritual consolation.

One of the characteristics of the experience of spiritual consolation is "genuine happiness and spiritual joy" (Ganss 1991: 205). We tend to forget that joy is central in the Christian life. The kingdom of heaven is something that people are committed to "out of joy" as Jesus says in the parable of the treasure buried in a field (Matt 13:44). Near the end of his life, Jesus tells his disciples that as the Father has loved him, so he loves them and to remain in his love. He tells them these things, he says, "so that my joy may be in you and your joy complete" (John 15:11). Even suffering and death cannot extinguish this joy. Jesus tells the disciples that although they will grieve because of his death, he will see them again and their hearts will rejoice and "no one will take your joy away from you" (John 16:22).

The experience of spiritual consolation is also effortless. As Ignatius puts it, the experience is "gentle and easy, like water falling into a sponge" or like "coming into one's own house through an open door" (Ganss 1991: 207). It feels like obstacles are being removed so the person can move forward in doing good. But this effortlessness is usually preceded by disciplined attention and practice. The retreat that Ignatius is famous for is called the Spiritual *Exercises*, after all. During the retreat the person spends a lot of time "considering" and "reflecting" on his life, doing imaginative prayer with the gospel accounts of the life of Christ, and engaging in other prayer exercises. These exercises are intended to free the person from attachments so that they are able to experience God's love and respond to the leading and promptings of the Spirit. As was mentioned, these promptings will be experienced as gentle and easy. There will be a sense of "coming home" to oneself and one's place in the world. From a theological perspective, the reason for this is that the spirit of the person and the Holy Spirit are moving in the same direction, so there is a "syncing" up or matching.

When a person is experiencing spiritual consolation, they are very much aware of God's presence and usually have a lot of energy and ideas about how to help others. They are not focused upon themselves. In this sense, the experience is egoless. For Ignatius, such egolessness is crucial in the spiritual life. As he put it in his *Spiritual Exercises*: "For everyone ought to reflect that in all spiritual matters, the more one divests oneself of self-love, self-will and self-interests, the more progress one will make" (Ganss 1991: 80).

For Ignatius, one's major decisions should be made in relation to and building upon experiences of spiritual consolation. This makes sense, given that during such experiences the person is experiencing in a concrete way God's leading and guidance in their life. It is important to highlight that spiritual consolation, which can be experienced during times of prayer, will also be experienced in the activities of daily life—while teaching, writing, attending to a patient in the hospital, doing scientific research and in other activities. In fact, experiences of spiritual consolation in such activities of daily life are an important way a person knows they are in the kind of working God is calling them to.

There are also analogies between flow and the notion of "wu-wei" in Confucian, Taoist, and Zen Buddhist traditions. According to Edward Slingerland (2014: 7), wu-wei is "a dynamic, effortless and unselfconscious state of mind of a person who is optimally active and effective." Of course, at the head of these three traditions stands Confucius, whose life was thought by his followers to exemplify wu-wei. When a local ruler asked Confucius' disciple Zilu about him, Confucius said "Why not just say something like this?":

> He is the type of person who becomes so absorbed in his studies that he forgets to eat, whose joy renders him free of worries, and who grows old without being aware of the passage of years. (Slingerland 2003: 61)

The elements of flow are very evident in Confucius' self-description. He is joyful and is not distracted by worries, which is what allows him to be so absorbed in what he is doing that he forgets to eat. And time passes by without his noticing it.

Many of the stories that the Taoist poet Chuang Tzu tells provide us with examples of people who exemplify wu-wei. In his poem "The Woodcarver," he tells the story of a woodcarver who was asked how he created such a beautiful bell stand. The poem is the woodcarver's reply:

> When I am getting ready to make a bell stand, the most important thing is not to exhaust my energy [qi], so first I fast in order to still my mind. After I have fasted for three days, concerns about congratulations or praise, titles or stipends no longer trouble my mind. After five days, thoughts of blame or acclaim, skill or clumsiness have also left my mind. Finally, after fasting for seven days, I am so completely still that I forget that I have four limbs and a body. There is no more ruler or court. My skill is concentrated and all outside distractions disappear. Now I set off for the mountain to observe, one by one, the Heavenly nature of the trees. If I come across a tree of perfect shape and form, then I am able to see the completed bell stand already in it: all I have to do is apply my hand to the job and it's done. If a particular tree does not call to me, I simply move on. All that I am doing is allowing the Heavenly within me to match with the Heavenly in the world—that is probably why people mistake my art for the work of the spirits! (Slingerland 2014: 22)

Fasting is a common practice of the religious traditions of the world. Notice here that the woodcarver is fasting especially from praise, titles, money, and concern about how others will regard his work. Because his skill is entirely concentrated on what he is doing, he doesn't have attention available to also be aware of himself ("I forget that I have four limbs and a body"). The ease with which he seems to do the work has to do with his being in sync with "the Heavenly," which is present in his own life and in the world.

Indeed, wu-wei in Confucian and Taoist traditions (and Zen) have to do with the person being in right relationship with Heaven. Slingerland points out that Heaven in these traditions does not refer to a place or even to the existential reality of being in the presence of a deity. In the way Chuang Tzu is using the term, Heaven refers to the high god who is the source of all value or goodness. The Way (Dao) has various meanings, but one of them is the right way to live, faithfully doing the will of Heaven. According to Slingerland (2014: 42), "Wu-wei is fundamentally linked to Heaven. Wu-wei works because to be wu-wei means that you are following the

Heavenly Way ... Wu-wei means becoming part of something larger: the cosmic order represented by the Way."

Conclusion

Mihaly Csikszentmihalyi recognized very early in his research that flow experiences are analogous to religious and spiritual experiences. In this chapter, I have brought flow experiences in sport into dialogue with experiences and insights from some of the religious traditions of the world. The religious traditions considered have in common the view that when we are not attached to external goods such as riches and fame and can let go of egocentric concerns we are able to live in right relationship with the transcendent source, with other people and the world in general. There are many ways in which the resources of the religious traditions of the world complement what we have learned from research on the flow experience. Both meditation and fasting are practices that free the person of attachments to riches and fame and egocentric concerns and help them to be in the present moment and concentrate on what they are doing. The emphasis on love and compassion in the religious traditions complements the notion of union with one's surroundings and adds depth and richness because of its personal character. The religious traditions also highlight the importance of being in right relationship to the transcendent, understood either as God or Heaven, in order for people to experience life as "flowing."

Study Guide

A helpful way for students to learn about the flow theory is to write a short paper describing an experience they have had of flow and how the elements mentioned in the article were present in their experience. Students can learn to apply what they know about flow theory in a practical setting by developing a practice plan for a youth sports team with young people of a certain age and skill level. It is also important for students to understand how flow theory provides us with new insights into the dynamics of the Christian life and opens up the possibility for dialogue with other religious traditions.

Study Questions

1. Describe an experience you have had of flow while participating in sports or other activities. Mention explicitly at least three of the elements of flow discussed in the article.

2. How would you coach a youth sports team so that they would enjoy playing and be likely to experience flow? Develop a practice plan that incorporates some of your ideas.
3. What did you learn from the Christian reflections in this chapter about sports and spirituality?
4. What did you learn from the Confucian, Taoist, or Buddhist traditions about sports and spirituality while reading this chapter?
5. Is it important for Christians to engage in interreligious dialogue with members of other religions? Why or why not?

Further Reading

Csikszentmihalyi, M. (1990), *FLOW: The Psychology of Optimal Experience*, New York: Harper and Row.

Ganss, G. (ed) (1991), *Ignatius of Loyola: The Spiritual Exercises and Selected Works*, New York: Paulist Press.

Kelly, P. (2012), *Catholic Perspectives on Sports: From Medieval to Modern Times*, Mahwah, NJ: Paulist Press.

Chapter 5

HISTORICAL RELATIONSHIP BETWEEN SPORT AND CHRISTIANITY

Andrew R. Meyer

Introduction

Over the centuries, sport and Christianity have operated as two highly influential and important cultural forces. From St. Paul's use of sporting imagery in the New Testament, to the Puritans' negative association of games and sport with sinful behaviors, through to today's use of athletes as evangelical icons, sport and Christianity have been associated in a variety of different ways. Yet by the nineteenth century, the blending of British Victorian ideals with the emerging Olympic and physical health movements created a justifiable Christian usefulness for sport in the modern world. This chapter discusses the relationship between sport and Christianity over time, introducing readers to the ways in which Christianity has variously viewed sporting pursuit through the ages. In doing so, it explores how these changing relations provide a vehicle through which we might better understand and analyze how sport and Christianity interact today.

At the outset, it is important to know that sport has not always been a global or commercialized or professionalized phenomenon. Meanwhile, although Christianity has changed and developed as a world religion over time, its ethos and core messages have remained consistent for two millennia. We must appreciate that modern-day sport is the product of a long and intricate process of social construction which has served to create and shape popular sporting practice at the local, national, and international levels (Guttman 1978).

Evidence of the social significance of sport is common place. For example, the now-extinct Mesoamerican ball games included practices of human sacrifice because of the game's connection with religious ritual (Wittington 2001). In turn, the ancient Olympic Games were contested by nude male athletes, reflecting their delight in the physical body (Sansone 1988). Moreover, lacrosse, a stickball game of indigenous North American peoples, was culturally appropriated by Ivy League universities in New England (McCulney 1974). Our experience of modern sporting forms is no different.

Yet, how is it that a frivolous physical and entertaining activity like sport has even become an academic subject worthy of consideration alongside a major world religion like Christianity? Can these cultural activities, with such widely different objectives, be understood to have any meaningful relationship? Much has been written in recent years about the sport–Christianity relationship. Some religious scholars have suggested that any comparisons between sport and religion (particularly Christianity) are faulty from the outset because of the fact that as cultural entities they share relatively little in common. Sport is a cultural activity that is good for health, entertainment, and cultural expression; Christianity is a general belief system and world view from which its advocates derive explanations of the meaning of life and find moral codes for living a purposeful existence. However, McClelland (2009) suggests that discounting the vitally important part that sport has played in Christianity over the past two thousand years runs the risk of dismissing the role it has had in promoting the Christian faith throughout its history. From the outset, Christianity has had a relationship with sport (Watson and Parker 2013). Indeed, in every culture Christianity has flourished, it has had to face the presence and popularity of sport.

Thus, to consider this relationship in any depth also requires an exploration of what sport is and how it has changed over time. For instance, when discussing sport during the initial centuries of Christianity in the Roman Empire, "games" (*ludic*) referred to theatrical performances while the concept "circus games" (*circenses*) referred to chariot races (Lee 2000: 151). During the Middle Ages, the term "sport" referred to uncodified games played by commoners and nobility alike, such as by AD 1500 two versions of golf were in existence: one for commoners (deemed lowly) and a higher form of the game enjoyed only by nobility (Hamilton 1998). Of course, there were codified tournaments of the Middle Ages, replete with jousting and suits of armor, familiar to us through the Legend of King Arthur and his knights. By the late nineteenth century, sport had adopted a much more codified form with rules and governing structures as we know them today. For the purposes of this chapter, I consider "sport" to equate to activities of physical competition.

Sport, Jesus, and St. Paul

Historically speaking, Jesus of Nazareth's preaching about the arrival of the Kingdom of God and his messiahship was seen as a disruption and challenge to the power of the ruling Jewish priestly class. In fact, it is well known that during the life of Jesus, there were many men who likewise lived in Judea claiming to be the messiah for God's People (Aslan 2013). This savior was expected to be a sovereign, perhaps like King David, who would save the Israelites from the clutches of the Roman Empire and fulfil God's promises to the chosen people. But Jesus was not a worldly ruler or someone of great status. Instead, he was the son of a carpenter who eventually hung from a cross as a salvific sign of God's power and wisdom (1 Cor 1:23). Because, as St. Paul declares, "the foolishness of God is wiser than human wisdom" (v. 25), many Jewish authorities rejected Jesus' message. Hence, most early Christian converts were non-Jewish (Gentiles).

Jesus lived during the Roman occupation of Judea, which was roughly between BC 63 and AD 313, and more specifically during a period of political and social unrest between Roman occupiers, ruling wealthy Jews and Jewish priests, and poorer Israelites. As a young man, Jesus lived in Nazareth, a small village a few kilometers from the thriving cosmopolitan center of Sepphoris. This city was itself a burgeoning hub, heavily traveled by people of diverse ethnicities and religions. It is likely that Jesus experienced the diversity of Sepphoris, and would have been familiar, not only with the political and social perspectives of his day, but also with a range of popular cultural activities, such as Roman theater and sport. While there is no record of Jesus experiencing, or directly mentioning, leisure activities (i.e., sport or games), sporting metaphors are clearly used by the first-century preacher of Jesus' message and primary author of the New Testament, Saul of Tarsus, better known as St. Paul.

Paul's use of sporting metaphors suggests his knowledge of his intended audience. Scholars have pointed to the fact that Paul used sport, and sporting terms, to connect the teaching and message of early Christianity to those listeners who might be drawn to it—particularly the Gentiles in Palestine and, more specifically, the Romans. In addition, the geographical location of Palestine was at a crossroads of commerce and culture, allowing early Christians to evangelize travelers and tradesmen who then spread their message throughout the Roman Empire. Paul, and other early disciples, understood the importance of connecting the message of Jesus to the everyday experiences of potential converts, which included sport. Because the early Church believed that Jesus was the Christ, God's anointed, who came to earth to reveal God's love and save humanity from sin (John 3:16), they preached about a man who actually was easy to identify with: this Son of God walked the earth, shared meals with friends, and washed others' feet as a sign of service. As an ordinary man, Jesus was relatable those around him. The use of sporting metaphors by Paul made Jesus' message even more attractive, connecting well-known experiences of sport with this new concept of God's Son among us (i.e., the incarnation).

Early Christians, like the Jewish population from which they emerged, were governed by the Roman Empire. Because of this, Roman social practices, including competitive games, would have been known to the early Christians. While many of us today are familiar with the sporting practices of the ancient Greeks (i.e., the Olympic Games), Roman expressions of sport were significantly different. It is commonly held that the ancient Olympic Games were contests between individual athletes that had emerged during ritualistic religious festivals to demonstrate the nearly divine-like abilities of competitors. On the other hand, Roman sports, especially by the time of Jesus, were events for the masses, held in stadiums for spectacle. Here, slaves and prisoners were pitted against trained athlete executioners (gladiators) for the entertainment of spectators. While the Greek Olympics occurred as they had for centuries before and during Jesus' life, it was the Roman sporting spectacles that would have been most popular when first-century Christians began to evangelize. It is interesting to note that the Olympic Games continued nearly 400 years after the crucifixion of Christ and ended when Theodosius I, a Christian Roman emperor, outlawed pagan practices throughout the Empire, which included the Olympic Games (Lee 2000).

The social importance of sport and games in the Roman Empire, from which Christianity emerged, is well documented. Grand stadiums were built as spaces for gladiatorial contests, reenactments of famous battles, and as central gathering places during Roman festivals and pagan religious events. Roman sports also demonstrated their usefulness as socializing events, a purpose that included aspects of punishment, entertainment, and collective national identity. This was clearly different from the religious focus of the Olympics. Roman sporting displays were also used for political purposes where the power and dominance of the Roman Empire were on full display. Slaves, prisoners, and gladiators fought to the death in front of thousands of civilians. These spectacles demonstrated to the masses what would happen to any individual or peoples that opposed the political might of the Rome. Such events were more about public execution and the demonstration of military strength than anything else. The notion that sports represented some kind of sacrificial homage to the gods or exhibitions of excellence was not present in Roman world of Jesus' day.

These sporting spectacles also served as a socializing process, often for conquered peoples far away from Rome itself. As these festivals often reenacted Roman military victories, they served as educational events and reminders of the Empire's collective history, reinforcing the mores and values of the dominant culture. These Roman sporting events cultivated a social history and appreciation for the glories of the empire, and in doing so broadcasted socially important ideals that reinforced Roman identity on conquered peoples. This would have been the sporting landscape that Jesus and his followers experienced during the first decades of Christianity.

Paul's use of sporting analogy in the New Testament (see, e.g., 2 Timothy 4:7; Corinthians 9:24–27; Philippians 1:27–30 and 3:12–14) reveals how he understood the necessity of using well-known social experiences as metaphors of Christianity's unique message, to not seem as outlandish to potential converts. Pfitzner (2014: 93) states that Paul's references to sport were particularly significant because sport was a universal activity through which the Christian messages of faith, perseverance, and discipline could be articulated. The early followers of Jesus targeted mainly non-Jews in the region, and thus non-biblical populations. These potential converts were either Pagan Romans or travelers with no knowledge of Jewish theology. Therefore, using Old Testament biblical messages and examples would not have been effective preaching method. Sport, however, would have been a much more universal vehicle through which to propagate the Christian message.

The early years of the faith were not easy times for Christians, persecuted as they were by both many Jewish Pharisees and Roman leaders. As such, the sporting metaphors served a secondary purpose which aimed to articulate the kind of faith required by the early Christians. For example, when Paul uses the term *running*, he is describing a universal physical activity which conjures up notions of increased effort and speed, coupled with focus and determined purpose. In addition to simply describing the act of running, Paul uses this metaphor to describe something of the very nature of Christian life (Brandl 2006). Like the *Suffering Servant* in Deutero-Isaiah of the Old Testament, Paul sees the focus and determination of the runner as commensurate with that which the Christian will need in keeping the faith during this time of persecution. In addition to the running, "the 'crown' of which Paul speaks, continues the Old Testament and early Jewish motif of the reward that awaits the righteous who suffer for pursuing God's will and wisdom" (Pfitzner 2014: 100). Here the crown depicts for early converts not only an understanding of the effort and determination of their own conversion, but also an appreciation of the "prize" at the end of that struggle. Paul's use of sporting and athletic metaphors as a means of speaking to potential converts was a useful and effective way to convey not only what their faith journey might look like, but also the ultimate meaning of their new life in Christ.

In the wake of its initial growth, early Christianity struggled for legitimacy alongside Roman paganism. Rome's first Christian Emperor, Constantine, who converted on his deathbed in AD 337, ushered in the slow demise and eradication of pagan rituals and practices (including sporting activities). At this time, pagan religions were understood to be "incompatible with correct Christian behaviors and practice" (Rizzi 2009: 41). In AD 476, the last Roman Emperor was defeated and the realm split into two halves: the Byzantine Empire to the east and the fragmented western region of Europe. Sporting venues in the west fell into disrepair and little record remains of sport-related activity following this collapse. While the disarray and struggle for survival dominated people's lives over the next few centuries, sporting activities would emerge, establishing new relationships with Christianity via the church's dominance in Europe.

Sport, Christianity, and the Middle Ages

The relationship between the Christian church (as a social, theological, and political entity) and sport during the Middle Ages is less clear than that during Greek or Roman times, or in the period since the nineteenth century. Social and political turmoil followed the collapse of the Roman Empire, yet sport continued to be a part of daily life. McClelland (2009: 34) provides a description of sport during the early centuries of this period (up to AD 900):

> The medieval reconstruction of civil society ... took at least partially ... the form of creating a culture of sport. The prevalence of sport at all levels of society is reflected in the frequency of its depiction in verbal and pictorial texts, not as a novelty but simply as an element of verisimilitude. The organization and regulation of competitive, ludic, physical activities and their orientation toward positive social goals were thus consubstantial with the new polity that, after ten centuries, consolidated the reconstruction of ancient Roman and Greek culture.

In Western society at least, by the start of the eighth century, social structures had come to include the well-known tiers of the European nobility system. Land owners and members of the aristocracy ruled over the peasants or surfs while the middle classes comprised tradesmen and business merchants. The loyalty of the serfs to the nobles was that of indentured servitude. They worked the land for themselves and their families and paid "rent" for the privilege of doing so. Life for most people during this time was consumed with daily activities relating to manual labor, harvesting and selling goods, and looking after what little people had.

Sporting entertainment for the ruling classes took the form of tournaments, incorporating military-like games with chivalric ideals. Tournaments were played for the nobility and by the nobility, with peasants tending horses and fulfilling other supportive tasks in the service of their landlords. Athletes, or knights, were often the secondary sons of the nobility, whose elder brothers were bestowed more meaningful ruling expectations. Tradesmen and merchants often watched and cheered the athletes on. In these sporting activities, Christian civility became fused with warlike sporting via a range of other activities such as fencing, hawking, archery, and early forms of golf. In one sense, it could be argued that Christianity had a clear impact and regulatory presence on upper class sport during the Middle Ages. However, while the popularity of the tournaments was imbued with Christian overtones, the Church was aware of and often openly hostile to these events (Huizinga 1924: 71). From the clergy's perspective, the "passionate character" and the "abuses resulting from" sporting activity were cause for concern. However, given the fact that sport was the domain of the middle and upper classes, the church had little recourse than to view such activities as social ills and evidence of the fallen nature of man.

Those of lower social status had their own sports that were played at festivals and religious celebrations, usually incorporating the consumption of food and alcohol. Mechikoff and Estes (2006: 109) state that "the apparent universality of ball games, their popularity with the peasant-serfs, the interest of the tradesmen and upper classes, their association with Christian holidays, and the long tradition of quiet acceptance of such games by church authorities" meant that these activities were widespread among medieval people. Indeed, while these games were at the very least violent and unruly, sport flourished during this time in Christian Europe.

By the time of the Renaissance in western Europe (approximately AD 1300–1600), sport had been split into *lawful* and *unlawful* activities, the latter usually associated with some sinful vice, such as gambling, drinking, fornicating, or violence. Activities deemed lawful, on the other hand, were bestowed with a sense of healthy living or militaristic utility. Yet, by the seventeenth century, Puritan and Sabbatarian religious movements had come to see sport and games as corrupt, frivolous, and trivial, and outlawed all such activities. The violence inherent to physical competitions, as well as the sinful assumptions associated with such activities, relegated sport and physical competition to be activities appropriate for children or for the unchurched. However, these rejections of sport were not universal within Christianity, which had become fractured after the Protestant Reformation (*c.* AD 1517–1648), and by the nineteenth century, sport and Christianity once again found themselves primarily in a more positive relationship.

Muscular Christianity

The importance of the mid-nineteenth century movement known as muscular Christianity cannot be underestimated when discussing its impact on the relationship between the Christianity and sport. This social, physical, and theological movement reflected Greek and medieval chivalrous values blended with nineteenth century Christian ideals around morality and social progress (Tozer 2016). Most profoundly implemented by elite English public schools, muscular Christianity was the underlying theological justification at the core of the Young Men's Christian Association (YMCA) and the modern Olympics. To this end, muscular Christianity ushered in an altogether more positive theological view of sport and physical activity, legitimizing sports' promotion within churches and by Christian preachers, pastors, and athletes themselves, who came to use sport as a vehicle for evangelization.

Muscular Christianity emerged from the writings of Victorian Christian Socialists, public school headmasters, and fictional authors. Most notably associated with the literary works of Charles Kingsley and Thomas Hughes, it embodied character traits such as masculinity, honesty, fairness, and physical fortitude, which were fueled by the necessity of maintaining the British Empire. Differing from previous Christian theologies that elevated care for the soul over the physical body, muscular Christianity was a holistic approach which encouraged care for both. As Kingsley said, we must "preach the divineness of the whole manhood" (Tozer 2016: 59).

In terms of its underlying values, muscular Christianity represented a new understanding of how participation in sports might encourage moral education and character building experiences (Lundskow 2008). The learning of important life lessons was central to its overall philosophy, including perseverance, endurance, and the value of competition. The encouragement of competition was based "on the moral grounds that games were a preparation for the battle of life and that they trained moral qualities, mainly respect for others, patient endurance, unflagging courage, self-reliance, self-control, vigor, and decision of character" (Freeman 1997: 127).

Contemporary sport theorists have detailed the pivotal role that muscular Christian ideals played in shaping Western perceptions of sport and physical exercise (Putney 2003). The blending of religion and philosophy in the nineteenth century created clear and justified connections between theology, sport, and physical activity. While Christian views historically describe the fallen and sinful nature of the physical body, muscular Christianity challenged such ideas.

For instance, Charles Kingsley details his version of a healthy and manly Christian in his 1855 novel, *Westward Ho!*, describing connections between manliness and godliness, where a healthy body was necessary for a healthy spirit. Thomas Hughes additionally illustrated muscular Christianity's attitude toward physical activity in his book *Tom Brown at Oxford* (1861). Scholars agree that it is the following conceptualization of muscular Christianity which reflects its core ideology:

> The least of the muscular Christians has hold of the old chivalrous and Christian belief, that a man's body is given to him to be trained and brought into subjection, and then used for the protection of the weak, the advancement of all righteous causes, and the subduing of the earth which God has given to the children of men. (Hughes 1861: 83)

This description of muscular Christianity details the wide-ranging impact the ideal of an athletic physical body had for influencing other areas of daily life during the Victorian era.

The influential role that muscular Christianity had on the progressive social movements during this time, such as the establishment of the YMCA, inner city sport leagues, and the perceived social benefits of the modern Olympic movement, is well documented. In this sense, the muscular Christian movement provided a theological justification for many of the mid- to late nineteenth century innovations in social organization, social care, and emerging scientific scholarship on human health. Sport and physical activity came to be understood as essential activities for overall health and well-being. Its authors not only promoted sport as a necessary activity through which important Christian character traits could be taught but aimed to benefit those of less means—a central message of Jesus (e.g., the Sermon on the Mount in Matthew 5–7)—and ensure that the physical body was well-cared for as the "house" of one's eternal soul.

Without doubt the muscular Christian movement shaped the relationship between sport and Christianity for the twentieth century and beyond.

Sport and Christianity today

When we look at the landscape of contemporary sport, we see more uniformity than difference. The modern Olympic movement helped facilitate this global perception of sport, one that seems to reflect universal "sporting" ideals rather than any one religious view. While different sports are played in different countries, from *futbal* to football, sumo wrestling to camel racing, or Iditarod to ironman, sport seems ubiquitous to every culture and every society around the globe. How then does Christianity fit into this modern sporting landscape?

As we have seen, many sports scholars recognize and acknowledge the role that Victorian muscular Christianity played in the shaping of modern sporting ideals, practices, and norms. In fact, it could be argued that Christians today have a stronger and generally more favorable view of sport than at any other point in history. However, many Christian leaders still bemoan the kinds of activities surrounding sport and examples of vice and un-Christian-like behaviors remain evident. Today, churches and para-church organizations, like the Fellowship of Christian Athletes, Athletes in Action, and Christians in Sport, overtly claim that those who play can come to know Jesus and His message through their sporting experiences. Many churches around the world have sports leagues, interact with local and international sports organizations, and see sport as a positive social activity not at odds with Christian ideals or teachings.

The influence of muscular Christian ideals is observable in a variety of organizations and popular sporting events. The YMCA was founded in London in 1844 and focused on the "moral and religious need of young men" (Baker 1994: 42). The effect of the YMCA in spreading the ideals of sport and physical activity cannot be underestimated; the "Y" is synonymous with sport and physical activity. As Baker (1994: 42) has argued, "especially in the United States, the YMCA lent institutional support to earlier, more theoretical muscular Christian preachments" as it translated "prophetic inspiration into organized for and ritual." Through basketball, the YMCA has delivered sport to every corner of the globe and today impacts hundreds of millions of people in 119 countries (YMCA Blue Book 2012). The reach and impact of this one organization alone demonstrates the positive impact that the sport–Christianity relationship can have.

Turning next to the largest Christian organization in the world, the Vatican has also fully embraced sport in the recent decades, hosting the first Jubilee of Sport in 1984. Since then, the Vatican has established the Dicastery for Laity, Family, and Life (2016) with its specific focus on sport, as well as hosting several other conferences including "Sport at the Service of Humanity" in 2016. In 2000, Pope John Paul II stated at that year's Jubilee of Sport that it was "a fitting occasion to give thanks to God for the gift of sport" (Lixey 2013: 250).

A third way that we can see sport and its relationship with Christianity today is through the use of athletes and sport to promote Christian values and ideals. One of the underlying efforts of the Christian Socialist movement, affiliated with muscular Christianity, was to push for better working conditions and higher standards of living for the English working classes during the Victorian era. We see these efforts persist through examples of athletes using sport and the social platform it provides to raise awareness about local, regional, and global issues (Meyer 2012). For example, in 1936, Jesse Owens was an antidote to Adolf Hitler's claims of white superiority at the Berlin Games; on the podium in 1968, Mexico City Olympic athletes Tommy Smith and John Carlos raised their fisted gloves to protest the plight of African Americans during the Civil Rights era; NBA superstar Erving "Magic" Johnson became the face of AIDS in the 1990s, raising awareness and acceptance of those afflicted with the disease; and in 2016, American football player Colin Kaepernick refused to stand for the playing of the national anthem in protest of police brutality toward African Americans. When we examine examples such as these and the power with which modern-day athletes yield over popular opinion on a variety of social issues, we see the lasting moral authority of muscular Christian ideals in contemporary social contexts.

Conclusion

If this brief examination and discussion about the history of sport and Christianity has shown us anything, it is that the relationship between these two cultural spheres is unpredictable and unstable. The nature of this relationship is founded upon historic and contemporary notions of sport, body, competition, God, social responsibility, and divine will. These ideas weave and wend their way into a myriad of other social, political, theological, and cultural pressures. To attempt to claim one firm definition of the sport–Christianity relationship would be futile. Rather, the history of the amalgamation of these two entities is a melting-pot of perspective and negotiation. From St. Paul to modern-day Christian athletes, the nature of Christianity's relationship with sport is complicated and diverse, ever evolving and never complete. In the final analysis, it is this diversity that makes the history of this relationship so dynamic and complex and which incentivizes scholars to pursue its trajectory.

Study Guide

This chapter attempts to draw the reader's attention to the social and cultural impacts of four significant time periods as they relate to the relationship between sport and Christianity. While no historical description will ever be complete, the reader will hopefully get a sense of how this relationship has been influenced by social, cultural, and political factors over time. Please feel free to help readers understand other factors that may have influenced the relationship between sport and Christianity, as you see fit.

Study Questions

1. How do you understand sport to reflect the social and cultural ideals of certain periods in history? How do you think modern-day sport reflects specific historical ideals and perspectives?
2. Briefly summarize the way that you understand sport to have been used to serve Christian perspectives throughout history.
3. What areas or aspects of religious life do you think are important to examine to understand the role of sport at any given time?
4. To what extent are the values of muscular Christianity evident in modern-day sport?
5. The relationship between Christianity and sport has changed over the centuries. What do you think this relationship will look like in 25 years? What about in 200 years?

Further Reading

Guttmann, A. (1978), *From Ritual to Record: The Nature of Modern Sports*, New York: Columbia University Press.

Meyer, A. R. (2012), "Muscular Christian Themes in Contemporary American Sport: A Case Study," *The Journal of the Christian Society for Kinesiology and Leisure Studies*, 2 (1): 15–32.

Watson, Nick, J. and A. Parker (eds.) (2013), *Sports and Christianity: Historical and Contemporary Perspectives*, London: Routledge.

Part II

SPORT AND CHRISTIANITY:
PRACTICES FOR THE HEART AND SOUL

Chapter 6

LIVED RELIGION IN SPORTS

Matt Hoven

Introduction

During a recent trip to Toronto, Canada, I heard two separate stories about a prominent player from the National Basketball Association (NBA) and a distinguished coach from the National Hockey League (NHL) who had each attended church services. Both stories were told with curious interest, and listeners appeared encouraged that high-profile sportspeople went to church. Yet, the stories also felt exotic and led to questioning about the substance of each person's religious faith—how did they integrate religious faith with their sporting endeavors? The same question can be asked in different circumstances. For example, when the Notre Dame Fighting Irish university football team attends Mass before a Saturday game, how does this influence the spirituality of players and coaches? Many of England's elite soccer teams, like Manchester City and Liverpool, were founded by churches; however, do these historical influences impact individual players today? When US sprinter Allyson Felix, winner of six Olympic gold medals in track and field, recites a biblical passage in the media, does she use it for motivation as a sprinter? On the surface, these examples reveal connections between sport and Christianity, but mere attendance at church services or the recitation of a biblical passage fails to fully capture the lived religion of sporting people today.

This chapter examines the spiritual practices of sportspeople through a sociological understanding of the term *lived religion*. In Part I, I rely primarily on Ammerman's (2014) research about lived religion to establish a framework for better understanding how people live spiritually outside of worship settings. In Part II, I use examples from the lives of elite athletes—as illustrative of Ammerman's work—to reveal how religious faith is lived out through various spiritual practices. The overall aim of the chapter is to present the diversity of Christian spiritual practices in sport, how these reflect the blurring of distinctions between sport and religion, and how churches nonetheless remain important places for educating people in spiritual practices.

Lived religion

Today's elite athletes have much at stake in sports. Climbing up the rankings within youth, collegiate, and professional sports is no doubt daunting, where the victor has the best chance of advancing and everybody will seemingly do whatever it takes to win. Competition can produce uncertainty and anxiety in the lives of athletes, where the gap between sporting existence and religious living (outside of sports) is smaller than one might think (Nesti 2010).

There are many ways to comprehend the relationship between sport and religion. In their book *Understanding Sport as a Religious Phenomenon*, Bain-Selbo and Sapp (2016) highlight Ninian Smart's seven dimensions of religion (e.g., ritual, doctrine, mythic, experiential, ethical, social, and artistic) as aspects for interpreting sports as religion: for example, in the mythical creativity of Brazilian soccer teams, or the emotional highs and lows of the New England Patriot's victory over the Seattle Seahawks in the 2015 Superbowl. Bain-Selbo and Sapp draw upon the work of Durkheim, a founding father of sociology, to exemplify how the rituals and community life of religion—that is, "collective effervescence"—can draw sportspeople together as displayed by fans of teams like the New Zealand All Blacks. In support of secularization theories, these authors conclude that, because the status of religious institutions is declining, "religiosity is diffused through our lives to greater and lesser degrees" (Bain-Selbo and Sapp 2016: 134). In other words, religion is not disappearing in the twenty-first century, but the clear division between conceptions of religion and the secular—in this case, sports—has blurred and thus requires a more careful examination of how sports interact with religion and vice versa.

In light of the fact that the role of religion in Western industrialized society is not as clear as it was 500, or even 100, years ago (C. Taylor 2007), some sociologists have begun to investigate how ordinary people act religiously in their everyday lives (i.e., lived religion). Ammerman (2016: 87) outlines that this area of study examines regular people, instead of religious professionals, to determine how ordinary people live spiritually outside of institutionalized religious settings. Orsi (1997: 7) explains that religion can still be seen as something unique and distinct from secular life, but that, in concentrating on the connection between experience and religion, "religion comes into being in an ongoing, dynamic relationship with the realities of everyday life." Thus, the focus of lived religion is not on authority found in religious traditions or the clergy but highlights how individuals freely choose to live out their spiritual lives. This kind of sociological work is not anti-religious or anti-institutional, because, as Ammerman (2016: 88) notes, institutional religion's influence on ordinary people should not be excluded or understood as disconnected from everyday life. Ammerman and others (e.g., Bergman 2014) are clear that they do not wish to separate spirituality from religion, as if institutionalized religion is devoid of spirituality or that it destroys personal spirituality. On the contrary, lived religion in the twenty-first century remains focused on ordinary *"domains of life where sacred things are being produced, encountered, and shared"* (original emphasis) (Ammerman 2016: 89), which often reveal a dynamic range of spiritual practices drawn from religious traditions.

Research in this field continues to take shape. In her mixed-methods study of the lived religion of ninety-five Americans of diverse backgrounds, Ammerman deduced several dominant cultural discourses that act as overarching categories to classify different spiritualities that extend beyond religious traditions. In other words, she finds spiritual commonalities among people in the twenty-first century instead of classifying people according to denominational differences, such as Baptist or Methodist. She distinguishes many cultural discourses, where people primarily connect spirituality to (1) the divine (theistic), (2) various naturalistic forms of transcendence (extra-theistic), (3) objects and bodies (embodied), and (4) everyday compassion (ethical). These categories focus on people's lived experience and freedom within their spiritual lives instead of being restricted to church attendance or basic religious practices like prayer. Using the above four categories as a conceptual framework, it is possible to facilitate greater understandings of how people engage religiously within the context of competitive sport.

Lived religion in sports

In line with this framework of lived religion, the remainder of our discussion engages with media interviews and stories of prominent modern-day athletes to show their human side and a spiritual dimension not typically highlighted in and through sports media. This particular use of lived religion is based upon my own research findings with fifteen-year-old student-athletes in Canadian Catholic high schools (see Hoven 2016; Hoven 2017; Hoven and Kuchera 2016). These findings operate as a pedagogical tool for better articulating what spirituality looks like in sports today. Several spiritual practices reflect personal authentication of the Christian faith, the possibility of existential depth for athletes, and even reveal connections to theological issues related to Christian spiritual practices in sports.

Theistic spiritual practices

Ammerman (2014: 28) describes three general ways that people report theistic spiritual practices: "it is about God, it is about practices intended to develop one's relationship with God, and it is about mysterious encounters and happenings that come to those who are open to them." By using theistic, Ammerman underlines the traditional connection to a higher power named God, as reported by her interviewees, that confirms the ways that people's practices relate to God. Reading the Bible and praying to God are two common examples; these and other practices shape people's lives.

Perhaps no athlete has been as dominant on the world stage—and as flamboyant before TV cameras—in recent years as the fastest human on Earth, Usain Bolt. While setting world records in sprinting, Bolt displayed a number of pre- and post-game spiritual practices: for example, in the starting blocks, he made the sign of the cross and pointed to the heavens, and then, when races ended, he often pointed upward and knelt in prayer. Further, he wore and kissed a miraculous medal, a devotional necklace in honor of The Blessed Virgin Mary. In interviews and on his Twitter account, Bolt professed his theistic belief: "I want to thank God for everything he has done for me cause without him none of this [would] be possible" (Farley 2015). He also tweeted about celebrating the true meaning of Good Friday and retweeted different inspirational scriptural texts. Elsewhere he stated: "My faith teaches me to believe in my ability and trust that hard work and determination will make me successful. It gives me confidence in my God-given talent and so I never set limits on what a human can do whether it is running, jumping or something else" (Cox 2016). Amid a highly charged and mediatized sporting context, Bolt offered many theatrical theistic practices that demonstrated how his Christian faith anchored his identity and sprinting—and which were not merely exhibitions for the media.

Another gold medalist from the London and Rio de Janeiro Olympic Games, American Gabby Douglas, described what it meant for her to win the Individual All-Around in Women's Gymnastics: "I give all the glory to God. It's kind of a win-win situation. The glory goes up to him and the blessings fall down on me" (Seigneur 2012). Upon returning to the United States after her victory in London, she explained: "I thought I could put together all those Scriptures … that I kept reading … God gave me this amazing talent, and of course I want to represent him … I've [since] watched myself at the Olympics … and I saw my mouth moving— that was me praying … When the judge's hand goes up I am praying, and there are little Scriptures I like to quote. That keeps me motivated" (Seigneur 2012). Here Douglas explains how she engages biblical verses during an actual event; these remind her of her God-given talent and identity in Christ. Although Douglas highlights how her athletic success reflects her religious faith, not all athletes enjoy competitive success. British sprinter Christine Ohuruogu, former Olympic and World Champion in 400-meter track, has explained the importance of prayer in athletics: "Sometimes people think because you pray and do all the right things as best you can, everything is going to be brilliant all the time. It's never like that at all. But you do realise there's a bigger picture and it puts things in perspective" (Premier Christianity 2016). Ohuruogu goes on to admit that devastating losses in track over the years have challenged her to make changes to her performance preparations; further, she testifies to the fact that undertaking a major loss can be a "wake-up call" and can serve to refocus belief in God. In the above examples, prayer re-orders priorities, can inspire, and can give rightful praise to God.

Both Ammerman (2014) and Hoven and Kuchera (2016) found that those who were more closely affiliated with a religion used more spiritual practices in sports. In the above three examples, the spiritual practices reflect specific Christian, theistic practices—like prayer, making the sign of the cross, and wearing a Marian medallion (see also Czech et al. 2004, Czech and Bullet 2007, Egli et al. 2014)—and reflect a meaningful personal spirituality for these three athletes. C. Taylor (2007: 506–513) explains this personalization of spirituality as a twentieth century development in an age of authenticity, where some in

Western societies no longer employed institutionalized forms of spirituality and sought spiritual expressions that resonated individually. This shift can pit religion against spirituality, where religion is rendered inflexible, doctrinal, hollow, and ritualistic, and spirituality is seen as altogether more personable, meaningful, and expressive. This dichotomy, Taylor argues, does not hold water. In the cases of three athletes above, their infusion of Christian practices buoys their lives above the flatness of everyday existence and shows how theistic practices can support a personal quest. Further, instead of understanding these athletes' spiritual practices as "self-indulgent activity" (Coakley 2001: 474) that attracts the attention of television cameras, these actions can be seen as a way of spiritualizing sporting endeavors and engaging theistic traditions to make deeper personal meaning in sport.

Extra-theistic spiritual practices

Ammerman (2014: 34) explains that extra-theistic spiritual practices are not usually directed toward God but give "attention to transcendent connections to others, the sense of awe engendered by the natural world and moments of beauty, life philosophies crafted by an individual seeking meaning, and the inner core of individual self-worth." Connections to something beyond ordinary life, a lifting of the spirit, are experienced by athletes seeking deeper meaning in their sporting lives. Extra-theistic practices, which often engage nature, are broadly constructed and thus are not necessarily an endorsement or contradiction to Christian institutional practices.

Extra-theistic spiritual practices are perhaps most visible in extreme sports, like surfing and rock climbing, where participants undertake challenges in natural settings instead of artificial atmospheres such as urban arenas. Watson and Parker (2015: 263) discuss the increased popularity of these sports and suggest that one of the reasons for this "is the apparent need of those concerned to escape from the increasingly materialistic, paternalistic and utilitarian Western lifestyle." This can coincide with the trend to seek out spirituality without religion, as the authors explain: "This goes hand-in-hand with the wider cultural revolution that has seen a gradual shift away from organised religion toward a much more inclusive and eclectic understanding of 'spirituality' and 'well-being'" (263–264). This focus on spirituality is captured by Edwards, a publisher of a surfing magazine for women: "[Surfing] is about balance, blend and unity. It is about being a part of, not about dictating or ruling it. The Zen of surfing is about being mindful of the energy you are joining forces with, not conquering it" (Bron 2007: 936). The wholeness, harmony, and even ecstasy surfers experience with the ocean (reflected in the term *soul surfing*) can intermingle with different religious traditions: Asian, indigenous, and even monotheistic religious beliefs and practices. For instance, Bethany Hamilton, a practicing Christian and famed US surfer whose arm was bitten off in a shark attack, speaks about the spiritual side of the sport. She has a passion for surfing "rooted in her soul" and understands this passion "as a gift from God," who enabled her to continue surfing despite her disability (Hamilton, n.d.). While surfing subcultures are not all Christian, or explicitly tied to a particular religion, they can and do hybridize with or borrow from religious traditions (Bron 2007).

The power of these extra-theistic practices in sports is also evident in transcendent experiences related to death. At both the elite and local levels of sports, it is common to find athletes dedicating their play to deceased loved ones, such as American Major League Baseball player Dee Gordon who tearfully hit a first at-bat home run after the tragic death of his teammate José Fernandez in 2016, or US Olympic gold medalist Billy Mills drawing on his deceased father's inspiration to win the 10,000 meters in Tokyo in 1964 (Percy 2016). Another example is US national soccer player Clint Dempsey, who has played for teams in both the English Premier League and Major League Soccer and who dedicates his play to his sister who passed away during his early teens. Because Jennifer was older and a talented tennis player, Clint's parents pulled him out of club league play so they could focus their time and money on their daughter. But when Dempsey's sister died of a brain aneurysm at sixteen, he returned to the club team with greater motivation: "Before she passed away, we had talks about death … And I remember her telling me that if something ever happened to her, she'd help me score goals" (Drehs 2006). After her passing, Dempsey vowed to look into the sky and think about her whenever he scored. His brother Ryan reflects on the significance of Jennifer for Clint: "When something like that happens, your perspectives change … Clint would go out and practice twice as much. He'd work twice as hard. He wanted to do it in her name, in her glory. So he dedicated everything to her" (Drehs 2006). Dempsey does not speak publicly about his Catholic faith but, in this instance, finds a sporting expression to connect with his departed sister. Here death draws Dempsey to his sister and his belief in the afterlife.

Sports' ability to activate extra-theistic spirituality is infinite, but it is worth keeping two key issues in mind. First, Watson and Parker (2015: 277) endorse the power of sporting experiences in and through extreme sports contexts which, they argue, "can be seen as forms of deep play, an avenue to well-being and growth, even spiritual expressions in an aesthetic, creative sense that provide opportunities for meaningful, therapeutic and exhilarating activities." However, for these authors such experiences are not on par with Christian mystical experiences because they do not confirm the otherness or transcendence of God. Despite the importance of this criticism, these extra-theistic practices can support belief in God's work in the world and thus support the gospel message. Theologian Patrick Kelly (2011: 168) confirms this stance and finds that "the joy of playing, absorption in the activity, effortlessness, the experience of selflessness and unity with others and an altered sense of time" opens athletes to transcendence.

Second, individual attempts to make personal meaning in sport can result in extra-theistic practices that may be superstitious. Athletes perform superstitions, as explained by Dömötör, Ruiz-Barquin, and Szabo (2016), to control elements of chance or unstable factors amid many psychological tensions faced in sport—such as the threat of losing or injury. Although players may accept no causal link between winning and, for instance, wearing their opponent's shorts to bed the night before a game (as in the case of former NBA all-star Jason Terry) or having athletic trainers physically slap them before games (as did former National Football League [NFL] player John Henderson), many still follow these routines (see tennis star Rafael Nadal's complicated pregame and preserve routines). A tennis star placing trust in the height of his socks may seem somewhat irrational for Christians and non-Christians alike, but these personal rituals psychologically can offer comfort amid sporting tensions through their placebo effect (Dömötör, Ruiz-Barquin, and Szabo 2016). While sport psychologists endorse different preperformance routines (PPRs) like meditation and visualization, personally meaningful rituals highlight the human need for something beyond oneself: reaching out for support from others, including a Creator (Hoven 2019).

Embodied spiritual practices

Sports engage the whole body. They can arouse all the senses: the smell of the pitch, the sight of the field, the sound of play, the physical touch-up against opponents, and, of course, the taste of defeat. Sports embody cultures with established sets of rules for people gathered. The element of embodiment is especially important to sports because of their physicality, where spiritual practices can be embodied and can express extra-theistic and theistic spiritualities. In fact, while Ammerman (2014) highlights the embodied-ness of many practices, Hoven and Kuchera (2016) incorporate it as a separate category because of sports' physical nature and many examples of embodied practices that were reported by young athletes: making the sign of the cross before a foul shot in basketball, experiencing sports as an escape or stress reliever, engaging nature, using special postures like volleyball players huddling after a point, wearing special clothing like a sibling's pair of football gloves or a meaningful jersey number, and using spiritual ascetics of sacrificing time, effort, emotions, and diet to improve oneself and the team.

Examples of embodied spiritual practices reported by the high school athletes in Hoven and Kuchera's (2016) study can also be found in elite sport (as shown above). A case in point is five-time world champion Formula One (F1) British racing driver Lewis Hamilton. Hamilton participates in a sport heavily reliant on scientific precision yet explains how his tattoos embody and anchor his faith:

> I love my ink … They all have a meaning. I'm very strong in my faith, so I wanted to have some religious images. I've got Pietà, a Michelangelo sculpture of Mary holding Jesus after he came off the cross … The compass on my chest is there because church is my compass … On my back I have the cross and angel wings: rise above it, no matter what life throws at you. And also, you know, Jesus rose from the grave. (Wilson 2017)

Hamilton's tattoos act as inspirational artwork that draws from his faith in God and the church to lift his spirits and his game.

Embodied forms of spirituality are not new to Christianity and, in fact, draw inspiration from the central teaching of Christ's incarnation: "the Word became flesh and made his dwelling among us" (Jn. 1:14). This doctrine, celebrated on

December 25th when the northern hemisphere embodies much darkness, commemorates the embrace of the physical world, of creation, by the Word of God. The church confirmed this biblical teaching in the fifth century at the Council of Chalcedon: Jesus Christ is "one in being with the Father, as touching his Godhead, one in being with us, as touching our humanity" (Marthaler 1993: 117). The Christian faith then, instead of being opposed to the physical world, embraces creation's goodness as revealed by the Son of God's incarnation. This means that instead of separating creation from God's saving work in Jesus, Christianity affirms an ancient Jewish approach that confirms the goodness of the physical world (i.e., Gen. 1:26–27). This embodied faith is most evident in sacramental practices established and endorsed by Jesus: his baptism, his sharing of a common meal at the Last Supper, and his many physical healings. Different Christian traditions embrace the practice of sacramentality to varying degrees; nonetheless, there is a common belief that God speaks through the physical world—as found in Jesus' instituting privileged embodied practices as sacraments.

For sporting participants, belief in the incarnation and sacraments means that created things in God's good creation can potentially speak to the Creator's creative design and goodness. This is particularly important for athletes who through play can integrate bodily existence with spiritual practices. As a point of contrast, for instance, seeing sports simply as entertainment can diminish these practices: Hillman (2016) argues that an overemphasis on consumption (i.e., sports fans bombarded with advertising) creates superior sports consumers instead of inspired fans who play sports more often.

Ethical spiritual practices

Interviewees from across the religious spectrum reported to Ammerman (2014: 82) the importance of ethical actions as spiritual practices: "To reach beyond one's own interests and to act with compassion was a spiritual discipline for some." She describes this dimension as "living a virtuous life, one characterized by helping others, transcending one's own selfish interests to seek what is right" (45). It should come as no surprise that acts of kindness, compassion, and justice are included in the practice of living religiously. In the case of sports and its competitive nature, Scholes and Sassower (2014) highlight how it can demand a greater sense of purpose and call for a code for living. The need for ethical codes in sport is evident in many coaching philosophies that demand players' virtuous actions, like ones spelled out by basketball's John Wooden or Canadian ice hockey's Father David Bauer. Hoven and Kuchera (2016) report that student-athletes in their research spoke of various ethical practices in sport: helping an injured teammate or opponent, pulling up a player who fell on the field of play, or protecting a weaker teammate. Furthermore, athletes reported how conventional sporting socialization encouraged ethical actions toward teammates—for example, sacrificing oneself for the team's needs—but also endorsed less virtuous actions toward opponents—for example, gamesmanship, trash-talk, and cheating (Hoven 2016).

Ammerman (2014: 82) notes that "practices of love and charity were the most common of these moral spiritual practices" for her respondents compared to acts of justice that sought "to attack the roots of the world's ills." In sports today, many elite athletes support charitable organizations and host high-profile events, acting as sponsors for worthy public causes. Several global icons such as Brazilian-born soccer star Neymar, tennis' Serena Williams, and basketball's Lebron James have their own charitable foundations and work with wider humanitarian organizations like UNICEF to help the vulnerable. Yet some athletes also act spiritually by challenging deeper problems of social justice that move beyond the bounds of charity. Such is the case of US Special Olympian Loretta Claiborne who, despite being discriminated against for her ethnicity, intellectual disability, and partial blindness, was inspired by faith and the faith of others—like Reverend Martin Luther King, Jr.—and overcame various personal and societal obstacles to become a marathon runner, and advocate for the intellectually disabled. She believed this: "Martin Luther King Jr. once said, 'Faith is taking the first step even when you don't see the whole staircase.' My message to everyone with intellectual disabilities is to have faith ... Women at one time weren't recognized that they could be in the workforce. But they had faith" (Gleeson 2015). For Claiborne, sports acted as a place for her to overcome injustice and encourage others through her bravery.

Many stories confirm sports as a space for social justice: for example, the legendary Muhammad Ali and his protest about the Vietnam War, or the political stand made by American Olympic sprinters Tommie Smith and John Carlos during the national anthem at the Mexico City Games in 1968. More recently, the protest of American NFL football quarterback Colin Kaepernick has echoed the concerns of Smith and Carlos. Starting in 2016, Kaepernick knelt during the American national anthem in support of the Black Lives Matter movement, which publicly challenged the high rates of African American deaths at the hands of law enforcement officers in the United States (Newkirk 2017). Before his protest, Kaepernick had enjoyed success on the field and spoke about the importance of his faith embodying his beliefs through multiple tattoos of a selection of the Psalms and other faith-related images (King 2013). The deep, personal meaning of these tattoos, along with his ability to influence a large group of people as a consequence of his public status, in part led to his actions. A call to a more just society for people of color became instantly controversial with those who saw Kaepernick's kneeling during the national anthem as disrespectful—including US President Donald Trump.

Works of kindness, mercy, and justice can be found in the lives of many sports personnel. The above examples may seem contradictory—for example, how can an athlete protest police brutality when he himself disrespects the national anthem and a nation's flag? Yet athletes may ground their ethical decisions in a deeper purpose or religious teaching. Theologically Jesus offered many ethical teachings about how to treat one's neighbor (as found in the story of the Good Samaritan in Luke 10:25–37) or one's enemy (as taught in the Sermon on the Mount in Matthew 5:43–48). Because competitive sports present numerous ethical dilemmas, athletes inevitably face tensions between particular ethical standards of Christianity and the competitive world of sports.

Conclusion

This chapter has highlighted a range of spiritual practices enacted by athletes: for example, pointing to the heavens, making the sign of the cross, reflecting on the purpose of prayer, exhibiting tattoos, helping a teammate, or openly questioning issues of injustice. By looking at sports through the lens of lived religion, we find athletes engaging in spiritual practices that give existential purpose and meaning in athletic endeavors. The intermingling of Christian practices within the sporting world, which blurs boundaries between sports and religion, can enable athletes to find the sacred in the created world (i.e., for Christians, the principle of sacramentality) and need not pit religion against spirituality. Scholes and Sassower (2014: 149) point out that "new interpretative horizons open up [and] allow for novel applications" for people bringing Christian practices to sports or when sports provide opportunities for Christian spirituality.

Ammerman (2014: 301) confirms this thinking by "recognizing the permeable boundaries of all institutions," where sport and religion are not clearly distinct in people's lives and religious institutions cannot assume authority over all things spiritual or religious. She argues that spiritual practices are shaped by social interactions with others, which allows for elements of religious (or sporting) identity to carry across distinctions of different fields. Thus, for the athletes featured here, these spiritual practices are not created individually; rather, they are socially constructed through interaction with family, friends, coaches, and ministers. Of course, institutional religion does not solely shape the identities of athletes, and determining religious identity, sociologically speaking, is not as simple as declaring that one is baptized. By accepting findings from lived religion and the apparent diversity of religious living today, we see that actions cannot necessarily be judged as sacred or profane on the surface and that they may be both sacred and secular at once (Ammerman 2014).

Using lived religion as a conceptual framework to better understand spiritual practices in sport provides a wider viewpoint for envisioning Christian practices in sports and more accurately captures the influence of faith overall. When only prayer or attendance at a chapel service are understood as Christian practices, personal development and the use of faith in sport are overlooked and religion is understood narrowly. What then are the consequences of a lived religion approach for churches? Ammerman (2014: 291) draws the following conclusion: "There is a strong relationship between participation in religious communities and engaging in spiritual practices in everyday life; spiritual community and spiritual practice are in a dynamic relationship with each other." Belonging to a religious community remains important for being educated in spiritual practices. Ammerman (2014: 302) adds: "In nearly every systematic comparison we have attempted to examine, people who attend services more frequently are different in ways that go beyond demographic differences or differences based on the type of religious tradition or differences based on the individual's levels of spiritual practice and virtuosity." While some research highlights innovative spiritual practices arising from sports themselves (Cipriani 2012; B. Taylor 2007), Ammerman found that people's spiritual practices often are connected to their religious backgrounds. As she concludes, the more engaged people are in the spiritual conversations and actions of their local congregation, the more likely they are to use that language and live out those actions in their own lives.

The sociological study of people's lived religion uncovers the diversity of spiritual practices in the twenty-first century. While this approach does not encompass the whole of a religious tradition like Christianity, it importantly reveals how it is lived outside of churches and religious institutions. Instead of simply accepting the cliché that "sports are more than a game," research and the above sporting examples highlight a transcendent element to sporting life and the possibility of finding God in sports.

Study Guide

The four categories drawn from Ammerman's work enable us to categorize different spiritual practices in sport. Instead of these practices appearing strange, they become understood as lived (religious) athletic expressions in competitive sport. The point then is to capture the diversity of Christian spiritual practices in sport, how these reflect the blurred distinctions between sport and religion, and how churches nonetheless remain important places for educating people in spiritual practices.

Study Questions

1. What Christian spiritual practices have you tried or witnessed in sports?
2. Complete an Internet search on one of the above named athletes or an athlete of your choice. What else can you learn about their spiritual lives in sports?
3. How does the blurring of the distinction between sports and religion enable Christian spiritual practices in sports?
4. According to Ammerman, why do churches remain important for supporting Christian practices used outside of church?
5. Different Christian traditions engage extra-theistic practices more than others. What kinds of comparisons can you make between these traditions in your experience or based on your knowledge?

Further Reading

Ammerman, N. (2014), *Sacred Stories, Spiritual Tribes*, New York: Oxford University.

Hoven, M., & Kuchera, S. (2016), "Beyond Tebowing and Superstitions: Religious Practices of 15-Year-Old Competitive Athletes," *International Journal of Children's Spirituality*, 21 (1): 52–65.

Watson, N. J., & Parker, A. (2015), "The Mystical and Sublime in Extreme Sports: Experiences of Psychological Well-Being or Christian Revelation?" *Studies in World Christianity*, 21 (3): 260–281.

Chapter 7

RUNNING AS LITURGY

Doug Hochstetler

Introduction

In her book *The Cloister Walk*, Kathleen Norris (1996: 266) writes: "Good liturgy can act like an icon, a window into a world in which our concepts of space, time, and even stone are pleasurably bent out of shape. Good liturgy is a living poem, and ceremony is the key." With a background steeped in the Protestant faith, in her adult years Norris explores and develops an appreciation for the monastic traditions, spending time participating in a Benedictine community. She finds value in the repetitive nature of the cloistered life, where the daily routine includes both aspects of ceremony amid the mundane. She observes that this structure has much in common with an artistic life: "both are attempts to pay close attention to objects, events, and natural phenomena that otherwise would get chewed up in the daily grind" (266). An advocate of movement, Norris realizes the spiritual nature of physical activity. After spending time in monastic life, and becoming immersed again in the daily routine of "normal life," she misses the ceremony and community that the Benedictine order provides. In its place, Norris writes, "My instinct is to keep as much of the monastery in me as possible. Now I honor the coming of the dawn with a long walk instead of going to church, but small difference, if I can turn it toward prayer" (267). Unlike Norris, my background does not include any time period immersed in monastic life. Nonetheless, I appreciate the veracity of her experience and intuit a similar relationship between movement and the spiritual life. While Norris looks to walking as a potential opportunity to cultivate prayer and liturgy, my own practice of running holds similar potential.

In this chapter, I contend that running, for some people, can be an important liturgical practice. While I leave open the possibility for running to function in similar ways in other faith communities, I focus primarily on the Christian faith tradition, and the place of running as a potential liturgical form. I do not claim that running is, or should be, the only form of liturgy for practicing Christians. While running on Sunday mornings may, at times, bring about a liturgical sense in the way I describe below, I still maintain that corporate worship, engaged community discipleship, and more traditional forms of liturgy, such as communion (or

Eucharist), are an essential part of the Christian faith tradition which cannot be totally replaced by the act of running. Furthermore, running is not the only movement form that makes possible this connection to the liturgy. That said, the nature of running is, for some people at least, conducive to worship and the type of space and activity needed to enter into communion with the Divine.

The nature of liturgy

In order to progress, I want to outline the nature of liturgy. I use the term "liturgy," following Lysaught (2008: 9), in a very broad manner to mean "the panoply of ways in which we, individually and corporately, worship God, come into God's presence and find ourselves participating in the divine life." In this way, while liturgy includes Sunday worship and religious sacramental acts, it also includes less formalized moments that may similarly bring about a sense of worship and entering into God's presence.

While the very nature of liturgy is sacred and central to the Christian faith, it is, as Lysaught (2008: 4) explains, "a complex, grace-filled, and ultimately mysterious practice." Note the connection between liturgy and "practice." The usage of the term "practice" is important here in the sense that a practice denotes actions performed repeatedly. Thus, these are not once-and-done bucket list kind of performances, but rather acts which constitute one's being and take on a certain identity of sorts. Here the use of practice runs similar to MacIntyre's (1984: 187) usage, whereby a practice entails "any coherent and complex form of socially established cooperative human activity through which goods internal to that form of activity are realized." Those in a monastic setting exemplify life structured around liturgy, with time spent throughout the course of the day for prayer and reflection. For example, Norris' (1996) liturgy schedule during her retreat setting included morning prayer at 7, noon prayer at 12, Eucharist at 5 pm and vespers at 7 pm. In his book section on *Steps into Unceasing Prayer*, Richard Foster (1992: 126) writes: "We do not leap into the dizzy heights of constant communication in a single bound. It comes over a period of time in measured practical steps. The first step is that of outward discipline. This is how we gain proficiency at anything."

Through these practice moments, or what might be termed ritual, the ordinary acts have the potential to become something more. The mundane and everyday occurrences take on a different level of meaning. Put another way, Ross (2015: P8) contends that "*ritual* does for behavior what *poetry* does for words; religious deeds grace ordinary activities the way poetic language elevates commonplace communication." Ross goes on to explain, "Ritual identifies and establishes meaning that already abides — unnoticed until then — in a person's routine behavior" (p. 10).

Courtney Martin (2016: 216) writes that through acts of ritual "we taste the sacred; through rites of passage, we devour it ... In the Celtic tradition they call these 'thin times' and 'thin places' – moments when the barrier that separates the earthly and the divine becomes porous." Like the religious acts noted previously, certain activities seem to have characteristics that give rise to the "thin places." For example, Foster (1992: 126) contends, "Washing dishes, making beds, waiting in supermarket lines – all can call us to prayer. Jogging, swimming, and walking can remind us as well." Formal faith traditions include a continuum of movement-oriented liturgical practices, from the highly animated services of the charismatic churches to the more staid intentional movement of formalized liturgical actions (e.g., taking the bread and wine, kneeling, performing the sign of the cross). In fact, by their very nature, liturgical acts involve an element of physicality—eating, drinking, reading, singing, or praying. Despite the dualistic viewpoint of many Christians—who view the "body" as somehow less valuable or worthy than the "soul"—our physicality permeates our very being and likewise impacts our identity. Foster (1992: 116) drives home this point when he writes:

> I do not have a spirit: I am a spirit. Likewise, I do not have a body: I am a body. The same is true for you … It is high time we restore a Christian incarnational understanding of the body. God's grace is mediated to us through the bodies. We worship God with our bodies. We pray with our bodies.

Not every moment of liturgy, however, may be experienced as grace-filled— thus the mystery and complexity of these spiritual practices remain. Even those committed to a cloistered life experience the Divine only occasionally, brief encounters amid the other, quite ordinary, time. Yet, amid the mundane acts of taking the bread, sipping the wine, kneeling to pray, reading the psalms, or singing worship hymns, the mystery of liturgy brings one closer to the ultimate source and opens the possibility for grace and wholeness to appear. Similarly, the act of running holds both the mundane and the grace-filled moments.

Liturgical possibilities through running

Part of the appeal and nature of running involves putting the participant in literal space and places in time—invitations for receptivity, as it were. To this point, Bogard (2017: 257) writes: "While some grounds make the sacred more accessible, and in some grounds we are more clearly invited to connect, if the sacred is anywhere, it is at our feet. We are in contact with it every time we walk [or run] out the door." As one settles into the rhythm of the run, with repetitive breathing and foot patterns, the runner has opportunity to receive and observe. The very act of running, typically outdoors and away from our concerns of work and "normal" life, provides the opportunity to enter God's presence. This daily discipline may lead to a more open and receptive stance, where one becomes increasingly aware and attentive to the natural world and to the nature of the run. While running, it is possible to sense God's presence through a sunrise, the natural surroundings of a trail run or run through farmland, or through this reflective stance come to realize a sense of gratitude or humility. Furthermore, this receptive attitude relinquishes the desire to control one's environment. Foster (1992: 144) tells a story of an individual who goes to a private retreat and encounters a "jogging monk." The monk counsels the man in attempts to focus on scripture passages in a meditative way and says, "Don't manipulate God; just receive. Communion with him isn't something you institute. It's like sleep. You can't make yourself sleep, but you can create the conditions that allow sleep to happen."

Part of this receptivity occurs as the result of the running act and transactional nature. For some runners, the more traditional Christian prayer poses—in a seated position with hands folded, eyes closed; or on bended knee—may seem too confining or rigid. Rather than praying from a static point, running provides a grounded position, albeit in a constantly changing format. In her article *Running Is Moving Meditation,* Christina Torres (2016) describes her realization of the meditative, and indeed liturgical, qualities of running:

> I surprised myself. While I'd always considered myself a mindful person, I often had trouble meditating. I would get distracted by my phone, or bugs, or the wind, or how thirsty I was or how hot I was or a million other things. Running was not the zen, silent space I imagined I could meditate in. With my feet pounding and arms pumping, how was I finding inner calm? Then, I realized God had been meeting me with moving meditation for years.

In order to grow in one's faith, and similarly, to develop as a runner, one must live in such a manner to emphasize the importance of these human projects. Indeed, this requires a sense of intentionality for sure. In the book *The Monk Manifesto,* Benedictine oblate Christine Paintner (2015) outlines seven principles dedicated toward living with purpose. These principles include (1) finding moments for silence and solitude, (2) radical acts of hospitality, (3) cultivating community, (4) cultivating awareness of one's relationship to nature through a healthy asceticism, (5) being fully present with one's work, (6) rhythms of rest and renewal, and (7) life as continual conversion and transformation.

Those who run on a daily basis, those individuals who indeed self-identify as runners in a deep way, may not consider themselves monks by any fashion. Yet, the daily ritual of running affords many of the same commitments found in Paintner's *Monk Manifesto.* Carving out moments of silence and solitude enables an attentiveness to hearing another voice (for those who run alone), cultivating community (for those who find nourishment in group runs, with the opportunity for developing and deepening friendships), experiencing healthy asceticism (note the qualifier here that discourages overcommitment or identification), and rhythms of renewal (times spent apart from others and work).

The practice of running holds potential for liturgical moments in part because the daily ritual provides a touchstone of sorts. Writing about the place of a labyrinth in the Christian tradition, Artress (2006: 14) contends, "Each of us must find our own touchstone that puts us in contact with the invisible thread ... Walking a sacred path means we know the importance of returning to the touchstone that moves us." To runners, the act of running is most certainly the touchstone in their lives, the practice, which puts them in contact with that invisible thread. They may not fully realize just what running can do for them and may take stabs at trying to verbalize this impact. On a spiritual level, however, this touchstone literally grounds us on a daily basis. Running provides a vehicle to return, day after day, to the activity which serves to move us and we realize its importance. In his book *Poverty Creek Journal*, Gardner (2014: 5) chronicles his daily run and its place in his life, where running takes him to literal places from which he experiences life around him:

> The first event most mornings is the pond—its surface, the light on it or not, the hills beyond peering down. A half mile through the woods, and then this open space. I've been doing this run for almost ten years. I gather myself here, resume a sort of open-ended conversation from the day or year before and then plunge back into the woods.

This ongoing conversation may focus on the transactional relationship between self and other—including God, nature, and other people—and an opportunity to reflect on the self in terms of personal meaning and direction. While the pond may be part of Gardner's daily routine, the experience—when viewed through an attentive lens—provides a never-ending mode of understanding. The pond itself changes, at times almost imperceptibly, impacted by wind or temperature changes, and over the course of a year and change of seasons. The runner, too, brings her own narrative to the daily run, and this intersection between the runner's life course and the pond may give rise to new insights and possible liturgical moments. The ongoing conversation may focus on the transactional relationship between self and other (e.g., God, nature, other people) and may allow for personal reflection as well.

This act of running, which serves as a potential touchstone for the runner, enables the participant to shift into a different realm of human existence, one potentially tuned toward liturgy. In *Mere Christianity*, author C.S. Lewis (1952: 153) writes:

> Good things as well as bad, you know, are caught by a kind of infection. If you want to get warm you must stand near the fire: if you want to be wet you must get into the water. If you want joy, power, peace, eternal life, you must get close to, or even into, the thing that has them. They are not a sort of prize which God could, if He chose, just hand out to anyone. They are a great fountain of energy and beauty spurting up at the very centre of reality. If you are close to it, the spray will wet you: if you are not, you will remain dry. Once a man is united to God, how could he not live forever? Once a man is separated from God, what can he do but wither and die?

Running, like other human projects, has a certain infectious quality, at least for some individuals. The thirty-something office worker, who embarks on a Couch to 5k training program, may finish the race with a desire to run another one, or to join a running club, or perhaps even train for a longer race. In this case they have caught the running bug, so to speak.

On a run, one meets the ground on every step, an action different from experiencing the world from the comfort of a recliner, or from the seat of a bicycle. While it is certainly possible to enter into worship from chairs and upon bikes, the act of running (or walking) provides an avenue for experiencing the Almighty in a different fashion, one which some individuals find appealing. An example of such liturgical approach might be what Artress (2006: 141) terms a "body prayer," the process of where "We sense our feet firmly planted on the ground, our legs, pelvis, torso, arms, neck, and head flowing with energy and life. When we are grounded in our bodies, we are stabilized and can receive information more accurately."

The act of running does not necessarily guarantee a worshipful experience. Even for those individuals who embark on a daily run with expectations of meeting God, the sublime may not necessarily appear; or at least the runner may not perceive this to be so. That said, one's stance toward the run creates conditions such that a meaningful experience may arise. For the parishioner who does not feel like attending church, the service may nevertheless become a worship time, but the chances are less so if one's attitude is not in keeping with the intent of a worship service. Yet, going through the ritual of entering a sanctuary and taking part in the service may indeed provide an avenue for a liturgical experience. While the runner may not necessarily feel like running (or worshipping) on a given day, the very act and discipline of heading out the door puts one in a position where liturgy becomes possible.

For running to be contemplative in nature, pace is an important part of the process. The exact speed, however, differs in terms of individual runners and corresponding fitness levels. One runner may struggle to run at an eight-minute/mile pace for any length of time while another runner may embody the fitness level to run at this pace for hours on end. For the novice runner, extending oneself to the point of gasping and wheezing for breath to complete a thirty-minute run, the attention and focus may be simply enduring the run as opposed to any "higher" objective. For the advanced runner, a pace near exhaustion may also preclude the likelihood of experiencing the run as a contemplative experience. This is not to say, of course, that high-intensity running is not valuable for many reasons. If one's intent is finishing a particular speed workout, or a race, it is not likely that the runner's focus will turn toward worship. There may be occasions when the runner, in the course of completing a marathon or other event, may offer prayers to the Almighty, pleading for strength and help during this time of suffering and pain. This notion of prayerful petition is different from a more meditative stance of openness and receptivity.

American philosopher Henry David Thoreau (2012), while not advocating for liturgy per se, did advance the importance of moving at a particular pace. He termed this form of speed and effort, one conducive to a mindful attentiveness, as "sauntering." Thoreau identifies two possible origins for the term, the first a reference to a form of walking with a particular purpose—a term with origins from the Middle Ages used to describe individuals walking toward "the Holy Land" (557). The second derivation of sauntering, he wrote, came from the term *sans terre*, meaning "having no particular home, but equally at home everywhere" (p. 557). In running parlance, the equivalent of Thoreau's sauntering may be a "recovery pace." While this pace differs for individuals at different fitness levels, it is roughly the speed at which they might be able to carry on a conversation (Hanc 2005). At this pace, the runner may be more receptive to contemplative thoughts as opposed to focusing on withstanding pain or completing a workout.

In the context of running and liturgy, it is logical to think that solitary runs may be more conducive to liturgical experiences as compared with group runs. This is true to the extent that solitude creates a space and time to potentially leave behind the noise of the world. During his time at Walden Pond, for example, Thoreau (2012: 306) wrote that "Some of my pleasantest hours were during long rainstorms … when an early twilight ushered in a long evening in which many thoughts had time to take root and unfold themselves." For many in the twenty-first century, the harried pace of daily life is anything but "sauntering" and includes a constant barrage of noise and continual interruptions. It is difficult to remove oneself from the stimuli of technological screens, to allow any sense of solitude or silence to take over. While solitude does certainly provide an open ground for liturgical experiences through running, this does not mean that group runs, or runs with a partner, may not also provide opportunities for liturgy. Courtney Martin (2015) describes her husband's running routine and how one particular run with a close friend provided the opportunity to share about a recent death. Martin recounts this moment and recognizes the change in her husband, describing this run with his friend as "holy space":

> My husband and one of his closest friends go on long runs in Redwoods Park near our house together these days and talk about their chaotic, wonderful lives. One afternoon, John came back and there was something different about him. It was like he was moving through the world with more reverence, with more breath and light and less dogged direction. He said, *"Today, Peter and I talked about the death of his son."* Peter's son, Lars, died at just three weeks old. He and his wife have since had another gloriously healthy baby who is almost two, and have another on the way. They're resilient, courageous people. They've experienced the worst of life and continue to make the best. I don't know exactly what John and Peter said that day, but I know it made John more fully human. They made a ritual out of their sneakers in the dirt and their eyes straight ahead, sweat and tears — I can only guess — intermixing, the unimaginable spoken and heard, the forward momentum of their legs and their hearts. It must have been a muddy, sacred thing.

By engaging in the seemingly mundane acts of everyday, we allow for grace and holy moments to appear. This brings to mind a poem by Mary Oliver (2004: 58–59), *Mindful*:

Every Day
  I see or hear
    something
      that more or less

kills me
  with delight,
    that leaves me
      like a needle

in the haystack
  of light.
    It is what I was born for—
      to look, to listen,

to lose myself
  inside this soft world—
    to instruct myself
      over and over

in joy,
  and acclamation.
    Nor am I talking
      about the exceptional,

the fearful, the dreadful,
  the very extravagant—
    but of the ordinary,
      the common, the very drab

the daily presentations.
  Oh, good scholar,
    I say to myself,
      how can you help

but grow wise
  with such teachings
    as these—
      the untrimmable light

of the world,
  the ocean's shine,
    the prayers that are made
      out of grass?

Running helps put us in a position where it becomes possible to see or hear—
to notice life around us in the form of natural surroundings and our inner muse.
While these encounters with nature may appear ordinary and even drab, the
very act makes the experience of which Oliver speaks possible. Practices such
as running hold the potential for enabling an attentive stance toward the world.

When on the run we are (often) away from others, away from work world, in touch with nature, in touch with the rhythms of our body, in touch with our inner muse, and, potentially, in touch with the Other. Despite this potential, we may run through awe-inspiring natural surroundings and yet be consumed by emotional turmoil. The individual weighted down by workplace personnel issues, for example, may find it exceedingly difficult to focus on the immediate surroundings. Thoreau (2012: 561) echoed this thought as he lamented his ability, at times, to focus: "But it sometimes happens that I cannot easily shake off the village. The thought of some work will run in my head and I am not where my body is, – I am out of my senses." Rather than beholding "the untrimmable light" around us while running, we may instead become filled with thoughts of worry, despair, hate—thoughts of the past or future instead of the present. These are missed opportunities, periods that may provide for physiological growth and progress but very little in the way of spiritual connections. As Oliver (2004) reminds us, to view the world in ways to behold the "untrimmable light" requires a certain aspect of spiritual discipline. It may be too tempting to ponder things that are not delightful, to observe and dwell on the revolting aspects of others, to perpetuate stubbornness and selfishness, to allow our inner musings to become merely navel gazing exercises. When approached in this way, the contemplative nature of running broods a form of solipsism instead of movement toward spiritual growth or true community.

Running as a spiritual discipline

Engagement in regular acts for the purpose of contemplation and ultimately liturgy potentially changes one's nature and identity, not unlike running-related acts that bring about physiological and psychological changes. Lysaught (2008: 12) contends that liturgical practices function to train adherents toward specific Christian skills and abilities: "faith, hope, charity, patience, humility, bearing with one another, prudence, truthfulness, temperance, peacemaking, mercy, reconciliation, a hunger and thirst for justice and righteousness, the ability to bear persecution, compassion, the directing of all things to the Father, and so on." It would be a stretch to contend that running would or could bring about all of these potential spiritual skills and abilities. That said, the act of running on a regular basis creates the potential for runners to become more Christ-like. For example, while on the run one may encounter an overwhelming sense of gratitude, for God's grace and for the love and support of other people. To return to C.S. Lewis' imagery of the fountain, the more time present near the fountain, the more one may grow in discipleship as a Christian.

Running may not be the liturgy of choice for all Christians, of course, but it may and can be especially appealing to a certain type of individual. Consider the differences in religious traditions and their approach to their religious practices, specifically the Benedictine order as compared with Jesuit order. Gardner (2014: 140–141) explains that "each Benedictine monk vowed 'stability,' to live out his remaining years in the monastic house he joined ... Jesuit prayer was individual, on-the-go, and self-regulating – like the *examen*." Just as Jesuits used this type of prayer because it met their needs, so too may running and praying fit with contemporary times. Those with sedentary occupations, for example, may find the repetitive, but movement-oriented, nature of running conducive to meditation and contemplation. These individuals may relish the opportunity to exercise, as it were, while simultaneously benefiting from, and appreciating, the opportunity for solitude, reflection, and perhaps even liturgy.

On a personal level, running puts me in the position for examen to occur—at times I enter this state intentionally and, at times, as the Spirit leads, so to speak. As I run, my thoughts shift over numerous items—thoughts of self, thoughts of relationships, praying for other people, times when I come up short, regrets, ideas for projects, wanting to do much better, realizing my shortcomings, having good attentions. I wonder if I may be at my best or most optimistic or most compassionate or most well-intentioned while in this state of running examen. I intend to spend more time with my kids and wife, intend to speak lovingly and not react judgmentally, and intend to pray more often and spend more time in scripture. When I finish the run I slip back into another routine—the routine of life not necessarily in examen or self-reflection, but the "normal," for me at least, life of work and home life, mortgage payments, youth sport schedules, and home repairs.

Because endurance pursuits such as running lend themselves to quiet introspection (and potentially examen and liturgy), some people choose not to run (or swim or bike) for this reason. They may believe endurance sports provide *too much* time to think and potentially examine. Contrary to the purpose of examen, these individuals may prefer not to spend *too much* time in their own presence. For some people, this self-reflection may be viewed as too risky. In his recollection of an intentional retreat spent alone in a Wisconsin cabin, Parker Palmer (2016) responded to a friend who asked him if he liked spending time alone. "It depends," Parker said. "Sometimes I'm my best friend. Sometimes I'm my worst enemy. We'll see who shows up." For those individuals not comfortable with the inevitable alone time found in running, they may gravitate toward team sports, other individual sports, and physical pursuits, or they may choose a sedentary mode of existence.

While helpful as a spiritual practice, the periods of examen one experiences while running should be more than merely self-examination. The purpose should not end with a continual inward focus or so-called navel gazing. This time of examination and self-tuning needs to be drawn back into community, toward improvement for self and others, for individuals and institutions—an act of grace. On the run we have the time and space for examen, the opportunity to do some inner work, so to speak, with the intention to become not only more Christ-like, but also to demonstrate the cash value of our Christ-likeness in our daily walk as we act and interact with our friends, family members, colleagues, and neighbors. In this way the periods of self-reflection lead to a sense of what American pragmatists refer to as meliorism, of improving upon the current version of life. This has parallels with the Christian notion of the kingdom of God: running may provide the opportunity, through self-reflection and liturgy, for bringing about the kingdom of God here on earth, using our hands and feet to do God's work.

In this way, the life of a runner, one committed to mobility, aligns with the Jesuit model for religious life. Running is a kind of engaged fieldwork, a time spent outdoors (or perhaps on the treadmill) as part of one's daily routine. The runner may hold a largely sedentary job for the bulk of the day, but the run itself provides an opportunity for an active respite from the norm. Undoubtedly, some religious adherents from various faith traditions may gather for communal prayer at fixed hours (Muslims and Jews come to mind here) or quiet themselves individually for prayer and devotion (perhaps Christians who say "grace" at mealtime). Even so, running provides an opportunity for those adherents "committed to mobility"— those who find running to be a meaningful way to experience life and liturgy.

Conclusion

In conclusion, perhaps now more than ever, it is important to carve out space and place for liturgy and potential connections between ourselves and the Other. Amid the too often harried pace of the twenty-first century, we need opportunities for renewal and retreat, for self-reflection as it impacts not only our personal lives, but also the lives of those around us. Running provides the opportunity for liturgical moment at regular times during our daily lives. It is not often that running appears on a list of "spiritual practices." This list might include more sanctioned activities such as yoga, labyrinth walking, or journaling. That said, for some people running has the potential to be experienced as a spiritual discipline and form of liturgy. While running is not for everyone, it is for some people, when practiced as such at a particular pace and with an intention directed toward, or at least open to, running as a form of liturgy.

Study Guide

The notion of spiritual disciplines holds great meaning for adherents of the Christian faith. Some of these disciplines tend toward individual growth while others contribute to Christian community. Some common spiritual disciplines include solitude, prayer, fasting, singing, reading scripture, and so forth. At times movement forms such as walking meditation, labyrinth walking, or yoga make the list of spiritual disciplines. In this chapter, the topic focuses on how running, when pursued in a certain manner, may be experienced as a form of liturgy conducive to spiritual growth.

Study Questions

1. To what extent, and in what ways, may disciplines help contribute toward spiritual growth?
2. How have spiritual disciplines—including movement forms such as running or walking—impacted your own spiritual growth?
3. What is it about the act of running which may potentially lead toward an increased stance of receptivity?
4. In what ways have you experienced grace or other instances of "holy space"?
5. To what extent does running exhibit both the "common, the very drab" and the potential for experiencing "the untrimmable light"?

Further Reading

Rohr, R. (2009), *The Naked Now: Learning to See as the Mystics See*, New York: Crossroads Pub.

Stevens, J. (2013), *The Marathon Monks of Mount Hiei*, Brattleboro, VT: Echo Point Books.

Tetlow, E. (ed) (1987), *The Spiritual Exercise of St. Ignatius Loyola*, Lanham, MD: University Press of America.

Chapter 8

ATHLETICS AS SACRIFICIAL OFFERING

Lillie K. Rodgers and F. Clark Power

I was his delight day by day,
Playing before him every moment,
playing in his inhabited world,
delighting in Adam's offspring.
Proverbs 8:30–32

Introduction

In the creation account from the Book of Proverbs as translated by Brown (2012: 28–29), Wisdom appears as a young girl, playing at God's side and among humankind. Play, an activity of the embodied spirit, is a primal feature of God's creation. It is through Wisdom's play that creation germinates, matures, and bears fruit. In this chapter, we describe athletics as a form of play, an activity of the embodied spirit, which discloses God's abiding presence to and delight in human activity. Based upon this, we reveal how athletics can be an embodied, human response of worship, or sacrificial offering, to the Creator.

As Kelly (2012) argues, play is far more than a refreshing break from the tedium and stress of work. It is not for the sake of something else, of something more serious and important. Play is by definition activity engaged in for its own sake (*ludere causi ludendendi*). Athletics, we argue, is a species of play, although its professionalization and privatization at all levels often obscure and distort its essence. In its pure form, the experience of athletics, we claim, has the potential not only to unveil God's caring presence in human life and development but also to inspire committed lives of love and sacrifice for the common good.

Play is rightfully distinguished from work or serious activity engaged in for some instrumental purpose, such as earning a living, serving in the military, or taking on political responsibility (Huizinga 1955). Yet, as anyone who has played a sport knows, the acquisition of the stamina and skills demanded by sport requires hard work. Athletics educates the soul as well as the body through practice and discipline; sports are physically and mentally demanding, and the necessary mastery of mind and body to play sports can only be acquired through effort over time. What makes athletics ultimately play and not work is that the effort is for the sake of play itself. In examining peak experiences in sports, Jackson and Csikszentmihalyi (1999) found that athletes' most joyful athletic experiences are in a psychological state of "flow" or of "being in the zone." Csikszentmihalyi (1990: 4) describes flow as a "state in which people are so involved in activity that nothing else seems to matter; the experience is so enjoyable that people will continue to do it even at a great cost for the sheer joy of doing it." Athletes in the zone are performing at their very best, yet they often describe their experience as "effortless." They see themselves as being fully focused, free, and confident. Jackson and Csikszentmihalyi (1999) point out that the flow state requires the prior acquisition of refined skills and full concentration. Paradoxically, hard work is a necessary condition for flow. Only through discipline, or what the ancient Greeks and Church Fathers called *ascesis*, can athletes acquire the mastery of body and soul that makes flow possible.

In describing the work involved in play, we do not mean that the effort of acquiring skills and training for competition is not itself a component of play. The hard work of athletics is joyful and rewarding because it is undertaken as preparation for the game, the race, the match. The good effects of the development that sport demands of us do not stop with the game but, indeed, prepare us for the rest of life—for work and civic engagement.

Returning to the passage from Proverbs, we see Wisdom and all of creation as developing in and through the delight of play. Play educates through practice and discipline. It also educates through social interaction. The Wisdom story in Proverbs focuses not only on the origin of God's creation (which begins with Wisdom) but also on creation's unfolding through continuous divine and human interaction led on by Wisdom. Brown (2012) calls Wisdom God's "play partner" (28), but she is ours as well, as Brown explains, "[Wisdom's] activity engages God and the world in the mutuality of play, holding creator and creation together through the common bond of delight" (33).

Brown (2012) unpacks the social dimension of play by drawing on the insights of Jean Piaget and other developmental psychologists, who describe play as the way in which children construct their socio-moral world. Play is an expression of children's freedom and creativity. At the earliest stages of play, children transform ordinary objects, like boxes and stones, into boats and boulders. Through hats and costumes, they become superheroes, doctors, and zookeepers. They are then introduced to competitive games, like tag and chutes and ladders, where they discover that rules and fair play are constitutive of competitive play. Games demand a new level of social understanding, cooperation, and sense of justice. These activities entail taking another person's perspective and balancing their self-interest with another's. This process of role-taking culminates in the development of the "golden rule" at the cusp of adolescence.

Although all kinds of human experiences contribute to socio-moral development, childhood play is special because it arises out of children's sense of freedom and self-direction, and it culminates in the development of autonomy. Children initiate and control their play. Although they learn to regulate their play by following rules, they come to understand that the rules of their games are social constructions, which they can change through negotiation with their peers. Proverbs depicts the essence of play as it is experienced in childhood and in adulthood (when and if we create the time and space for it).

As Brown elucidates in his commentary, play has a vertical as well as horizontal dimension. Wisdom is God's playmate and our own. In fact, Wisdom brings the divine and human together. One of the most remarkable features of the creation story in Proverbs is its depiction of God as a caring, even "doting" parent, who "childproofed" creation to make it "safe" for play (Brown 2012: 33). Unlike the Yahwist (J) account of creation in Genesis (see 2:5–3: 24), there is no fall from paradise or focus on the origins of sin, suffering, and death.

Proverbs does not deny the harshness and limitations of life but reminds one of the goodness and trustworthiness of God and all creation. Play is only a small and precious part of human life, most of which is consumed by the weal and woe of life. Moreover, play requires a measure of safety and leisure unavailable to many because of the harsh circumstances of life. As Paul puts it, "We know that the whole creation has been groaning as in childbirth right up to the present time" (Romans 8:23). When one plays, timeless as the experience is, it does not last forever. It ends when the buzzer sounds, we cross the finish line, or the inning ends. Athletics gives us an intimation of immortality, nothing more.

Renaissance scholar and former Commissioner of Major League Baseball, Bartlett Giamatti (1989: 14), describes participation in sport, whether as a fan or an athlete, as "religious," pointing to our capacity for leisure and work as well as our desire to find happiness together in community: "Sports represent a shared vision of how we continue, as an individual, team, or community, to experience a happiness of an absence of care so intense, so rare, and so fleeting that we describe the experience as religion." Note that Giamatti does not equate sport with religion. In fact, he is careful to separate the two. Yet he finds that the happiness one seeks and often finds in sport can open a window into our humanity at its very best. Athletics at its best reflects the human desire for perfection, both individual and social, in a deeply flawed world.

In his enthusiastic "*apologia*" for sports, Michael Novak (1994: 224) states that "participation in sports is a foretaste of the eschaton." This bold theological assertion may seem strange even to the most avid sports fan among us. Novak is saying more than that sports and religion have many similarities, such as rituals and emotional involvement. He elaborates, "To participate in the rites of play is to dwell in the Kingdom of ends. To participate in work, career, and the making of history is to labor in the Kingdom of means" (40). Novak draws a sharp distinction between play and work, the Kingdom of ends and the Kingdom of means. Like Giamatti, he regards play as respite from our ordinary world of labor and anxiety. But he goes further than Giamatti in suggesting that play reveals our ultimate destiny, which is to be one with God and each other in the Kingdom of God. What implications does such an understanding of play have for us here and now? Both

Giamatti and Novak suggest that we have a responsibility to ourselves and to the human family to create the conditions in both our interior life and our external social structures that protect and nourish our rites of play. Christians understand that the Kingdom of God is both already and not yet (see 1 John 3:2; Hebrews 2:8–9). As we see in Proverbs, Wisdom's play is by its nature inviting and inclusive. All of us are called to play in the Kingdom of ends, and our task this side of the eschaton is to welcome all into the game.

The human person: Unity of body and soul

The anthropology underlying our vision of athletics is one that sees the human person as a fundamental unity of body and soul. Christianity took root and grew in a Greek culture heavily influenced by Platonism, which saw the body as a tomb or prison for the soul. Christianity had to work hard to defend the dignity of the body within a unified conception of the human person. Within the early Church especially, dualistic movements repeatedly emerged, with Gnosticism, Manichaeism, and Docetism as some of the most threatening (see *Catechism of the Catholic Church* 2002: 285). Dualism also was at the heart of later controversies within the medieval Church, such as those regarding the use of sacraments and sacred images within worship. Yet ultimately, prominent Church theologians—from Augustine to Aquinas—arose to combat the dualism of their time. They appealed not only to the doctrine of the creation of matter and spirit but also to the mysteries of the incarnation and resurrection.

Overall, there is no room within the Christian tradition for a Platonic disdain for the body, as if the body somehow is "under" the soul. In fact, there is no room for dualism at all. Instead, the orthodox anthropology of the Christian faith is one of unity between the body and soul. Macquarrie (1983: 53) thus argues that the human person is neither an "animated body" nor an "embodied soul" for neither term adequately expresses one's true anthropology. Most fundamentally, he writes, there is an "irreducible category, namely, that of 'person,' which is a unity."

Sacramentality and the body

A central characteristic of the Catholic-Christian tradition, but which is incorporated in other churches—like those in Eastern Christianity and forms of Anglicanism—is its emphasis on creation as mediating God's presence:

> No theological principle or focus is more characteristic of Catholicism or more central to its identity than the principle of sacramentality. The Catholic vision sees God in and through all things: other people, communities, movements, events, places, objects, the world at large, the whole cosmos. (McBrien 1994: 1196)

In other words, at its very heart, Catholicism is a "sacramental" Church, for humanity accesses God in and through created reality. Because of a vision of the unity of body and soul, it follows that human beings perceive God through the signs and symbols of creation.

Avery Dulles (1980: 55–56) calls this the "symbolic structure of revelation." He writes:

> Revelation never occurs in a purely internal experience or as an unmediated encounter with God. It is always mediated through an experience in the world. More specifically, it is mediated through symbol—that is to say, through an externally perceived sign that works mysteriously on the human consciousness so as to suggest more than it can clearly describe or define.

While humanity can connect with God through the mind and soul, this only is made possible first by bodily existence, which Mitchell (2006: 175, 187) calls "the meeting place between God and humanity ... the privileged site of God's self-communication." This is a sacramental view of the body; the body is the "sacrament" of the person in that it makes present a deeper, invisible reality. In the words of Avery Dulles (1980: 55–56), "Religious awareness," therefore, "paradoxically, requires a turning *to* the world." Indeed, it requires a turning *to* the body, *through* the body. Christianity is inherently sacramental because God self-discloses through physical, created reality. All "spiritual" experiences are made possible in and through the body.

Asceticism and bodily sacrifice

The term "asceticism" comes from the Greek word "askesis," which refers to the training regimen to prepare for athletic competition. Such training involved abstaining from certain foods and vigorous exercise (Cunningham and Egan 1996). As a result of Platonic influences, asceticism became a means of freeing the soul from bodily appetites. Early Christian writers, such as Jerome and Augustine, pictured the body as the source of temptation and in need of subjugation. Throughout the history of Christianity, spiritual writers often encouraged the mortification of the body through practices ranging from abstinence and fasting to self-flagellation.

The martyrs did not operate out of a dualistic ontology, whereby the body was seen as unimportant and thus could be cast off to free the soul. No, it was what they endured bodily that allowed their biographers to use athletic metaphors to describe the martyrs. For example, according to his hagiography, Pionus—a third-century martyr who was burned at the stake—upon reaching the amphitheater, "gladly removed his clothes as the prison keeper stood by. Then, realizing the holiness and dignity of his own body, he was filled with great joy ... those of us who were present saw his body like that of an athlete in full array at the height of his powers" (Cardman 1993: 98–104, 149). Similarly, the author of the account of the martyrs of Lyons and Vienne depicted Blandina as "a noble athlete" who "although small and weak and greatly despised, she had put on the great and invincible athlete Christ, and in many contests had overcome the Adversary and through the conflict had gained the crown of immortality" (Kelly 2012: 101). Lastly, Ignatius of Antioch encouraged Polycarp to embrace his persecution and eventual martyrdom as "God's athlete" (Kelly 2012: 99).

While the Roman state showed disdain for the bodies of martyred Christians— casting the bodily remains to dogs, and burning bodies and throwing the ashes into the Rhone River, so that they could not be buried—the Church found profound beauty in the martyrs' bodies. According to Keenan (1994: 337), "while the state made these [martyred] bodies objects of attack and derision, the Church depicted them as gloriously triumphant ... [for] in martyrdom the Christian finds freedom, not from the body, but from death; the martyr's body triumphs."

Within this early tradition of martyrdom emerged the origins of Christianity's willingness to see the body as the means of worship, as previously mentioned. More specifically, this worship took the form of imitating Jesus' self-sacrifice. Second-century bishop Ignatius of Antioch (1885: 73), for example, while traveling on the way to his martyrdom in Rome, where he would be given up to the lions, referred to himself as the "wheat of God" who longed "to be found a sacrifice to God." In sum, the martyr's body was revered, rather than defiled, by death, and the martyr became a sacrificial offering of worship, in imitation of Jesus' own suffering and death.

Beginning with Cyprian and later as Christianity aligned itself with the state during the reign of Constantine, the ascetical imitation of Christ transferred from the "red martyrs," who shed their blood, to the "white martyrs," who died to the world and its allurements without physical death (Kinnard 2006). These white martyrs became the monastics, who separated themselves from the world and devoted themselves to prayer, bodily discipline, and work.

According to Athanasius' biography of Anthony, who is considered the founder of monasticism, Anthony's daily routine was as physically demanding as any athlete's (Bouyer 1963). He spent whole nights in prayer, without sleeping (a discipline called "watchfulness"); when he did sleep, he lay on a thin mat or on the bare ground. He maintained an austere diet of bread, salt, and water; he ate only once a day at most, sometimes less when fasting. Even more important than these disciplines, however, Anthony's central task each day was his manual labor: basket weaving. Commenting on Anthony's life, Bouyer (1963: 309) writes, "Work, work which brings sweat to the brow, is the primary form of asceticism, the necessary basis for all the others ... However, throughout his life of labour itself, the monk applies himself to a new task which is properly his own: prayer, a prayer which tends to become constant." Herein lies the origins of the motto of the Benedictine Order—*Ora et labora*, prayer and work. Indeed, prayer and work, especially the bodily work of the monastics, are partners that cannot be separated.

Overall, for the ancient monastics, the ideal was not a "wholly spiritual asceticism," as if ascetical practices were distinct from the body. The ascetics did not reject the body as sinful. In Bouyer's (1963) words, the monastics like Anthony "had no contempt either for creation or for the body. It was precisely, we might say, because they did not misprise the latter that they knew how necessary it is to master it." Ascetical practices were situated in the context of the goodness of creation and the need for purification and integration after the fall. By sacrificing inordinate desires and attachments, for the monastics, or their very lives, for the martyrs, the ancient ascetics reformed the soul by way of the body, showing the inseparability of body and soul.

Positive regard for the body in spite of its implication in sin continued into the medieval period, where a look at devotional practice reveals an outright affirmation of the body as the privileged site of spiritual endeavors. Medieval Christians traveled on pilgrimages, walked in processions, put on mystery plays, and created great works of art, among other devotions. All of these activities, which were ostensibly physical in nature, were believed to be undoubtedly *spiritual*. In addition to the above list, Christians during the medieval period were known for playing sports on Sundays and feast days. And by the late fourteenth century, the humanist and Jesuit schools included games and sports as an integral part of their curricula.

However, there was a noticeable shift in the Church's approach to athletics within modernity, due in large part to two factors. First, in the sixteenth century, the Puritans emerged and proposed a new understanding of work and leisure. According to their theology, godliness was associated with one's work, and leisure activities were viewed with suspicion. Athletics in particular often was associated with sin. Second, the Enlightenment and thinkers like Descartes of the seventeenth century reintroduced a dualistic framework where body and soul were seen as opposites: the body as material and unthinking, and the soul as immaterial and thinking.

However, this approach to athletics has gone out of style more recently, with the Church recovering its authentic theological anthropology. Pope John Paul II (2000), for instance, encouraged people to regard athletics with esteem for what it can offer to the human person's integral development, including one's spirituality. In his words, "Athletic activity, in fact, highlights not only man's valuable physical abilities, but also his intellectual and spiritual capacities. It is not just physical strength and muscular efficiency, but it also has a soul and must show its complete face." A more in-depth theology of athletics can help foster our self-understanding as fully corporeal, fully spiritual beings—revealing that the body and soul cannot be separated from one another.

The athlete's vocation of sacrificial offering

As we have noted, a theologically robust approach to athletics must be built on several basic principles of theological anthropology. First, sport, which is fundamentally play, has intrinsic value as an expression of human freedom and dignity. Second, the experience of sport as play affirms the goodness of creation and humanity's ultimate purpose and destiny to be happy with God forever. Third, like sexuality, sport demonstrates the beauty of the body and the goodness of bodily delights. Fourth, sport cannot escape the ambiguities of human existence. Although athletics can bring out the best in humanity, it also can become pernicious, serving the interests of power, prestige, and wealth.

We believe that the best way to keep athletics in perspective is by developing a spirituality of sport. Christian living requires sacrificing one's own needs and desires for the good of the other. Paradoxically, it is in the complete giving of oneself in love that true happiness is found, and this paradox of giving and receiving is experienced through sport. The *ascesis* of athletic training demands a sacrifice of body and spirit, and the roles of teammate and opponent demand a sacrifice of the ego to foster the common good of athletic competition. The goodness of sport, understood theologically, is not that it provides us with an "escape" from our everyday cares and preoccupations, but that it immerses us more deeply into our shared vocation of sacrificial love.

This understanding of athletics stands in contrast to the common experience of sport, during which sport becomes an idol and its performance an opiate that satisfies the self at the expense of the other. Its artificiality—evident in its rules and conventions, which mark it off from the rest of one's experiences—should guard us from mistaking sport for life. And yet, all too often sport elicits a devotion meant only for God and becomes a cult, which detaches its followers from responsible life as members of the human community (Giamatti 1989).

To be authentic, athletics needs a spirituality that connects the experience of sport including its *ascesis* with the Christian vocation of sacrificial love, particularly to the poor and others in need. The vocation of the Christian athlete is one of self-offering with a consciousness that one's whole self, including one's play, is a gift to be shared with others as an offering of thanksgiving and adoration. In his letter to the Romans (12:1), Paul urges the congregation "to offer your bodies as a living sacrifice, holy and pleasing to God, your spiritual worship." The word "sacrifice," which comes from the Latin *sacrificium,* can be translated, "to make sacred or holy." With this in mind, athletics as sacrifice is the transformation of the ordinary gifts of one's talents, energy, and freedom into a holy offering—to God and to our sisters and brothers who have a God-given right to play. This vocation of the Christian athlete entails freeing oneself of ego-driven desires to become a disciple of Christ, modeling oneself upon Christ's *kenosis* or self-emptying.

This spirituality of athletics has important implications for how and why one competes as well as for one's life beyond sport. In its simplest form, the goal of athletics is not to glorify oneself but to glorify God. Competing hard and winning are a part of God's grace working through us; however, winning is not the penultimate or sole goal. For example, the interdenominational ministry Athletes in Action instructs athletes to imagine that they are playing for an "Audience of One"—God—for the purpose of glorifying God alone.

To this spiritual notion of playing for a divine audience, we hasten to add that the play that glorifies God must include beneficence to one's neighbors. Christian spirituality is never an exclusively private affair. As 1 John 4:20 instructs, we cannot love God whom we do not see without loving our sisters and brothers whom we do see. Our personal relationship with God must always open our hearts to those on the margins; otherwise, it becomes an empty gesture or even a form of idolatry (see Matt 25:40–45). When we see play for what it is—God's gift to all—then we can never be content knowing that so many adults as well as children cannot play because they are hungry, sick, at work, or have no safe place to gather; the freedom and leisure that make play possible are not meant to be the privilege of a few. The Christian athlete's vocation thus is to be connected with Christ and with others, particularly those on the margins, through the sacrificial offering of one's bodily efforts as spiritual worship.

Conclusion

In this chapter, we have developed a framework for both a theology and a spirituality of athletics as play. Using the creation story from Proverbs 8, we have argued that when we experience the happiness of play, we experience God's love for us and our destiny to play with God in the eternal Kingdom. We also have emphasized that sport is an experience of freedom that involves the body as well as the soul. Given this framework, we criticized both religious and nonreligious attempts to denigrate the body as evil and play as idleness. Our intention is not to present sport as a religion, nor to persuade Christians to become sports fanatics, but to understand how the body necessarily mediates our relationships with each other and God. Any bodily action—from kneeling in prayer, to going for a run, to singing, painting, or playing the piano—can be a spiritual act of worship. Christians should embrace their physical activities, regardless of how athletic or physically exerting they are, as inherently spiritual opportunities. As the theological anthropology argued for in this chapter demonstrates, Christians truly are "the most sublime of materialists," as Karl Rahner (1977:183) claims, for what one does with the body cannot be separated from what he or she does with the soul.

Yet, just as the intention is not to turn everyone into an athlete, this chapter also does not call for the spiritualization of sport, as if athletes should focus on prayer for each and every second of their athletic pursuits. In other words, the runner does not need to consciously pray throughout his or her run; no, the run itself becomes the prayer—the offering, the gift of oneself, and one's efforts for the glory of God. Recall from earlier that worship involves not mere interiority and intellect but the "prayer of the body itself." As Peter Berger (1970:60) puts it, "The experience of joyful play is not something that must be sought on some mystical margin of existence. It can be readily found in the reality of ordinary life. Yet within this experienced reality it constitutes a signal of transcendence, because its intrinsic intention points beyond itself".

It should thus come as no surprise that theologians such as Romano Guardini see the liturgy and thus all Christian worship as a form of play. In an essay he wrote on the eve of World War II, Guardini encouraged Catholics "to play the divinely ordained game of the liturgy in liberty and beauty and holy joy before God" (1997:70). Similarly, according to "Play Theologians" like Hugo Rahner and Jurgen Moltmann, when humans encounter play in and of itself, they participate in the divine life. All play, Rahner (1972) contends, "is an attempt to approximate to the Creator, who performs his work with the divine seriousness which its meaning and purpose demand, and yet with the spontaneity and effortless skill of the great artist he is, creating because he wills to create and not because he must" (28). In this way, play becomes "an anticipation of heavenly joy; a kind of rehearsal, fashioned into gesture, sound or word of that Godward directed harmony of body and soul we call heaven" (8). Quite simply, humanity at play preempts the heavenly dance. Similarly, the athlete at work meets the divine.

Athletics at its best, when it accords with its ultimate purpose, is to glorify God and sacrifice for others. Lost in their love of the game, athletes truly encounter God, sharing in God's delight and worshipping through the sacrificial and spiritual offering of their bodies. Just as importantly, athletes must connect their sacrifices with a concern for others, whether that be their teammates, their opponents, or others for whom they offer their efforts. In this way, sport builds the Kingdom of God on earth and unites members of the Body of Christ.

The conclusions of this chapter are not the result of pure theological research or intellectual ponderings, but the combination of such research and ponderings with the push-and-shove of real-life experience. More than any other area of our lives, the realm of athletics has proven to be the most fruitful avenue for the development of our Christian faith and character. While for so many today, athletics is a means to achieve personal glory, for many of us, athletics has been a continually humbling reminder of our weaknesses. As a walk-on basketball player in college, undersized and a half step slower than my teammates, I (the lead author) rode the bench for four straight years, thus learning that sport wasn't about just me. With time, prayer, and the gentle coaching of my Christian mentors, I learned the value of self-sacrifice—whether I was running sprints at the end of practice or cheering on my teammates from the bench during a game—out of a desire to glorify God and to give generously of myself to my team, regardless of my personal success.

Long-distance running has proven to be just as verdant a training ground for sacrificial offering as the basketball court (and its sideline benches) once did. The monotony, the pounding, the physical strain of miles upon miles is but the smallest reminder of Christ's own journey with the cross. A favorite spiritual practice is to run a race as a prayerful offering for someone in need, or even to have each mile dedicated to a specific intention. Overall, using our bodies through athletics reminds us to be grateful and places us in right relationship with others and with God—the God who gave us the ability to run, who sustains us as we play, and who looks upon us with delight as we use our gifts joyfully with others in mind.

Study Guide

Drawing on Proverbs 8, we argue that sport is play and that God made us to and for play. These ideas may seem strange to many readers who think about sport as entertainment or a way to stay fit and God as a serious lawgiver and judge. We do not deny that sports are a form of entertainment and that they serve many different purposes. Yet we hope you will reflect on the nature of sport itself and what makes sports so enjoyable for both the fan and the athlete. Sports are games to be played for the sake of playing, even for scholarship and professional athletes. Sports are human creations, expressions of our freedom as God's children, made in the image and likeness of our Creator. As Novak (1994) points out, sports at their best can offer us a foretaste of the "eschaton," pointing us to the Kingdom of God when we will experience complete happiness as a human community in God's presence. Sports not only bring us exquisite delight but also elicit extraordinary devotion, engaging us—body and soul. The consciously Christian athlete accepts the discipline, the *ascesis*, that sports demands not out of a disdain for the body or a desire to overcome the limitations of mortality, but as an offering to God. Sport played with gratitude and surrender to the will of God can bring us to a greater awareness of God's love for us. It can also lead us to a heightened consciousness of our connectedness to the human community, especially to those who live on the margins of society.

Study Questions

1. What is the nature of "play," and how can play become sacrificial in a way that aligns it with its God-ordained purpose?
2. What are some examples of dualism between body and soul in contemporary society, or within athletics more specifically?
3. What is meant by "sacramentality," and does your church community hold to this belief, even in a limited way? How does sacramentality impact how one understands athletics?
4. What sacrifices do athletes make in sport, and how can these have a religious parallel to ancient martyrs and monastics in the Church?
5. What is the "vocation" of the Christian athlete, and how is this vocation lived out?

Further Reading

Kelly, P. (2012), *Catholic Perspectives on Sports: From Medieval to Modern Times*, New York: Paulist Press.
Novak, M. (1994), *The Joy of Sports: Endzones, Bases, Baskets, Balls, and the Consecration of the American Spirit*, Lanham, MD: Madison Books.

Chapter 9

INTEGRATING FAITH: SPORT PSYCHOLOGY FOR CHRISTIAN ATHLETES AND COACHES

Trevor J. Egli and Matt Hoven

Introduction

Robert is a captain and starting quarterback on his American high school football team and is known by both his teammates and his coaches as someone who identifies as a Christian. He regularly attends worship services with his family, as his parents are leaders in his particular church, and he has even attended multiple summer camps hosted by the Fellowship of Christian Athletes. In preparation for his games, Robert writes Bible verses on his wristbands and participates in reciting the Lord's Prayer before leaving the locker room for the start of each game. However, after reciting the Lord's Prayer, he often provides his teammates with an emotional pep talk laced with several obscenities to degrade the current opponent. Robert encourages his teammates while at play, but he is often both verbally and physically abusive to his opponents. He believes these acceptable parts of the game enable victory on the field. Despite his team's on-field success, Robert's mood depends on his individual performance, in particular his statistics, which will negatively impact his behavior for days following a poor showing on the gridiron.

Is Robert a mentally tough athlete? How well did this athlete integrate his faith in sport? As a player or coach, you may be able to relate to this story from your own sporting experiences, where a religiously devoted person seemingly lives a double life on and off the field of play. You may have goals for yourself, but they may never seem good enough, or maybe you struggle to maintain your emotions during competition. Overall, the story is more common than you might think for both men and women, especially since I have encountered similar situations while working with Christian athletes in a sport psychology consulting relationship. Early on in our working relationship, a frequently stated primary goal of these athletes is the integration of the Christian faith into their sporting experience. In the example of Robert, we might be able to see that his identity is performance based—that is, outcomes of his sporting performance impact his daily mood and even his self-perceptions. In addition, using vulgar language and excessive aggressive behavior, he engages in the culture of sport that he may find unacceptable in other areas of his life. However, I believe that how a Christian athlete or coach integrates their faith within sport is a task that can be learned and practiced and oftentimes is not given much deliberate thought. Robert may benefit from such practices.

There are many faith-based athletes who find living out their faith difficult in the midst of competitive sport, like the fictitious Robert in the story above (see, e.g., Stevenson 1991). As a certified mental performance consultant (CMPC) (the first author) who has worked with a number of Christians, I hear athletes saying that they want to please and glorify God through their sporting experience, but their behavior, like Robert's, is not always consistent with those desires. As Paul stated in Romans 7:17–19:

> As it is, it is no longer I myself who do it, but it is sin living in me. For I know that good itself does not dwell in me, that is, in my sinful nature. *For I have the desire to do what is good, but I cannot carry it out.* For I do not do the good I want to do, but the evil I do not want to do—this I keep on doing. (New International Version) (emphasis added)

I believe Paul's stated dilemma—that his understanding of himself is often not reflected in his actions—is true of many athletes and coaches today. Although this may be true at times, I also believe it is possible to glorify God in our sporting experiences and carry out our desires to please God within this context. More specifically, as a Christian mental performance consultant, I believe participation in sport and the integration of faith with psychological skills have the power to provide an avenue for spiritual formation and holistic growth for any sportsperson. In light of the example of Robert above, the chapter will first present a brief summary of the relevant research related to Christianity and sport psychology before presenting a Christian sport psychology model. I will also include practical suggestions for how Christian sportspersons may utilize psychological skills to enhance their personal faith.

Christian athletes and coaches in sport

There is very scant sport psychology literature that engages Christianity (Egli, Czech, Shaver, Todd, Gentner, and Biber 2014a). Stevenson (1991, 1997) has completed two studies that examined the athletic experiences of Christians in elite sport. In his first study, Stevenson (1991) looked at how Christian athletes understood their identities as a "Christian" and as an "athlete" within the context of sport. Thirty-one athletes involved in Athletes in Action (AIA), a Christian sport ministry, were interviewed and categorized into one of three role-identity types based on their behaviors and spiritual understanding. The categories included segregated, selective, or committed. As one might assume, the segregated Christian athletes often compartmentalized these two identities based on context. Many spoke of how they were uncertain of how to integrate the two. Selective

Christian athletes brought their Christian faith into sport; however, the cultural norms of sport, such as excessive violence or a willingness to do anything to win, were often deemed acceptable and took precedence over their religious faith. This was the most common experience for the Christian athletes in the study. Committed Christian athletes, according to Stevenson, put their Christian identity above all other identities, including that of an athlete. Despite this commitment, they still discussed struggling to resist being consumed by the culture of sport. Some athletes even left sport because of this dilemma.

Stevenson's (1997) second study on Christian athletes was concerned with understanding their major struggles in elite sport, as well as their coping strategies with these struggles. Similar to his first study, he interviewed thirty-one Christian athletes within AIA. Five common themes of difficulty emerged from the data within elite sport. These included (a) the importance placed on winning, (b) the importance placed on social status, (c) navigating the relationship with the team and coaches, (d) treatment and relationship with opponents, and (e) the expectations of others outside of sport. These struggles led these Christian athletes either to experience a "crisis" within their sport or to find greater purpose behind their involvement. Ultimately, these dilemmas and consequences led these athletes to turn to their faith for solutions and gaining perspective. This entailed some having a greater commitment to sport and wanting to win more than ever, but in doing so they accepted the cultural norms of sport. Others were led to act in a more "Christian" manner within sport. This approach impacted their behavior in their desire to follow the rules, maintain proper emotions within sport, and use their status within sport as a platform for sharing Christ. Three Christian athletes chose to leave sport altogether, as the culture of sport strained their faith and they were unwilling to compromise this central principle in their lives.

Similar to Christian athletes' faith integration struggles, Bennett, Sagas, Flemming, and Von Roenn (2005) found comparable difficulties in their case study of a Division I, elite college coach, who openly felt tensions toward his Christian faith within elite sport. More specifically, his drive to win, pressures to maintain or increase social status, and his overall behavior in sport proved the most challenging for him. His solutions to these dilemmas were threefold: (a) disconnecting from his coaching identity in sport, (b) using a "take it or leave it" mentality toward coaching, and (c) acknowledging God's control over all areas of his life. All in all, this coach realized that he had to avoid certain areas of competitive sport in order to salvage his identity and his Christian faith.

Although all three studies mentioned above (Bennett et al. 2005; Stevenson 1991, 1997) were conducted with elite athletes and an elite coach, it may be safe to assume Christian athletes and Christian coaches at all levels experience similar dilemmas. One should also recognize that we do not fully know how these Christian athletes turned to their faith or what exact spiritual practices the coach employed. As I mentioned in the opening story, having the presumably right intentions and beliefs does not necessarily lead athletes to their desired outcome. These studies provide us insight into the experiences of Christian sportspersons, which demonstrates the challenge of faith integration.

Because this literature does not offer a practical approach to how Christian sportspersons might narrow the gap between intentions and behaviors, I next present one approach of Christian faith integration through engagement in sport psychology.

Sport psychology and Christian faith

Unlike the fields of psychology and counseling, which in some cases offer spiritual and religious approaches to their work (Meier, Minirth, Wichern, and Ratcliff 2010), sport psychology has yet to offer such perspectives. Although spirituality and religion are seen as "taboo" in the sport psychology training (Egli, Fisher, and Gentner 2014b), there is evidence that athletes are interested in practicing sport psychology through their faith tradition (Egli and Fisher 2016; Mosley, Frierson, Cheng, and Aoyagi 2015). Therefore, in hopes of developing similar practices within sport psychology, I offer how sport psychology can draw support from Christian traditions. The following discussion of how sport psychology can be integrated with Christianity draws from sport psychology research and other resources focused on understanding and engaging with spiritual and/or Christian sportspersons, and the author's personal experience as a CMPC working with this particular population.

When choosing to include a Christian worldview in sport psychology, it is important to recognize how one views the relationship between psychology and theology. Some argue that psychology and theology are polar opposites, while others see common ground between them yet do not confirm the validity of religious beliefs or experiences (Carter and Narramore 1979). Furthermore, these two fields may be seen as having points of contact with each other while remaining distinct from one another. Here, theology and sport psychology approaches can fuse together for the benefit of athletes. Christian counseling literature labels this an integrative model, as biblical theology and psychosocial sciences are mutually supportive and work together for athletes (Carter and Narramore 1979). As a mental performance consultant and as one who believes that God is the fountain of all truth (Hebrews 12:2), I know many places of congruence between psychology and theology. Taking this approach means that consultants have (or should have) thought about their assumptions, such as their image of God, the nature of human beings, scripture, sin, forgiveness, and hope (Clinton and Ohlschlager 2002). Although these beliefs may be viewed differently by consultants, they themselves must be aware of their own understandings to avoid projecting their own viewpoint on others.

A primary goal of traditional sport psychology consulting is to help athletes and coaches become more consistent and better sporting performers through implementation of psychological skills training that increases self-awareness. This is also true of a Christian sport psychology model, but it has a concurrent goal of helping athletes and coaches respond to larger questions of identity and meaning, along with developing as persons of faith (Nesti 2004). This is done by integrating psychological skills and spiritual disciplines within the sporting experience: when Christian sportspersons include this training, they can transcend ordinary experiences in sport and provide an avenue for spiritual formation.

Psychological skills training and spiritual disciplines

Weinberg and Gould (2015: 248) declare: "Psychological skills training refers to learning to systematically and consistently practice mental or psychological skills for the purpose of enhancing performance, increasing enjoyment, or achieving greater sport and physical activity self-satisfaction." Similar to physical training, mental skills require time and effort by participants to produce positive results. Some common psychological skills include managing anxiety or energy levels, goal setting, imagery, self-talk, communication, attentional control (focus), as well as others (AASP 2017). For example, athletes can learn to create a positive mantra or phrase they can say to themselves that will boost confidence or calm their minds, or they may learn diaphragmatic breathing to relax themselves during a stoppage in play. Integrating elements of a sportsperson's religion with psychological skills is a process some sport psychology scholars believe to be beneficial when athletes or coaches bring this lived aspect into the consulting relationship (Balague 1999; Egli et al. 2014 ab; Egli and Fisher 2016, 2017; Watson and Nesti 2005).

Psychological skills training requires discipline on behalf of the athlete and can support the use of spiritual disciplines. In his classic text *The Spirit of the Disciplines* (1988: 68), Willard defines spiritual disciplines as "activities of mind and body purposefully undertaken, to bring our personality and total being into effective cooperation with divine order." He discusses a multitude of spiritual disciplines in his book and categorizes them as either "disciplines of abstinence" or "disciplines of engagement." Acts such as solitude, fasting, frugality, and chastity are considered disciplines of abstinence, whereas study, worship, service, and prayer are considered disciplines of engagement. It is also important to note that Willard cautions his readers about the difficulty of practicing these spiritual disciplines:

> The need for extensive practice of a given discipline is an indication of our *weakness*, not our strength. We can even lay it down as a rule of thumb that if it is *easy* for us to engage in a certain discipline, we probably don't need to practice it. The disciplines we need to practice are precisely the ones we are *not* "good at" and hence do not enjoy. (138) (his emphasis)

A spiritual discipline leads us to rely on God's grace and not solely on our own strength. Being disciplined requires effort and oftentimes requires us to do something we might not want to do. However, if we know *why* we're enacting such disciplines, then we may experience more success in their efforts.

Christian practices in sport psychology

Bringing Christian practices to sport psychology is about more than using mental processes to become closer to God. Looking at Willard's (1988) above definition of spiritual disciplines, they include "activities of both mind and body"; however, this involves more than just changing how we think or becoming mentally tough. In Matthew's Gospel (6:21), Jesus says, "For where your treasure is, there your heart will be also." The heart is where people draw their emotions and deepest desires from. Our behaviors and actions reflect, even in a distorted way, what is in our heart. And our "treasure" can be seen in our habits, and "no habit or practice is neutral" (Smith 2009: 83). Habits, cultivated over time, move either toward or away from the love of Christ. Smith (58) describes our habits as:

> inscribed on our heart through bodily practices and rituals that train the heart, as it were, to desire certain ends. This is a noncognitive sort of training, a kind of education that is shaping us without our realization.

Therefore, before sport participants may begin to change their actions or behaviors, they must understand their habits and where they are directed—as St. Augustine of Hippo has noted. Thus, for athletes and coaches who are willing to begin practicing psychological skills, it must start with knowing central questions about their intentions: Why do I play sport? Why do I work hard? Why do I respond to competition the way I do? Those Christian athletes and coaches working with a mental performance consultant who includes faith can thus enable them to examine their relationship with Jesus as the central "treasure" in their life and determine their openness to the transforming movement of God's grace.

With the space remaining, I will offer three ways Christian sportspersons might use such disciplines to grow closer to Christ within the context of sport. These will include prayer, study, and practicing the presence of God.

Prayer. Willard (1988) describes prayer as a discipline of engagement because it requires action on the part of the prayer. Watson and Czech (2005), thus, defined prayer as "adherents' religious practice of communicating with God" (27). Sport psychology researchers have found that prayer is not uncommon for Christian athletes (Czech, Wrisberg, Fisher, Thompson, and Hayes 2004; Hoven 2019; Mosley et al. 2015; Park 2000; Vernacchia, McGuire, Reardon, and Templin 2000) and Christian coaches (Egli, Czech, Shaver, Todd, Gentner, and Biber 2014).

Czech et al. (2004) have conducted the most comprehensive research on how Christian athletes experience prayer. They interviewed nine elite collegiate (i.e., NCAA Division I) Christian athletes and discerned four major themes from the data. They described the first theme as *performance-related prayers*. Athletes used prayer as a method to cope with the stresses of their sport, including for their safety and the ability to play their best. Next emerged the theme of *routine*. Primarily, this referred to Christian athletes praying before, during, or after practice and competition in a format that was rarely deviated. The third theme was *thankfulness*, which one co-participant explained as a way for him to be motivated and give 100 percent effort during his performances. Lastly, the theme of *God's will* emerged. This reflected the athletes' understanding that their performance outcomes were "under the influence of God's will" (8), which offered them a balanced, yet supported perspective. Czech et al. (2004) were able to provide informed insights into how Christian athletes experienced prayer; however, little is known about the experience of Christian coaches.

Building on this research, Egli et al. (2014a) asked a similar question of elite collegiate (i.e., NCAA Division I) Christian coaches. Six coaches were interviewed and four themes emerged: (a) *relying on God's guidance*, (b) *roles of coaching*, (c) *prayer types*, and (d) *subtle influence*. *Relying on God's guidance* reflected a need for seeking God's wisdom when team issues arose, trusting God's will, and trusting God as a way for coping with the job stress. The second theme, *the roles of coaching*, demonstrated the use of prayer as a way to remember the impact they had on their players, as a method of preparing for each day, and as a way to put success into perspective. *Prayer types* described the context in which they experienced prayer, which included both individual and team prayer. The fourth theme of *subtle influence* was a way for coaches to gain perspective on how their Christian faith impacted their teams, as their goal was never to proselytize but to have the light of Christ shine through them as a coach—thus creating a subtle influence.

Athletes and coaches have different roles within sport; however, there are similarities among Christians praying in these positions. For example, prayer is often used as a method of coping (Czech et al. 2014; Egli et al. 2014b; Park 2000). Sport psychology consultants have expressed that conversations that turn to spiritual topics can become more impactful when prayer is utilized (Egli et al. 2014b). In addition, the routine of prayer is a powerful tool for athletes and may even be used as a method of team cohesion (Egli et al. 2014a). Theologically speaking, sportspersons should try to constantly foster the practice of prayer and ensure that a faith-based practice not merely becomes a method of mental preparation—in effect, distorting the original intention of prayer. It is beneficial to approach Jesus with the same desire as the disciples and ask, "Lord, teach us to pray" (Lk. 11:1). Willard (1988: 185) states: "The more we pray, the more we think to pray, and as we see the results of prayer—the responses of our Father to our requests—our confidence in God's power spills over into other areas of our life." Learning to pray is an ongoing process and may be helped by practical guides written by Peña (2004) and Lipe (2015) and should consider potential moral dangers of prayer in sport (Hochstetler 2009). Prayer may be practiced as a discipline by itself, but it is often practiced with other disciplines and activities, such as study and meditation (Willard 1988).

Study. It is not uncommon for athletes and coaches to constantly study their sport. This may include watching films to learn about opponents, watching their past performances to determine areas of correction, or reviewing plays and strategies. While this form of study is often helpful for athletes, Christian sportspersons also can consider the discipline of study as engaging "with the written and spoken

Word of God" (Willard 1998: 176). The writer of Psalm 119 reflects the importance of this practice. Similar to prayer, Willard (1988) discusses study as not only a discipline of engagement but also the "primary discipline of engagement" (176). He goes on to say that it is an essential practice that can be done individually or "under the ministry of gifted teachers who can lead us deeply into the Word and make us increasingly capable of fruitful study on our own" (177). Reflecting on relevant scripture passages is another method sport psychology consultants have used with Christian athletes to help them integrate their faith into mental training (Egli et al. 2014b). It is important for sportspersons to cautiously integrate scripture into one's lived situation—here drawing on a sound biblical commentary may prove essential. The goal of studying engages the mind and heart in deeper reflection on athletes' identity in sport and beyond, supporting the whole person and not simply offering to "fix a problem" or improve sporting performance. As the mind and heart continue to be transformed by God's Word, a more complete transformation of the sportspersons' lives, including their sporting activities, is possible. As prayer may be included in their study of Christian scripture, both may be part of practicing the presence of God.

Practicing the presence of God. We know from Stevenson's (1991) study that not all Christian athletes name personally experiencing God within their sporting experience. Although some might state having had spiritual experiences, it still may not include a conscious connection with God. For example, Watson and Nesti (2005: 229) state that a spiritual experience may entail "an athlete's close relationships, or extraordinary and self-affirming moments in life such as winning an Olympic medal, or securing a personal best." This may not be directly connected to a lived Christian faith, yet the practice of experiencing the presence of God can awaken athletes to God's omnipresence at all times.

Brother Lawrence, a French monk living in the 1600s, is known for his ability to practice this spiritual discipline (Lawrence 1724/2013). Because of a lack of education, his primary role in the monastery was to serve in the kitchen, which, at first glance, isn't the most highly esteemed position. However, in even the most mundane tasks, Brother Lawrence sought to be in communion with God. Even though the kitchen was something "to which he had a natural aversion, he proceeded to do everything there for the love of God, praying continually for God's grace to do his work well" (Lawrence, 1724/2013: 16). When others sought his guidance on how to achieve this constant communion with God for which he was known, he provided the following advice: "Please remember that I have recommended that you meditate often on God, day and night, during business and recreation. He is always near you and with you; do not leave Him alone" (51). He recognized the transcendent presence of God, which can imbue sport. As Psalm 139:7–8 proclaims: "Where can I go from your Spirit? Where can I flee from your presence? If I go up to the heavens, you are there; if I make my bed in the depths, you are there." Instead of dividing life into pieces, which can or cannot include experiences of God, Brother Lawrence and the Psalmist confirm God's constant love and concern for all people at all times—and offer another way to integrate faith into sporting activities.

Conclusion

At the beginning of this chapter, I presented a case study of a football player named Robert. He was an example of someone who could use psychological skills training to sort out several internal and external issues. Even if Robert did talk to himself (self-talk), try to manage his emotions (emotional control), think about his next play (imagery), and have goals in mind (goal setting), these attempts do not necessarily mean that his intentions were carried out effectively.

As a Christian mental performance consultant, I am able to help athletes and coaches use psychological skills training to help them with their overall sporting experience. When working with Christian athletes, a consultant can pray before, during, and after an event. Engaging scripture to help guide what is said and done ensures that the consultant is being responsible to their clients and their own faith commitments.

Whether you attempt to apply the principles above on your own or work with a trained professional, I would challenge you to begin the journey of integrating your Christian faith with sport psychology practices. Ultimately, the goal of working with any athlete or coach in a sport psychology consulting relationship is for the athlete or coach to be able to self-regulate one's thoughts, feelings, and behaviors (Weinberg and Gould 2015). Including the Christian tradition in this relationship requires an additional step but allows sportspersons to incorporate practices that support the treasure they find in Jesus.

Study Guide

The goal of this chapter is to present a sport psychology model that uses a Christian framework. Unfortunately, the field of sport psychology does not have spiritual and/or religious models. It is valuable for Christian athletes and coaches to reflect on their own sporting experiences and how well they can integrate their faith into sport. Sharing personal experiences, both successes and failures, is a means to support one another through the above practices. Of course, integrating faith into sport has many moral challenges, especially at elite levels. However, there is conceptually a Christian way to engage sport psychology that draws from psychological skills and spiritual disciplines, which can transform the lives and sporting lives of Christians in sport.

Study Questions

1. Did you ever have a moment in sport where you could echo what Paul says in Romans 7:18, "For I have the desire to do what is good, but I

cannot carry it out"? If so, why do you think you were unable to do what was "good" in that moment?

2. Based on Stevenson's (1991) research study with Christian athletes, which role-identity group do you most identify with? Please explain.

3. Willard (1988) believes that "the disciplines we need to practice are precisely the ones we are *not* 'good at' and hence do not enjoy" (p. 138). Do you agree with his sentiment? Why or why not?

4. In Matthew 6:21 Jesus says, "For where your treasure is, there your heart will be also." Reflecting on your habits and actions within sport, what do they say about your "treasure"?

5. How have you experienced prayer in sport? Can you relate to the experiences of any of the Christian athletes' uses of prayer listed in Czech et al.'s (2004) study? What about Egli et al.'s (2014a) study with Christian coaches?

6. Where do you most often experience the presence of God? What actions or disciplines will you take to help you experience the presence of God within your sport?

Further Reading

Egli, T. J., & Fisher, L. A. (2017), "Christianity and Sport Psychology: One Aspect of Cultural Competence," *Journal of the Christian Society for Kinesiology, Leisure, & Sports Studies*, 4 : 19–27.

Willard, D. (1988). *The Spirit of the Disciplines: Understanding How God Changes Lives*. New York: HarperCollins Publishers.

Part III

SPORT AND CHRISTIANITY:
PRACTICES FOR THE MORAL LIFE

Chapter 10

SERVANT LEADERSHIP AND SPORTS COACHING

Don Vinson and Andrew Parker

Introduction

The body of literature concerning the relationship between sports coaching and Christianity raises a number of questions about whether or not competitive sport might be considered a legitimate vocational field for Christian coach practitioners. Indeed, this literature has offered limited theoretical clarity for Christian sports coaches seeking a sound and legitimate foundation for their professional practice. In this chapter, the role of the coach is considered broader than the pedagogical function of helping athletes learn technically and tactically. Instead, we focus on the overarching concept of leadership and, in particular, servant leadership, with a view to offering Christian sports coaches an operational framework in relation to their practices and responsibilities regarding athletes and teams, predominantly in the competitive sporting domain. The central aim of the chapter is to provide insight into the connections between servant leadership and sports coaching and, in particular, the ways in which servant leadership behaviors might manifest themselves in and through coaching practice.

There has been considerable debate over the years concerning leadership theory and sports coaching. Common to all contemporary writing in this area has been the focus on follower-centered, or shared, models of leadership, that is, those that reject the authoritarian and domineering depictions of leaders in sport, which are commonly portrayed (and often lauded) in the media. Perhaps the most prominent body of scholarship has come from Chelladurai and colleagues and has concerned the development and refinement of the multidimensional model of leadership as part of a broader and sustained contribution to the field (see Chelladurai 1990, 2007, 2013; Chelladurai and Saleh 1980). Chelladurai and Saleh (1980) proposed that the alignment of required, actual, and preferred coaching behavior leads to group satisfaction and enhanced performance, with the specific actions of the coach being dependent upon the situational, leader, and member characteristics. As Chelladurai and Riemer (1998) later acknowledged, however, the multidimensional model lacked both specificity and actionable strategy, leading them to turn to transformational leadership (TFL) as an alternative. TFL is best understood through the augmentation hypothesis, that is, that transactional behaviors such as praise or payment of financial bonuses essentially reward or punish followers for exceptional behavior. Such transactional behaviors are then supplemented and enhanced by more transformational behaviors, which can be described under the headings of inspirational motivation, individualized consideration, intellectual stimulation, and idealized influence (Bass and Riggio 2006). In recent years, the prominence of TFL in sport has increased considerably, and a growing body of research has demonstrated a wide range of benefits in relation to such approaches. For example, TFL has been shown to be impactful in the development of task cohesion (Arthur, Woodman, Ong, Hardy, and Ntoumanis 2011), athlete well-being (Stenling and Tafvelin 2014), personal, social, cognitive, and goal-setting skills (Vella, Oades, and Crowe 2013) as well as athlete satisfaction, effort, and intrinsic motivation (Arthur et al. 2011; Charbonneau, Barling, and Kelloway 2001; Rowold 2006). Despite this impressive array of potential benefits, the principal focus of transformational approaches is on the superior achievement of organizational goals. In this view, the benefits to individuals, while crucially important, are not the ultimate driving factor (Bass and Riggio 2006; Smith, Montagno, and Kuzmenko 2004). For example, a national governing body of sport might advocate TFL with the ultimate aim of meeting or exceeding the organization's Olympic medal target as outlined by their nation's funding agency. Such a goal is ultimately focused on the number of medals won, rather than on the holistic personal development of the individual athletes.

Alternatively, servant leadership places the individual at the heart of the developmental process; the needs of the followers outweigh the emphasis on organizational goals (Kim, Kim, and Wells 2017; Smith et al. 2004). This focus on individuals represents a principle more compatible with a biblical, Christ-like perspective (Grudem 1994). Furthermore, the term "servant" resonates strongly with Christian teaching, including the infamous incident in which the disciples, James and John, approach Jesus requesting to sit at His side in heaven—Jesus responds that they should first seek to become a "servant of all" (Mark 10:43–45). The scholarly construct of servant leadership has been principally attributed to Robert K. Greenleaf (Page and Wong 2000). Greenleaf (1977: 7) described this concept by stating thus:

> The Servant-Leader is servant first … it begins with the natural feeling that one wants to serve, to serve first. Then conscious choice brings one to aspire to lead … the best test, and difficult one to administer is this: Do those served grow as persons? Do they, whilst being served, become healthier, wiser, freer, more autonomous, and more likely themselves to become servants? And, what is the effect on the least privileged in society? Will they benefit, or at least not further be harmed?

As Walker (2010: 113) has argued, central to the concept of servant leadership is that service precedes the desire to lead, and in this sense such a philosophy "cuts directly across the attitudes that prevail in so much of life and leadership in contemporary society. It insists on the moral priority of the other; it demands that leadership is not self-serving but other-person-centred." Walker goes on to point out how such ideas have been eagerly accepted and accommodated by those within the Christian faith whose calling to serve has come to form the mainstay of their religious identity. So too have such ideas fueled an increasing emphasis in recent years on pastoral care and leadership within broader ministry circles. In a secular sense, there are also connections here with the work of sociological scholars whose theoretical offerings have focused on the intrinsically oppressive nature of institutional power and the collective and individual inequalities that more traditional versions of leadership might sponsor. In contrast, the servant leader is one who considers their position of responsibility to be one of stewardship, that is, holding a position of trust in order to develop others by foregoing their own self-interest (Greenleaf 1977; van Dierendonck 2011). Indeed, consideration of the power relations between leader and follower is crucial to understanding Greenleaf's (1977: 9–10) perspective:

> A fresh critical look is being taken in these times at the issues of power and authority, and people are beginning to learn, however haltingly, to relate to one another in less coercive and more creatively supporting ways ... A new moral principle is emerging which holds that the only authority deserving one's allegiance is that which is freely and knowingly granted by the led to the leader and in response to, and in proportion to, the clearly evident servant stature of the leader.

Perhaps most importantly for Greenleaf, servant leadership should not involve an attitude of subservience or submissiveness; rather, the servant leader resolutely sets out to ensure the flourishing of every follower to be of unique value to the organization.

Various authors have sought to model servant leadership in a number of different ways (e.g., Barbuto Jr. and Wheeler 2006; Patterson 2003; Russell and Stone 2002; Spears 1995; van Dierendonck 2011) in order to generate insightful and practical understanding of the philosophies, beliefs, and behaviors associated with its authentic outworking. In attempting to synthesize work in this area, van Dierendonck (2011) distilled six key characteristics of servant leadership that he felt resonated across the various conceptions published in the field to date. These comprised: (i) empowering and developing people, (ii) humility, (iii) authenticity, (iv) interpersonal acceptance, (v) providing direction, and (vi) stewardship. van Dierendonck (2011) combined these key characteristics with the antecedents of the leader's predisposition to serve, a consideration of culture, and the leader's individual characteristics to produce a conceptual model of servant leadership (Figure 10.1). The outcome was a modeling of the expected outcomes of servant leadership around six broad concepts, which comprised high-quality leader–follower relationship, a positive psychological climate, self-actualization, enhanced follower job attitudes, better performance, and improved organizational outcomes.

Measurement in servant leadership research has also featured a number of differing approaches. Perhaps the most prominent is the work of Paul Wong and

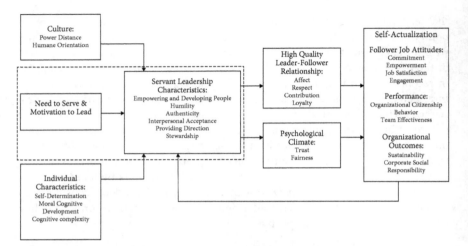

Figure 10.1 A conceptual model of servant leadership (van Dierendonck 2011).

Don Page (e.g., Page and Wong 2000; Wong 2004; Wong and Page 2003) who produced the (revised) Servant Leadership Profile (RSLP), a sixty-two-item instrument comprising seven factors (empowering and developing others); power and pride (inverse factor); serving others; open, participatory leadership; inspiring leadership; visionary leadership; and courageous leadership) derived via principal component analysis. In contrast to the Servant Leadership Survey (van Dierendonck and Nuijten 2011), the RSLP is a self-report tool that was validated to reflect followers' perceptions of their leader's behavior and beliefs. Other measures of servant leadership have been developed such as the Servant Leadership Assessment Instrument (Dennis and Bocarnea 2005), the Servant Leadership Questionnaire (Barbuto Jr. and Wheeler 2006), and the Servant Leader Behaviour Scale (Sendjaya, Sarros, and Santora 2008), yet none has reliably and consistently established a measure or factor structure that fully captures the breadth of servant leadership characteristics or has become the predominant tool of choice within the field (van Dierendonck and Patterson 2010). Arguably, the RSLP remains the most widely used tool and has formed the basis for the limited survey work that has been conducted in the field of sport (Hammermeister et al. 2008).

One example of such work is that of Hammermeister et al. (2008) who developed the Revised Servant Leadership Profile for Sport (RSLP-S) by recruiting 251 collegiate athletes to complete a modified version of the RSLP and conducting a subsequent factor analysis. This process reduced the number of items from sixty-two to twenty-two and from seven to five factors. Perhaps not surprisingly, it would appear that a great deal of the RSLP's insight and intricacy is lost when asking athletes to complete the instrument based on their perceptions of their coach's beliefs, motivations, and behaviors. One subsequent use of this instrument was by Rieke, Hammermeister, and Chase (2008) who recruited 195 collegiate basketball players to also complete a wide range of psychological inventories in an attempt to show the benefits of being coached by a servant leader.

However, Rieke et al.'s (2008) attempt to demonstrate a performance benefit was undermined by the use of a non-validated research tool (the Basketball Athletic Performance Questionnaire) and their relatively arbitrary designation of the terms "servant leader" and "non-servant leader" with no greater insight than establishing the former category had simply been scored more highly overall by their athletes than the other group.

How to attribute the label "servant leader" has proved challenging. Gillham, Gillham, and Hansen (2015) also utilized the RSLP-S to examine the relationship among servant leadership, coach effectiveness, and other social behaviors, providing rigorous evidence to suggest that athletes may perceive a stronger coach–athlete relationship if they consider their coach to be trustworthy, empathetic, and servant-hearted. Nevertheless, as Gillham et al. (2015) acknowledge, the evidence concerning the relationship between servant leadership and coach effectiveness was much less strong. Jenkins' (2014a, 2014b) attempt to review the concept in relation to legendary basketball coach John Wooden ultimately proved much more convincing in terms of pragmatism and paternalistic leadership. Furthermore, other sport-related literature based on a framework of servant leadership has highlighted the potential of such approaches in relation to the coach–athlete relationship (Burton and Welty-Peachey 2013; Kim et al. 2017). Azadfada, Besmi, and Doroudian (2014) further confirmed the benefits of athletes' perceptions of servant-hearted behavior from their coach in terms of athlete satisfaction; however, as with all of the other empirically based sports coaching works in this field to date, little, if any, insight has been offered regarding the beliefs, intentions, and motivations of coaches from their own perspective. The aim of the present chapter is to offer some form of corrective in this respect by providing empirical evidence from coaches themselves around the following questions:

- To what extent do the philosophies of Christian sports coaches reflect the theoretical foundations of servant leadership?
- To what extent does the intended practice of Christian sports coaches reflect the theoretical foundations of servant leadership?
- What sociocultural factors influence the philosophies and intended practice of Christian sports coaches?

To reflect the distinction between servant leadership and other frameworks, we will particularly focus on the theoretical foundation of other-person-centeredness. Before we elaborate on our findings in relation to these questions, we will initially turn to a discussion of methods.

Methods

Ethical approval for the study was granted by the University of Worcester (UK) Institute of Sport and Exercise Research Ethics Committee. The participants comprised 110 coaches ($N = 88$) and coach educators ($N = 22$) who responded to an invitation to complete an online survey (female = 24, male = 86). The participants were drawn from an extensive internet search for sports coaches openly proclaiming a Christian faith or working for an overtly Christian educational institution or charity. The search was restricted to coaches featured on websites published in English. Participants were also requested to pass on the email invitation to anyone they considered might fall within the stated inclusion criteria of being actively engaged in sports coaching or coach education and proclaiming a Christian faith. In addition, invitations were sent to the administrators of a number of national (UK) and international Christian sports organizations with a request that the email be forwarded to anyone meeting the inclusion criteria. Overall, 1570 named, individual, invitations were sent out, with 84 respondents from the USA or Canada and 26 from other countries including the UK.

Participants were asked to affirm that they accepted the Evangelical Alliance (UK) "Statement of Faith" (Evangelical Alliance 2014) and to complete demographic information including gender, nationality, and coaching role. Participants were then asked to complete the sixty-two-item RSLP (Wong 2004) and to respond to six open-ended (qualitative) questions, which comprised: (1) Please tell us about your coaching journey, (2) Please tell us about your coaching practice, (3) To what extent is there a relationship between your Christian faith and your coaching practice? (4) What is your personal approach to leadership within your sporting context? (5) What values do you seek to promote within the sporting environment(s) in which you operate? and (6) How do you evaluate your success as a sports coach? Respondents were also invited to add anything else they thought might be relevant in a free-text box.

The quantitative data were screened for potential violations of the assumptions relating to parametric data testing including consideration of boxplots and P–P plots through which outliers were eliminated. Groups larger than thirty were considered to be normal following the Central Limit Theorem (Field 2013), while smaller groups were checked through visual analysis of histograms via the Shapiro–Wilk test (Field 2013). Data were then analyzed at a univariate level including three independent variables (gender, coaching role, and nationality) each featuring just two categories. Only one violation of the assumptions was identified and was analyzed via the Mann–Whitney U test. All other variables were entered into an independent sample t-test. Due to there being only one violation of the assumptions and for the sake of consistency, all data are reported as mean ± SD. One-sample t-tests were utilized to compare the findings of the current investigation to previous studies. Where presented, effect sizes have been calculated via Pearson's r, using the cutoffs of 0.1 (small effect), 0.3 (medium effect), and 0.5 (large effect) (Field 2013). The internal consistency of the seven-factor structure of the RSLP was affirmed with Cronbach's α coefficients ranging satisfactorily between 0.73 and 0.86.

In terms of the analysis of the qualitative data, thematic and axial coding was used whereby the authors adopted a cyclical process of examination and inductive interpretation to draw out themes and meanings in response to the primary aims of the research and in line with the key themes and concepts identified from the existing literature (Charmaz 2002, 2014). Data were analyzed in four stages. First, responses were reread in full to facilitate data saturation. Second, each response was individually coded and indexed, whereby a detailed capturing of the different aspects of participant experience took place. Third, these experiences were then categorized into a series of overarching topics, which broadly encompassed the key issues emerging from the data. The final stage of analysis involved the formal organization of these topics into generic themes by further exploring the key issues around participant experience and framing those experiences within the context of existing conceptual debate (differentiated by respondents). These themes provide the general context around which both our quantitative and qualitative findings were viewed and around which our subsequent discussions are structured.

Christian sports coaches as servant leaders

Results and discussion

There were no significant differences evident when comparing the seven dimensions across gender ($t(101-107) = 0.02-0.63$, $p = 0.53-0.99$) or coaching role ($t(102-108) = 0.22-1.07$, $p = 0.29-0.83$). North American coaches and coach educators rated themselves significantly higher in terms of courageous leadership ($t(108) = 2.91$, $p < 0.01$, $r = 0.27$) and visionary leadership ($U = 715.50$, $z = -2.40$, $p < 0.05$, $r = -0.23$) than those from other nations although these only demonstrated a small effect. Furthermore, there were no significant differences evident within the other five factors ($t(105-108) = 0.05-1.49$, $p = 0.15-0.96$). While very few meaningful differences were evident when making comparisons within the sample, it is apparent when contrasting the findings of the present study to previous investigations that these Christian coaches and coach educators rated themselves more highly in all seven of the servant leadership factors. In Table 10.1, data are presented alongside equivalent self-rated scores in business settings (Rude 2004) and by Methodist ministers (Gauby 2007). In each case, the participants within the present study rated themselves significantly higher across each of the seven factors when analyzed via the one-sample t-test.

Table 10.1 Sample means (SD) for servant leadership factors alongside Rude (2004) and Gauby (2007)

Factor	Present sample	Rude (2004)	Gauby (2007)[a]
Developing and empowering others	5.98 (0.43)	5.65 (0.86)	5.53
Power and pride	2.83 (0.91)	1.77 (0.72)	1.06
Serving others	6.12 (0.54)	5.60 (0.80)	5.71
Open, participatory leadership	6.32 (0.38)	6.08 (0.57)	6.08
Inspiring leadership	6.02 (0.57)	5.27 (1.03)	5.17
Visionary leadership	5.99 (0.63)	5.66 (0.93)	5.25
Courageous leadership	6.25 (0.54)	5.89 (0.80)	5.97

[a] Gauby (2007) did not present SDs

Respondents in the present study scored themselves most highly for "Open, participatory leadership" and "Courageous leadership." The "Developing and empowering others" and "Visionary" factors were scored less highly, although still significantly higher than those reported in either Rude (2004) or Gauby (2007). Alternatively, "Power and pride" characteristics are inverse factors whereby lower scores are more akin to servant leadership principles; however, respondents scored themselves significantly higher in this factor when compared to previous studies. The inverse of "Power and pride" is "Vulnerability and humility," which might represent an easier concept to apply practically.

The significantly higher score in the "Power and pride" factor suggests that this element represents the one which our sample of Christian coaches and coach educators find the most difficult to resonate with in their professional practice. In sum, what these data suggest is that, as an operationalized concept, servant leadership resonated strongly with this particular cohort. Moreover, in terms of the existence of clear linkages between the quantitative and qualitative data, the development and empowerment of others appeared especially prominent as part of coaching practice. Hence, it is on this theme our qualitative analysis focuses.

Christian sports coaches developing and empowering others

There are various reasons why people become involved in sports coaching—winning, success, personal affirmation/gain—and yet for a number of the coaches in our sample, servant leadership was the underpinning principle of their sporting identities; therefore, the holistic health and well-being of their athletes were at the forefront of their coaching behaviors. More specifically, the development and empowerment of athletes as people was something that was evident in many of the coach responses to the open-ended question: "Please tell us about your coaching practice." It was not unusual, for example, for coaches to adopt a nurturing approach toward their athletes and to express the desire to impart and encourage wider lifestyle attributes and abilities as these two data extracts illustrate:

> I coach because I love seeing people achieve their goals, and gaining in their own self-belief and confidence. I hope that in my coaching I give out an air of confidence in my knowledge of the sport but, more significantly, that those I coach can see that I have their interests and abilities at heart and that I want to help them. As a coach, the most important elements of my role are honesty, fairness, understanding and setting the right example and I think if you can inspire people to be the best that they can and to work for others then you have coached well. I aim to create an environment in which people feel they can thrive, and in which they can achieve their personal and team goals.

> My key responsibilities are to nurture, equip, empower the players to do their best … I try to develop an environment where mistakes can be made without

condemnation or ridicule - failure leads to success - and where we can have fun but work hard and accomplish our goals.

In turn, coaches articulated the desire to influence the lives of their athletes beyond sport, that is, to emotionally and relationally transcend the conventional bounds of the coach–athlete relationship, with the intention of engendering certain character traits and values, which is consistent with previous research findings (Arthur et al. 2011; Charbonneau et al. 2001; Rowold 2006). One respondent talked of the desire to "help empower others to think for themselves and solve problems [by] slowly giv[ing] my players more and more responsibility." Another stated: "I believe it is my personal goal and duty to build well-rounded individuals on the field and in the classroom." Presenting something of a contrast to the "win at all costs" mentality of modern-day sporting practice (see Watson and White 2007), such an approach appeared to hold the potential to redefine coaching "success":

> I coach to inspire kids to be the best they can be. All coaches love to win and the world looks at our [coaching] record as a way to determine our success. I look at success as helping young men and women to grow into responsible adults and grow in their relationship with Christ. The team setting provides so many opportunities to learn how to get along with others and accomplish things as a unit. It is not about what each person can accomplish, but about what we can accomplish as a team. The growth is in the journey.

> I believe athletics have the potential to develop the character of a person. As a coach, it is my job to harness and extend the potential of each individual on my team, pushing them past their perceived limitations and helping them to accomplish their goals. In a Christian institution, I also place high value on personal, mental, spiritual, and emotional health and wellbeing, not just physical. Improvement and winning are always a plus, but encouraging an individual to have more confidence, overcome obstacles, and believe in themselves is much more important.

Given the religious demographic of the sample cohort, it is perhaps unsurprising that spirituality played a key role for many coaches in terms of their wider personal development narrative although holistic coaching foci have also been a prominent focus of secular work over the last decade (Price and Weiss 2013). Instilling a sense of importance around the centrality of God to life both within and outside of sport was seen as a key responsibility for some participants in the present study:

> I coached because I enjoyed the challenge and opportunity to help student-athletes to develop their sports skills, their interpersonal skills, and life skills, and to set goals and strive to reach them. And most importantly, while doing these things, to build relationships with each other and with God.

I try to encourage personal responsibility, gratitude, servant hearts, teammanship [sic.], and excellence in all that we do. We talk about living with no regrets, being strong women, and learning to have a voice. We acknowledge God as the giver of all good gifts, including our athletic ability, and we try to maximize our use of this gift. I try to care about the struggles of my athletes outside of the sport and help them. I believe the team considers me a tough coach, but I also believe they know I care deeply for them.

As one might expect, leadership skills were a key theme for many. One coach expressed a particular concern over the generational demise of such skills and the importance of sport in their promotion:

I coach to make a difference in the lives of young men. I believe that leadership skills are eroding in this generation and young men - particularly young Christian men - need this training and experience. Sport is a great way to reach them and train them.

Self-leadership also appeared frequently amidst participant responses being largely located alongside notions of responsibility, ownership, and discipline:

I coach to not only teach a sport, but to teach discipline, self-leadership, owning your role, and working well with others. This has developed over time as I have learned that by teaching the above qualities it helps with winning. So instead of just focusing on a win, you can develop a well-rounded athlete that can also produce. My key responsibilities as a coach is to engage the athlete in what is being taught, encourage them to grow as an athlete and an individual, and excel at every task they take on.

Conclusions

Our aim within this chapter has been to provide insight into the connections between servant leadership and sports coaching and, in particular, the ways in which servant leadership behaviors might manifest themselves in and through coaching practice. Our analysis of questionnaire responses from Christian practitioners suggests that where servant leadership features as a key point of reference, coaches adopt an athlete-centered approach, which translates into an intentional desire to develop and empower those with whom they work. Amidst an environment of trust and support, this, in turn, plays out in the promotion of a series of key values and attributes that have the potential to enhance the holistic development (emotional, relational, spiritual, physical) of the athlete and to impact their life beyond sport.

What these findings also suggest is that the sporting environment continues to pose challenges for Christian coaches and coach educators. While overtly focusing on the empowerment and growth of their athletes, respondents also acknowledged (albeit somewhat subliminally) the ever-present shadow of the importance of winning and the inevitability of the success of their role being judged by tangible and objective aspects. Such findings resonate with previous research (e.g., Bennett et al. 2005; Hunt 1999) and highlight the difficulties of striving to act in a vulnerable and humble manner within an environment that lauds notions of "power and pride." It is evident that further research is required to investigate the precise motives of Christian coaches and coach educators and to understand how these professionals deal with the overt and covert pressures of the secular sporting milieu.

Study Guide

We have seen that the theoretical underpinnings of servant leadership offer some strong foundational principles upon which Christian sports coaches might base their practice. However, the nature of sport will continue to present real challenges to practitioners who seek to put the development of the individual before winning or financial success. Addressing the following questions will enable you to revise your understandings of the key aspects of servant leadership and to consider for yourself the extent to which this particular leadership style offers Christian sports coaches a potential basis for their work.

Study Questions

1. What are the key characteristics of servant leadership?
2. In what ways might sport help promote servant leadership?
3. How can sports coaches incorporate servant leadership principles into their work?
4. In what ways might a servant leadership approach enhance athlete well-being?
5. How does servant leadership reflect Christian values?

Further Reading

Bennett, G., Sagas, M., Fleming, D., & S. V. Roenn. (2005), "On Being a Living Contradiction: The Struggle of an Elite Intercollegiate Christian Coach," *Journal of Beliefs & Values*, 26 (3): 289–300.
Greenleaf, R. K. (1977), *Servant Leadership: A Journey into the Nature of Legitimate Power and Greatness*, Mahwah, New Jersey: Paulist Press.
van Dierendonck, D. (2011), "Servant Leadership: A Review and Synthesis," *Journal of Management*, 37 (4): 1228–1261.

Chapter 11

SPORT, ENVY, AND THE CONUNDRUM OF COMPARISON

Brian R. Bolt and Chad Carlson

Introduction

Clutching her wounded leg, a distraught Nancy Kerrigan repeatedly sobbed the question, "Why?" She would soon get her answer. In the brief 1994 video, perfectly cut for social media long before there was such a thing, television cameras captured the American Olympic figure skating hopeful moments after being struck with a club in the corridor of an ice arena. Kerrigan had been practicing, so the assailant knew exactly where she would exit. With a clear path and no witnesses, he delivered one decisive blow with a police baton just above Kerrigan's right kneecap. Over and over, media outlets aired the dramatic clip of the injured and distressed Kerrigan still wearing her white performance dress, prompting all who watched to ask the same question as Kerrigan—Why? The unexpected answer: Envy.

Before long, authorities traced the attack on Kerrigan to her rival, Tonya Harding. Separated by only a year in age, Kerrigan and Harding grew up in the figure skating world together. Both were high-level performers, but early on Harding had the upper hand. At the 1991 US Championships, Harding was the first female to land a triple axel in competition while earning a perfect 6.0 score. Yet while Harding had been more successful on the ice, Kerrigan got all the attention. Kerrigan was tall, graceful, and photogenic, yielding her multiple sponsorships and endorsement opportunities. Harding, in contrast, was considered low class and unsophisticated off the ice. In the spotlight, Kerrigan sparkled in Vera Wang designer costumes, while a financially struggling Harding had to sew her own outfits (Oliveira 2017). The seeds of envy sprouted.

Harding's then-husband along with her bodyguard hired the attacker. They wanted to injure Kerrigan so that she would be unable to compete in the 1994 Olympics. Ultimately, this plan was unsuccessful. The baton missed Kerrigan's knee, resulting in a bruise, not a break. She healed quickly and went on to earn a silver medal in Lillehammer that same year. Harding also competed—her role in the attack was undetermined at the time of the Games—finishing a disappointing eighth in the competition. Harding was never criminally convicted for the attack. She denied knowing about the conspiracy. But the United States Figure Skating Association eventually concluded that she was indeed behind the attack and banned her for life.

It's easy to judge Harding. What she and her accomplices did was clearly wrong and tragic. She allowed her discontent to grow into resentment toward another person, and finally, her envy led to an act of violence. But she is not unlike the rest of us. Athletes, coaches, parents, and fans, if they are honest, will admit to moments and perhaps extended seasons of envy in and beyond sport. Looking through her eyes, it's not hard to see how Harding viewed her situation as unjust. She had performed as well as Kerrigan through most of her young career, but only Kerrigan was reaping fame and fortune. It didn't seem fair. Though few resort to violence, envious tendencies are in all of us. Indeed, we as authors admit to feeling envy in and about sport. We work at "rival" higher education institutions. And each of us coaches an intercollegiate sport. On our best days, we inspire each other to excellence, but too often we allow envy to take hold. And we both work at Christian colleges! In this chapter, we will explore what envy is, how sportspersons may be more susceptible to envy than others, and how Christianity offers much-needed antidotes to this deadly sin.

Envy and its allies

Scholars from different disciplines agree that envy's foundation is the comparison between oneself and another (Cohen-Charash and Larson 2017). In the comparison game, the envious person loses and often perceives a deep sense of unfairness, discontent, and hostility. Envy always includes a perception of one's own inferiority coupled with hostility toward the comparison target (Annoni et al. 2017).

Envy has a marquee presence in Christianity. It's one of the seven deadly sins, and envy's cousin, covetousness, is decreed as a commandment—something we *shalt not do*. Envy is the culprit for the Bible's first recorded murder. Cain envied the favor God gave to Abel's offering, so he killed him. A few chapters later in Genesis, we learn of the envy that Jacob's sons had for their younger brother, Joseph, because Jacob loved his youngest son the most. Like Cain, Joseph's brothers acted on their envy by conspiring to kill their brother but ultimately decided to sell him as a slave. Not surprisingly, Joseph and his brothers were no strangers to envy at home. Their family had already been torn apart by the intense, envious rivalry between the two sisters, Leah and Rachel, who had married their father. Leah was initially envious of Jacob's preference for her sister Rachel. Rachel became envious of Leah's ability to have children.

Both the Old and New Testaments are full of envy stories, the most famous and influential being Jesus's death. The religious leaders were envious of Jesus's increasing popularity and power. After he cleared the temple during the Passover celebration, "the chief priests and the teachers of the law heard this and began looking for a way to kill him … because the whole crowd was amazed at his teaching" (Mark 11:18, New International Version).

Though somewhat different, envy, covetousness, and jealousy are used interchangeably and often depicted with the color green (e.g., green with envy, jealousy the green-eyed monster). All three have the underlying root of discontent with one's situation in relation to that of another person, but there are a few important distinctions. Jealousy is mostly about protecting something you may have or own against a perceived threat. For instance, a woman may become jealous because she suspects her boyfriend is attracted to another woman or that the other woman is attempting to steal what is hers. Jealousy is an uneasiness that flows from a suspicion that what you have is in danger of being taken. Nick Jonas's song *Jealous*, for example, shows how one's perception of a situation can lead to jealous conclusions when he sings, "I don't like the way he's looking at you. I'm starting to think you want him, too."

Conversely, Taylor Swift's song, *You Belong with Me*, is an example of the beginning of covetousness. So is Rick Springfield's *Jesse's Girl*, in which he wonders, "Why can't I find a woman like that?" In both songs, the singers identify what they desire as the love and affection of a particular person, and they lament their inability to change their circumstances. Often this more innocent form of daydreaming stays in the world of playful fantasy. We notice something or someone of beauty or value that quickly sparks a desire. The sin of coveting, though, generally refers to an inordinate desire for something that someone else has and can lead to deadly consequences. King David coveted his military commander Uriah's wife because of her beauty. David had Uriah killed in battle so that he could have Bathsheba for his own (2 Sam 11). Coveting can be about a person, like Bathsheba, or it can be blatantly materialistic, referring to a possession that someone else has that you want for yourself, like Jacob wanting and then stealing Esau's birthright (Gen 27).

Perhaps envy presents the deepest shade of green because of the intensity of the desire. Like coveting, envy involves desiring what the other has, but the envious one also takes aim at the person who has the thing of desire. The envious person notices the good fortune of another and resents them for it. Starting from a relatively low sense of self, the envious mind builds an open and shut case against the person holding the object of desire, wallowing in deep bitterness and pain. Reducing the pain involves improving one's relative standing by either bringing oneself up or bringing the other down.

Sometimes bringing the other down is more satisfying and expedient. Tonya Harding envied the prestige and attention Nancy Kerrigan garnered from her skating, so she set out to take away her ability to skate. Removing Kerrigan from the Olympics would have improved Harding's chance of winning, but if getting the gold for herself were her only motive, she would have had to remove several other competitors as well. It is likely that the attack on Kerrigan was as much about hurting Kerrigan as it was about helping Harding.

King Solomon understood envy quite well, as he used its markers to solve disputes. In his magisterial role, two women approached him, each claiming she was the mother of a certain baby. Seeing no way to determine who the actual mother was, Solomon called for a sword to cut the baby in half. The true mother of course could not stand to see this happen, but the envious woman agreed to the ruling. Since she could not have the baby, she preferred that no one would (1 Kings 3:16–28).

Tiger Woods was the greatest golfer and one of the most recognized athletes and celebrities in the world at the time of his public scandal. As much as we revered Tiger for his abilities, many would admit to finding an odd sense of satisfaction at his humiliating public demise. This sense of pleasure at another's troubles or failures is the definition of the German word, *schadenfreude*, literally linking harm and pleasure. Schadenfreude is similar to envy. Sport philosopher Mike McNamee explains that with any of the "close cousins" of *schadenfreude*— envy, spite, resentment, and jealousy—"we must accept that the feeling is imbued with a judgment or an interpretation of their situation" (2010: 330). When we envy someone, we wonder about our situation in relation to theirs: why can't we have what he or she has, and even more, we hope they lose what they have. Even if success appears to be earned, as in the case of Tiger Woods, we can find comparative unfairness in a person's fortunate array of genetic gifts or life advantages. Tabloids capitalize on this knee-jerk, somewhat sordid, human reaction to great success. As Don Henley sings in his song *Dirty Laundry*, "people love it when you lose."

The comparative deficit that envy exposes eats at the heart. The Oscar-winning movie *Amadeus* is fictional but rings true as a portrayal of envy. The film is about two premier composers, Antonio Salieri, of whom few have heard, and the world-famous Wolfgang Amadeus Mozart. The two composers were contemporaries. Yet even though Salieri was accomplished and talented, he was tortured by the genius of Mozart. As Salieri toiled endlessly to produce good music, it seemed that creating brilliant music came to Mozart almost automatically and without effort. The film depicts Mozart as lazy, crude, and unworthy of such a special talent. In one scene, Salieri obtains a folder of some of Mozart's original pieces. He's told there are no duplicates, so he is holding Mozart's first drafts. As he frantically looks through them, the beauty of the music overcomes Salieri, but his face and body are at the same time writhing with envious, hostile emotion. The infuriated Salieri grumbles that the compositions "showed no corrections of any kind. Not one! He (Mozart) had simply written down music already etched in his head" (Zaentz and Forman 1984).

The target of Salieri's envy was the undeserving Mozart, but his real complaint was with God. Salieri knew he would never measure up to Mozart because he did not have the genetic gifts of the better-known composer. He simply was not as talented, and he was filled with hate to soothe his self-pity. This kind of hatred for another can naturally lead to hating God because God is ultimately responsible for bestowing the other person with such talent and its consequent success (Konyndyk DeYoung 2009). Why had God given this magnificent ability to someone as ungrateful and undisciplined as Mozart? Salieri plots to kill Mozart, but before he can carry out his plan, Mozart becomes terminally ill from excessive drinking and frantically trying to work himself out of financial debt. Even after Mozart's death, Salieri's life ends in a depressed state, obsessed with his own comparative mediocrity. Envy remained because of Salieri's comparatively low self-worth. Envy's existence feeds on comparison.

Envy in sport

Sport is one of envy's most fertile gardens, and the soil is rich. The competition of sport—me versus you, us versus them—is a near-constant invitation to compare. Before and after the actual prize is awarded, athletes compare talents, advantages, genetic traits, practice habits, and opportunities against those of competitors. Indeed, if not instinctive, they are encouraged to do so from many directions. French-American scholar René Girard argues that humans live, interact, and evolve through comparison. We learn how to behave by watching others, striving to be like them, and, in essence, to *be* them. We desire what others desire in large part because it is what they desire—a concept Girard calls mimetic desire. As we do so, it naturally leads to competition, what Girard (1996) refers to more critically as rivalry because it pits us against each other for often scarce goods and resources.

Desiring what others desire is part of sport. We want victory, and our opponents do, too. We want the number one ranking or the league championship that our opponents have. As we mimic others in sport, we become more like them. Indeed, Girard argues that our rivalries and the envy that comes from competing for scarce resources and goods demonstrate that we are much like those with whom we compete. Essentially, we are more likely to envy people who are similar to ourselves, or at least those whom we believe to be similar to us. Sibling rivalries or the competitions among those in close social circles embody this quality (Girard 1996).

We may marvel, for instance, at great entertainers like Tom Hanks or Beyoncé, and may wish to have the wealth of Mark Zuckerberg or the mental toughness of Serena Williams, but these whimsical yearnings rarely have much effect on us. Our true envy most often goes to those we can see and whose situation is only slightly better than our own. Sport brings similar people together and is very visible. As we progress in sport, the differences between athletes' abilities and accomplishments become smaller and smaller, as do the margins between winning and losing. Only fractions of points and measurements or hundredths of seconds often separate the performances of competitors vying for ultimate prizes and recognition. Like siblings in the same house, with the same parents, sparring for the same goods, envy makes its living on proximity and similarity.

But before teammates compare themselves with opponents, they compare with each other. Teammates compare things like playing time and a coach's attention. They perceive their own effort as greater than others or their faults as lesser. Coaches within the same athletic programs compare records, resources, and attention with fellow coaches. Teams compare fan attention and facilities with other teams. These comparisons are not unique to sport. They are found everywhere in society, including workplaces, educational institutions, politics, law, and families. But the public nature of sport and the fact that sport is fundamentally a contest for scarce goods make comparison and its consequences as natural as breathing.

It is important to pause here to make this clear; sport itself is not an act of envy. Joseph Epstein (2003: 7) points out: "Envy ought not be confused with open conflict." When teams or players compete for a prize, the sport is played based on cooperatively agreed-upon rules and terms. Players voluntarily enter the contest in public for all to see. In a game or sport, each athlete desires the prize, and each will work tirelessly to not only obtain it but also keep the opponent from possessing it. In fact, each will suppress instincts of care and concern for another in the middle of a contest. There will even be "in-game *schadenfreude*." Consider this: when a team needs one more point, one more run, one more goal for victory, it almost always occurs when an opponent fails in their task. A penalty kick saved by a keeper to win a football (soccer) game causes one team and its fans to cheer with glee, even though one person's great play represents the anguished kicker's failure. This is the essence of sport's zero-sum nature that perpetuates envy. One person or team's success means another's failure.

Outside of the context, one might think it cruel to celebrate the mistake of another. In most sporting situations, to be competitive, to aspire to win, to temporarily shelve one's care for another's pain during a game is not an unethical act, a sin, or envy, even though all the fundamental elements of envy are present. Even though sport itself is not envy, it is helpful to understand that sport has all the ingredients. Sport makes it almost too easy for us to be envious, and the vice's availability in sport often taints us morally.

Envy outside the lines

French economist Jeremy Celse has written prolifically on envy and recently turned his attention to its effects in sport. Qualitative scholarship on the character-building merits of sport—often formulated on a particular theory, personal experience, or anecdote—has been the focus of scholars from a number of academic disciplines. Most arguments position sport to have a favorable effect on human character, but since it is so hard to measure, few empirical studies exist that assess the influence of sport participation on athletes' attitudes, dispositions, and practices outside of sport. Using an experimental research design, Celse set out to explore "the dark side of sport" (2011: 37) by comparing athletes to non-athletes on measures of antisocial behavior consistent with envy. In particular, he wondered whether athletes, when compared to non-athletes, would be more likely to:

1. Be distressed by unflattering social comparisons.
2. Be consumed with negative emotions triggered by disadvantageous social comparisons.
3. Be prone to undertaking actions aimed at damaging the situation of their rivals.

In the experiment, each participant (Player A, for instance) played a mouse-clicking computer game and was told that they earned a certain number of Euros. Next, they were asked to rate their satisfaction with the amount they earned. In the following step, they were told the amount another player (Player B) earned, revealing that their own payment was lower. After hearing this, they were again asked to rate their satisfaction with the amount they earned. In doing so, the researcher was able to assess whether and how satisfaction changed after comparing it against someone else. Finally, the participants were told they could reduce the amount earned by Player B if they chose to do so. If Player A chose not to reduce Player B's amount, the game was over. However, if Player A chose to deduct from Player B, it came at a personal cost. As they reduced the amount from Player B by a certain fraction, Player A would also lose money. Player B would still earn more, but not as much more, than Player A. However, if Player A chose to reduce Player B's total by the maximum amount, then Player A and Player B would receive the same number of Euros, but both would get substantially less than was first provided. In other words, Player A would be willing to take home less money for the game provided they could damage the other player's earnings even more (Celse 2011).

Through a number of surveys, the researcher was able to separate what he called athletes and non-athletes. The results revealed that all participants were likely to express a decreased satisfaction when exposed to an unflattering social comparison ("Player B earning more than me"), but being an athlete increased the "probability for a subject to report a decrease in satisfaction derived from social comparisons" (Celse 2011: 38). Moreover, the results also revealed that athletes made more reduction decisions than non-athletes, and the more time athletes were involved in sport, the more likely they were to reduce the other player's amount (Celse 2011).

Though one experiment is not proof of a pattern, we do know that athletes are in the business of comparison. Even after victory the athlete cannot rest, as the next competitor is likely to bring a fresh challenge. To become virtuous, according to Aristotle in his *Nicomachean Ethics*, one acts virtuously over and over again (1105a:18–35). By its very nature, sport encourages comparison and judgment over and over again. It is no wonder athletes are prone to it—they have a lot of opportunities to compare.

The Kerrigan–Harding spectacle that we previously discussed enthralled onlookers because it was so extreme, but rarely does rivalrous envy evolve into such a public act of malice. Sport plays out in the spotlight; envy lurks in the dark. Envy becomes the lens through which we interpret our rival's actions and words. To the target of our envy, we attribute false motives, arrogance, and contempt. The envious person plots behind the scenes, conspiring to obtain that which is envied and taking pleasure in making sure the other person loses it. Their success is our offense, reinforcing preconceived narratives and birthing ruinous plans. "Envy often leads people to lie, because the envious are capable of using almost any means possible to destroy their rivals" (Campolo 1987: 94). Rather than a public attack, in sport the envious person is more likely to chip away at reputation, dismiss the other's ability or success as luck, question their integrity in victory, pretend it is not as good as it is, murmur, slander, and gossip. The words we use may seem innocent enough, and they may have a hint of truth, but the objective is the same: to slight, hurt, and lower the other to improve one's standing by comparison. And then, unfortunately, we rationalize.

Virtue and vice

The path from virtue to vice in an individual's life is well worn. In the modern world of sport, delusion easily warps reason, and new language twists trouble into triumph. In sport, we promote obsession by calling it passion; we commonly encourage misplaced priorities, naming it commitment; parental pandering is called child-centeredness; blind passivity is labeled loyalty, intimidation parades as strategic assertiveness, and idolatry as creative marketing. But what about envy? The repetitive cycle of schedules and seasons means teams and individual players will naturally compare themselves to those closest to them in skill and accomplishment. This repeated comparison forms a close knowledge of the others and a history of past victories and defeats, leading to the seemingly natural formation of rivalry.

As Girard argues, the problem with mimetic desire and rivalry comes "when our relentlessness (toward misdirected desire) makes the rivalry obsessive" (1996: 215). The offshoots of our relentlessness are things like envy, jealousy, pride, anger, and despair. We often fall into the trap of making our rivalries obsessive. Girard mentions that this is "a very general but not universal human failure" (1996: 215). It is natural for us to obsess over our rivalries. And these obsessions are often the beginning of a slippery slope. "The more we stumble against an obstacle [obsessing over our rivalries], the easier it should be to avoid further stumbling, but most frequently, the opposite happens: we stumble so much that we seem to be limping" (Girard 1996: 215–216). This paints a rather somber picture of humanity when connected to sport competitions and rivalry. In practice, we often obsess over our rivalries and continually stumble into allowing these rivalries to pull us into unethical, envy-perpetuating behavior.

A better way

As stated above, sport itself is not an envious act, and we do not suggest that athletes cease to participate in sport. But it is helpful to recognize that the constant comparison of sport could make a person more susceptible to envy. Sport comparison is natural and necessary. We regularly encounter teammates and opponents who are better than us, even if only by a small degree. We aspire to be like them, to be better than them. We need a comparison target, a way of determining whether or not we have truly become better. In sport, the final measurement is always the other person, team, or teammate. If Celse (2011) is correct, the mere practice of comparison makes athletes predisposed to envious behaviors. To not carry that practice through to other parts of life, and to keep envy from developing, is akin to watching only one episode at a time on Netflix—it is nearly impossible. Understanding that envy may creep in, especially in rivalrous situations, is a good first step to curtailing the early stages of envy.

Further, we belong to a faith tradition that asks us to strive to be better. While the identifying mark of a Christian is faith in Jesus Christ, "faith by itself, if it is not accompanied by action, is dead" (James 2:17, New International Version). Good deeds and right actions should accompany a deepening faith in Christ, all of which is aimed at the perfect model—Jesus Christ Himself. Thus, we are taught to compare, to seek the perfect model. Comparison is within the fabric of the Christian faith. And this is positive—an aspiration, when our object of desire and imitation is Christ. In theory, this is clear. In practice, however, it is much more difficult.

As Christians, we should prayerfully search our hearts and be honest with ourselves. This is not always easy because separating envy from more noble feelings of justice is not always a black and white distinction. What if the situation is actually unfair? What if the success of another is truly unwarranted? What if the target of my envy has achieved success through deception? What if, as Epstein describes, what feels like envy is "a clear dislike for someone authentically fraudulent?" (2003: 72). Are not then my efforts not only justified but morally courageous? And if it makes me feel good to see them fall, is not that just the satisfaction of things being set in right order? Epstein goes on to admit, "The distinction between schadenfreude and justice hunger is a tough call" (2003: 72).

Unfairness in sport is everywhere, and there are times when zeal for justice is appropriately placed. Yet we should be cautious in finding justifications that suit our envious tendencies. According to Rebecca Konyndyk DeYoung, "The hatred of the rival can be an elaborate cover up, ultimately, for the envier's sense of rejection and unworthiness in his own self-hatred. The commandment is to love your neighbor as you love yourself. The envier can do neither" (2009: 51). This gets to the heart of envy. The envious person finds self-worth, or aspects of it, apart from God, and when faced with a comparative deficit, welcomes envy as a vacuous form of temporary comfort. Social media "Likes" and "Followers" are modern self-worth traps, and so is the public world of sport. Sport is about results, and the outcomes of sport are public. After each event, athletes are generally asked whether they won. This is a well-meaning question, but it also indicates that a person's worth in a sporting environment is judged by wins and losses. Konyndyk DeYoung recognizes that it is not just in sport, though, where we compare ourselves to one another. Comparisons, whether public or not, pervade our lives. She suggests time away from competitive and comparative environments be filled with enjoying music, art, hiking, or other noncompetitive activities to remind us that all of life is not measured on an aptitude scale. To unlearn envy, she proposes investing ourselves daily in activities with common goals, where one person's increase does not diminish the share of another (Konyndyk DeYoung 2009).

Participating in sport without falling prey to envy-invoking comparison is possible in sport—a less radical suggestion than Konyndyk DeYoung's (2009). Sport philosopher Scott Kretchmar (1995) has argued that competitive sport includes two dramas: the first is how well one performs the skills and tactics tested in the sport and the second is how well one does in relation to one's competition. We so often focus on the latter and ignore the former. And yet, sport provides recurring opportunities to display one's abilities in ways that do not *require us* to focus on winning. Losing only makes someone a loser if the competitor is ignorant of the value of trying one's best, improving, and enjoying the experience. Following Kretchmar, ethicist Robert Simon defines competition in its best light as "a mutual quest for excellence" (2010: 27). Sport is at its best when each competitor says to the other, "I am going to do my best and I expect you to do the same. That way we can have the best experience possible." As such, the focus is not on comparison, dampening the pull of envy and its peers.

And yet, in practice, the modern social trappings related to the world of sport exist and have persuasive power. Indeed, they often entice athletes toward what we might call spiritual injury—a competitive misalignment caused by overexposure to unhealthy social pressures—believing that one is only lovable based on wins, records, and other successes. In Christ, however, our sport-worth does not equal our worth to God and others. Jesus visited the earth to die for both Olympic champions and recreation league failures. In 1 John 3:1, the apostle shouts the truth with the intensity of a full sports stadium: "See what great love the Father has lavished on us, that we should be called children of God! And that is what we are!"

Moreover, biblical writers are unequivocal on the subject, especially St. Paul: "Love does not envy" (1 Cor. 13:4). That is a tough standard, one that might make any of us think we cannot measure up. The good news is that it is true; we cannot measure up. Avoiding envy through our own will is foolish and impossible. The antidote to envy is love, the kind that we receive from the grace of God made evident in Jesus Christ. Leading with love in sport is not easy, but certainly not impossible. Seeing one's competitors not as opponents but as human beings loved by God is a start. Developing friendships with or showing respect for teammates and opponents can go a long way toward praiseworthy competition. Giving one's heart to Christ in a conscious way each time an athlete or coach enters the event might be a nice reminder of the way Christ loved amid life-threatening opponents. Maybe we can do the same thing amid much less survivalistic circumstances and opponents in sport.

The wildly popular book series *Harry Potter* weaves the story of Severus Snape, Harry's teacher and bitter enemy. From the beginning, Snape hates and mistreats Harry, and Harry does not understand why until told that Snape hated Harry's father, James, while they were both at school. The hatred boiled down to envy. When Harry asks about the origin of the rivalry, James's best friend Sirius tells him, "I think James was everything Snape wanted to be – he was popular, he was good at Quidditch, he was good at pretty much everything" (Rowling 2003: 670). In addition, Snape was in love with James's future wife, Lily. James had everything that Snape could never possess, and Snape hated him for it. Harry, then, became a living reminder of that which he had always wanted and could never have. Yet Snape's character is a complicated one, and in a final plot twist, it is revealed that he had been working for good all along. Snape helped save Harry from the man who murdered his mother. Though Snape could not suppress his hate and mistreated Harry, his love for Lily ultimately superseded his envy. Love can overcome envy.

Conclusion

We have argued that people in sport are more susceptible to envy than others, but that sport does not require us to be envious. Further, the moral traps lurking within sport can be avoided by heeding Christian principles—specifically the greatest moral trait, love. Love is not a chore when people are likeable, when they make us feel better, or when they make us look good. We like having people around who prop us up or make us feel worthy. But in sport, we will always have teammates and opponents who seem to get more than they deserve. We as authors know a championship coach who has brought her team to the highest levels of her sport. Her teams have won multiple championships (and lost just as many). They are really the "envy" of the sport. Yet every time her team makes it to the championship game, high on her priority list is to make a friend of the opposing coach, to give gifts, and to encourage the opposing coach and team. Sometimes her team goes on to win and sometimes they lose, but either way, the friendship remains. The deadly determination of envy is weakened when we practice acts of love for others despite being in the midst of a comparative rivalry, or maybe, especially then.

Study Guide

The authors offer three possible remedies for envy in sport. First is the most drastic—spend more frequent time in noncompetitive activities (avoid sport). Second is the most traditional—when engaged in sport, focus more on one's improvement, enjoyment, and quest for excellence than simply "beating" one's opponent (change sport). Third is the most Biblical—lead with love when engaged in sport (change oneself). Students may have interest in discussing the relative merits of these three options, especially considering the high emotions and quick-response nature of sports. Certain options may sound good in theory but be very difficult to execute when in the midst of a high-stakes sporting event.

Study Questions

1. What is envy, and how does it compare to covetousness and jealousy?
2. Describe a situation when you felt envy, or experienced someone envying you, in a comparative environment.
3. What about sport makes participants susceptible to envy?

4. What are some practical ways that you can avoid or dampen envy when you participate in sport or other competitive activities?
5. Can we ever have comparison—in a sport setting or otherwise—that doesn't lead to either envy or feelings of superiority? Why or why not?

Further Reading

Kretchmar, R. S. (1995), "From Test to Contest: An Analysis of Two Kinds of Counterpoint in Sport," in *Philosophic Inquiry in Sport*, ed. by W. J. Morgan & K. V. Meier, 36–41, Champaign, IL: Human Kinetics.
McNamee, M. (2010), "Schadenfreude in Sports: Envy, Justice and Self-Esteem," in *The Ethics of Sports: A Reader*, ed. by M. J. McNamee, 327–339, New York: Routledge.

Chapter 12

ORDO AMORIS: THE ESSENCE OF CHRISTIAN WISDOM FOR SPORT

Mark Hamilton

Introduction

Decades ago, rocker Pat Benatar released the song *Love is a Battlefield*, describing how she and her lover must continually fight for their love and fight to maintain their love. She sang about struggling to maintain control, questioning whether their love will last as they grow older and whether their hearts will surrender and remain open to each other. She passionately cried out, "Heartache to heartache we stand, no promises, no demands. Love is a battlefield." Yes, love is a battlefield, a battlefield of the heart. A war of devotion occurs internally in the human heart when objects and persons compete for the affections of our innermost beings. Little did Benatar know that she was testifying not only in personal terms but also in cosmic terms and that one aspect of the heart that is a zone of conflict is arranging the objects of its affections. She could have easily been singing about the manifestation of *ordo amoris* (the ordering of love).

Ordo amoris is a concept that was first developed by Augustine (AD 354–430), which he called the "brief and true definition of virtue"; it was central to his understanding of the good life. It is about knowing the proper value of the objects we love and then loving them rightly, orderly (*ordo*)—in accord with their true essential value. Understanding this and living it rightly are the core of true human, or rather, divine wisdom. Humans enter life with a self-consuming desire for happiness, and there are many objects "seeking" affections or loyalties that compete for primacy. David Naugle (2008: 57) writes, "The human mind and heart, then are a battlefield of ideas and affections, the greatest Armageddon, the true holy war."

A moral life is lived by a person who loves what ought to be loved properly. Evil and disharmony occur in loving things the wrong way, out of order, or not according to their inherent value. In this ongoing pursuit for meaning and serenity, one of the more popular contemporary means of satisfying the heart is through the sporting life. The love of sports seeks to own the human heart and often does so quite successfully. Sport competes for primacy over our affections;

and if not loved appropriately, there is no doubt that it can consume us, even to our destruction. This misaligned affection for sports can create numerous problems in human lives, relationships, and in priorities. This is because of the failure to rightly determine its real value according to the measure of virtue established by Augustine and explained further by Max Scheler in his essay "*Ordo Amoris*," and because of this failure, sports is morally "killing" us. The aim of this chapter is to develop the concept of *ordo amoris* and to apply it to the rudiments of our sporting affections while evaluating its moral impact.

Ordo Amoris *and the pursuit of happiness*

Since Aristotle (fourth century BC), it has generally been accepted in the West that happiness drives most, if not all, human activities. Humans attach their hearts to those things that they believe can satisfy their thirst for happiness. And though not everyone agrees on how to achieve contentment, most agree that it is happiness that humans most frequently desire. However, in a skeptical age where happiness can appear to be a relative good, there seems to be increasing doubts that there exists any single specific universal answer to this quest. Scheler (1973: 119) has suggested that, "modern man thinks that in general there is nothing fixed, nothing definite or binding, there, where he simply does not take the trouble to look seriously for something of the sort." Humans obviously love many things like food, partying, recreation, work, amusement, and exploration, along with meditating about abstract concepts. But no object or activity is viewed as essentially or objectively more valuable or meaningful than any other. It has not always been this way. Contrary to this "classically, among the great Western philosophers and theologians, happiness denoted the state of the genuine fulfillment of human nature that resulted from being properly related as a person to the truth of reality" (Naugle 2008: 10). Aligning one's affections to the true value of the world has historically been thought to be an achievable human ambition worthy of seeking after.

This belief in the objective value of the world that has been held throughout much of Western history was founded on the notion that objective value is based on the inherent worth that God has placed on the objects in existence. Western thinkers assumed the *ordo amoris* to be the core of the world order taken as a divine order (Scheler 1973: 110). There was, furthermore, a belief that a person's actual feelings and affections could "be in harmony with or oppose the rank-ordering of what is worthy of love ... (that one) can feel and know himself (or herself) to be at one with, or separated and opposed to, the ... world" (Scheler 1973: 111–112). The failure to arrange affections in this harmonious order, aligned with reality as God had made it, creates a lack of satisfaction, and restlessness, and possibly even evil. Scheler (1973: 113) goes on to observe the futility of this, stating: "The sensualist is struck by the way pleasure he [or she] gets from the objects of his enjoyment gives him [or her] less and less satisfaction while his [or her] driving impulse stays the same or itself increases as he [or she] flies more and more rapidly from one object to the next. For this water makes one thirstier, the more one drinks."

In contrast, Christian thinkers have proposed that there is something that is by its very nature supreme in value and should be the ultimate aim of our affections. Those who hold to an *ordo amoris* believe that there should be a clear hierarchy of our affections based on the inherent value of the objects of affection. This order would descend from the top down based on the object's intrinsic value beginning with love for God, which is love for the eternal, then for others, self, and things, which are temporal. "A love which is by its essence infinite, however much it is interrupted, however much it is bound to and particularized by the specific organization of its bearer, demands for its satisfaction an infinite good. In this sense, the object of the idea of God already underlies the thought of an *ordo amoris*" (Scheler 1973: 114). Thus, when *ordo amoris* is properly practiced, it creates a harmony between the world and humans based on how the world was structured by God. God created a world with many and various pleasures, but they are to be loved only in their proper relationship to the other objects of our affections. God is to be loved above all else, with each other object being loved in accord with its value as determined by God. This coincides with the belief that there exists an ethical structure in the world and objective moral laws inscribed on the human heart—"which correspond to the plane on which the world is constructed as a world of value" (Scheler 1973: 117).

In this view, each created entity has its own essence because of the way in which God has hierarchically made it under Him; thus, it is God who gives value and worth accordingly to all things and not humans. As Scheler (1973: 111) argues, "Man's love is restricted to recognizing the objective demand these objects make and to submitting to the gradation of rank in what is worthy of love. This gradation exists ... 'for' man, ordered to his particular essence." Even though each object is distinct and made by God, it cannot provide more for humans than its nature can provide based on its intrinsic value determined by God no matter how much humans would otherwise desire. Since objects and activities have an essential objective nature to them, determined by how God evaluates them, then these objects, including sports and games, are made to meet specific purposes or ends based on their nature. We should love things as they are viewed by God and as they are meant to be loved. Our hearts must align themselves in a right manner. We should love God, people, animals, places, and things the way they should be loved. In the words of Naugle (2008: 51), "Happy, then, is the person who comprehends and loves all things in their proper places in their proper ways," and if we do not, then our lives become topsy-turvy.

This view is rooted in Augustine's broad explanation for the ethical structures in the world:

According to Augustine, "There is a scale of value stretching from earthly to heavenly realities, from the visible to the invisible; and the inequality between these goods makes possible the existence of them all." God is one thing, angels are another, as are people, terriers, red oaks, squash, rocks, and dirt. Each item fits in God's overall scheme of creation. (Cited in Naugle 2008: 49)

This initially sounds like a metaphysical hierarchism, but it is much more. It is both a metaphysical and an ethical hierarchy. The essence of things in this arrangement is argued immutable and, as such, each is able when loved to provide the appropriate kind of satisfaction based on its nature. Augustine sees the universe as an ordered structure where the levels of being are levels of value, where the lower must be subordinate to the higher because this is the value God has placed on it. Augustine considers evil to result from a disarrangement of affections or a corruption of the good. It is a perversion of something good by twisting it or misusing it until it becomes evil by loving it in ways that it is not worthy of receiving because it is not according to its proper metaphysical value. Humans must make an accurate rational assessment of the worth of the objects of affection; the wise or good life results when one loves what ought to be loved properly. Evil and disharmony occur in loving things out of order. Augustine attaches his affections to things he believes would satisfy him and were fitting objects of his love, and because of the essential differences in the nature of these objects, the results of loving each would be distinct and different. Augustine (1996: 118) asserts that this requires humans to make a detached unbiased assessment to love the objects of affection

> in the right order so that you do not love what is not to be loved, or fail to love what is to be loved, or have a greater love for what should be loved less, or an equal love for things that should be loved less or more, or a lesser or greater love for things that should be loved equally. (Naugle 2008: 53)

Scheler *and* Ordo Amoris

This concept of providing a ranking order of the value of objects is of crucial concern to modern theistic ethics as well as the ancient period. Scheler (1973: 99) revives this idea of *ordo amoris,* noting that the "central problem of all ethics" is the establishment of the proper knowledge concerning the "ranking of everything which is possibly worthy of love in things, in accordance with their inner values." This ranking is from lowest to highest and goes from pleasure, utility, vitality, culture, and holiness as he claims this to be an objective order of values. According to Scheler (1973: 100), what and how one loves is the most central and important aspect of any human being. Humans are defined according to their passions or, as he states, "Whoever has the *ordo amoris* of a man has the man himself." It is the primary determinant of a person. Reflecting the Augustinian hierarchical approach to reality, Scheler (1973: 99) relates, "The highest thing of which a man is capable is to love things as much as possible as God loves them and in one's own act of love to experience the human act at one and the same point of the world of values. The objectively correct *ordo amoris* becomes a norm only when it is seen as related to the will of man and as commanded to him by a will," meaning the will of God who sets the objective value of the objects of affection as He has ordained them and as humans are directed to align their affections accordingly.

In recovering this moral principle, Scheler (1973: 98) describes how we live in a "vast world of sensible and spiritual objects which set my heart and passions in constant motion." These many items in this world and beyond compete for our affections. This is the battlefield warring for priority over my affections. Objects in the world cry out to us, "Love me, love me more than the others." And often the heart pauses, listens, and attaches itself to these temporal objects. This potentially creates problems as Scheler goes on to describe, "any sort of rightness or falseness and perversity in my life and activity are determined by whether there is an objectively correct order of these stirrings of my love and hate .... It depends further on whether I can impress this *ordo amoris* on my inner moral tenor" and how the failure to do so can lead to numerous difficulties.

Disordering our affections

There is nothing wrong with the created finite objects of the world. There was nothing inherently wrong with the forbidden fruit in the Garden. There is nothing intrinsically evil in sports. Complications arise, however, when a person does not understand the nature of the objects made and fails to order their affections according to the value of the object being loved. This, of course, is common as many "fail to grasp the unique character of each object, the place it should hold, and the purpose it is to fill in our lives" (Naugle 2008: 50). If someone does internally wrestle with and understand where objects find their position in the hierarchy and acts rightly, then wisdom is found and their love will be "correct and in order; if the positions change places, if under the influence of passions and drives the hierarchy of levels is overturned, then our love is incorrect and disordered" (Scheler 1973: 124). To love objects unfittingly is to disorder our affections. Those of us who live disordered lives are usually blind to our actions and are deceived. Pascal (1995: 132) observes that "those who lead disordered lives say to those who lead ordered ones that it is they who stray from nature, and believe themselves to follow it; like those on board a ship think people on shore are moving away." Our sinful revolt against God is the reason for this deception, penetrating our thoughts and affections. This is a struggle, even an internal war, over the greater good. "We are blinded to it in our sin, and we are deceived about it by the droppings of our cultures. Because we fail to understand things as they are, we love in a wrong way and with false hopes. In our blindness, our loves are woefully disordered" (Naugle 2008: 57). Scheler (1973: 124) describes this foolishness of not rightly evaluating the objects of affection and thus not responding with wisdom:

> Our spirit finds itself in "metaphysical confusion" when an object which belongs among those in any way and in any degree value-relative is loved in the manner appropriate only to objects of absolute value; that is, when a man identifies the value of his spiritual, personal core with the value of such an object to the extent that he stands to it basically in the relation of faith and worship and thus falsely deifies it, or rather idolizes it. At a particular level of value-relativity, an object of

lesser value can be preferred over another object of greater value. ... In this case
the love is not adequate to the object. These degrees of adequacy can increase
from blind love all the way to completely adequate or evident, clear-sighted love.

The heart, the organ of human emotion, becomes impaired when misdirected;
and when it is misdirected toward sports, sports become elevated to an object of
affection far beyond what it is able to deliver. No created object, including sports,
can satisfy the deepest longing of the human heart. Several millennia ago, this was
echoed by Solomon in the book of Ecclesiastes: he determined human activity
to be vanity even though these temporal objective objects of longing were as
attractive to Solomon then as they are to us today.

From this perspective, humans must remain conscious that created things
like sports compete for our affections. As Naugle (2008: 47) observes, "We must
be aware of happiness look-a-likes. There are many really good impersonators
out there" and sports is one of the great imitators. Naugle (2008: 47) goes on,
"We can all too easily confuse what we desire with what is desirable, satisfy the
superficial and starve the essential traits of our nature, love absolutely what we
should love relatively and love relatively what we should love absolutely. We can
be on a fool's errand after fool's gold." We confuse real goods with apparent goods
when sin and social pressures confuse human knowledge about happy, fulfilled
living. Secondary things then become primary things. For example, a young,
highly successful athlete might find himself in the following situation. He gets a
concussion at a late summer soccer practice. Yet his father wants him to head back
to school as soon as possible. The father informs the coaches and administrators
that his son will soon be returning to school and practice before he is medically
cleared. The father clearly wants the son to play as soon as possible, and he has
made himself blind to the possible risk to his son. Why is this? Because as much
as the father loves his son, he unconsciously loves what his son's success in soccer
does for himself more than anything else. Does the father love his son? Of course,
but his love for his son may get trumped by his love for what his son's success does
for his own ego.

We can be deceived or simply deceive ourselves, where we place our hope
on finding a nourishing life dependent on things (including sports) which,
according to Augustine, can never fully satisfy our own desires. Or we can seek
temporal love as finite human beings and allow that to overtake a love for an
eternal God. If God is removed from the position of deserved supremacy in
life, then sports or anything temporal has the potential to fill this vacuum and
becomes the new groundwork for life. A substitute foundation is laid, as Naugle
(2008: 64) states:

> [U]nder our feet (that is, until a hardship occurs, and we call upon God as our
> heavenly butler for a quick fix). Otherwise, we forget God amidst a multitude
> of legitimate pleasures in life—"Golf is life: The rest is just details." These things
> excite us and give us a sense of meaning and purpose, until their insufficiency is
> revealed. Meanwhile, we live as practical atheists rather than as adoring theists.

C.S. Lewis (1970: 280) writes about the tragic effect on a person when the disordering of affections occurs, "The woman who makes a dog the centre of her life loses, in the end, not only her human usefulness and dignity but even the proper pleasure of dog-keeping." This disordered way can become a path of self-destruction and a loss of what the original pleasure brings someone. Lewis (1970: 280) subsequently adds:

> It is a glorious thing to feel for a moment or two that the whole meaning of the universe is summed up in one woman—glorious so long as other duties and pleasures keep tearing you away from her. But clear the decks and so arrange your life (it is sometimes feasible) that you will have nothing to do but contemplate her, and what happens? Of course this law has been discovered before, but it will stand re-discovery. It may be stated as follows: every preference of a small good to a great, or a partial good to a total good, involves the loss of the small or partial good for which the sacrifice was made.

And more than likely, this deception will not be grasped by the individual.

Ordo Amoris *as applied to sport*

Ethical questions must be raised by Christians as we examine sport and competition from an eternal perspective with an understanding of evil and how this translates to sport. Unfortunately, many times we can live disordered lives through misplaced love of sport. What is the consequence of sport itself being victorious on the battlefield of life and becoming the primary object of our affections? Consider the parent who teaches, or passively accepts, that it is more important to regularly attend a weekend soccer tournament or to play in a Sunday morning golf league than it is to offer worship. What is this saying to children about the parent's *ordo amoris*?

No one ever exemplified a greater love for the game of baseball than has Pete Rose as he succeeded in becoming the all-time games played and all-time hits leader in Major League Baseball by the time he retired in 1986. Rose played twenty-four years in the major leagues and made seventeen all-star teams. He was one of the most popular and greatest players in baseball history and ended up even managing his hometown Cincinnati Reds. But Rose was eventually banned for life for betting on games while manager of the Reds. Rose may have played the game with as much passion as anyone who had ever played. But as much as he loved the game, he loved the thrill of the game multiplied through wagering on the game more than he loved the actual game. He ended up loving the game in ways that it could not deliver. Because his passions focused more on baseball and wagering than on a balanced love for the game and the people in it, this love became disordered and distorted. Rose ended up losing two families, being banned from Major League Baseball for life, failing to enter the Baseball Hall of Fame, and in becoming a shameful fallen hero because, like many great athletes who fall from grace, he could not rightly align his affections.

Contemplate the coach who decides that she will put everything into coaching and her athletic program's success to the extent that she spends fifteen hours a day coaching and sacrifices her time with her family and husband, leading to a divorce and the disintegration of family life. She makes a value-judgment that says, "I love my family but I really love my job," and "My desire to win at any cost overrides my love for my family." She pours herself into her sport, giving every spare minute to her team and her vocation as a coach, but neglects her family by missing her children's sporting events and watching footage of her team instead of being with family or finding time to pray. She still loves them, but in her actions it becomes obvious that she loves her job, loves her coaching, and loves winning more than she loves her family or God. She justifies this by her need to succeed and excel, but the order of her affections places coaching over family. There is a distortion or a disordering of affections, and the consequence is that her family suffers, her marriage suffers, and her spiritual life suffers. Her family senses that this is the order of her loves and that her love for sport is "killing her." And though she may deny this and believe that she can handle all of the consequences, her actions confirm the reality of her hierarchy of affections. She loves her job, her coaching, and her family, but actually loves sports more than her family or children—but to what end?

Humans are easily deceived often thinking that things of lower value are worth more than things of higher value. Athletes frequently love success more than virtue, leading to shortcuts such as the use of illegal enhancements or cheating, thus perverting their character. Consider the example of seven-time Tour de France champion Lance Armstrong, who loved winning so much that he cheated and sacrificed his virtue to be a champion. Many do not understand that this is a losing proposition. As Lewis (1970: 280) states, "If Esau really got the pottage in return for his birthright, then Esau was a lucky exception. You can't get second things by putting them first. You can get second things only by putting first things first … What things are first? Is of concern not only to philosophers but to everyone" (Lewis 1970: 280).

Correcting the disordering

A correct order can be restored by one of two ways—either by demonstrating the world's vanity so the heart will withdraw its overwhelming passions from objects that are not worthy of it; "or, by setting forth another object, even God, as more worthy of its attachment, so as that the heart shall … exchange an old affection for a new one," writes theologian Thomas Chalmers (1971: 1). The ultimate emptiness of the single-minded pursuit of objects of lower affection, like sports, needs to be rationally comprehended and emotionally felt. It is futile "to think of stopping one of these pursuits in any way else, but by a naked demonstration of their vanity" (Chalmers 1971: 1). This is the lesson it took Solomon so long to discover eventually declaring in the book of Ecclesiastes, "Vanities of vanities," he writes, "it is all striving after the wind." But it is very hard to admit this and let go of the wind.

The discovery of this emptiness is insufficient in itself. "To bid a man into whom there has not yet entered the great and ascendant influence of the principle of regeneration, to bid him withdraw his love from all the things that are in the world, is to bid him give up all the affections that are in his heart" (Chalmers 1971: 3). This is all he knows, and to ask him to give it up without discovering something more valuable is futile. This is a powerful description of the person void of God and missing an ability to make a correct moral assessment of what is most valuable. For Naugle (2008: 51), "The greatest disordered love of all is our confident but false hope that our love for things in this world, despite their goodness and desirability, can satisfy the need we have for loving union with God." This affection "cannot be expunged by a mere demonstration of the world's worthlessness. But may it not be supplanted by the love of that which is more worthy than itself? The heart cannot be prevailed upon to part with the world, by a simple act of resignation" (Chalmers 1971: 3). It can only really be expelled by a newer and greater love for God. This is to be the first, chief, and fountain of the affections (Edwards 1997).

Jesus is to be preeminent in life because He is preeminent in all things. Jesus "is the image of the invisible God, the first-born of all creation. For by Him were all things created, both in the heavens and on the earth, visible and invisible, whether thrones or dominions or rulers or authorities ... so that He himself will come to have first place in everything" (Colossians 1:15–18). Thus, love for Christ should be the first priority while everything else, including sports, is secondary. Jesus says in Matthew 10:37, "He who loves father or mother more than Me is not worthy of Me; and he who loves son or daughter more than Me is not worthy of Me." What does Jesus mean by this? He is speaking of the ordering of affections. It is good to love father and mother; it is good to love son and daughter. But it is not good to love father or mother, son or daughter more than one loves Christ. This is because what one loves first and foremost in life becomes one's God, and it must be asked whether it is able to fulfill that calling? Finite humans, such as parent or child, cannot, and neither can sport. The love for things must be subordinate to our love for God. Is it permissible to love other things than God, such as family or sports? Of course it is! But they are not to be loved more than the eternal, for they are temporal and not God. The eternal must be loved first and foremost; otherwise, life is lived upside down and evil results.

This is not eliminating our other loves. It is placing them in their rightful position of affection subordinate to things more valuable. It is the "overbearing of one affection by another" (Chalmers 1971: 3). This is in line with the creation mandate where the world or the activities in the world are redeemed when done to and for the glory of God. As Scheler (1973: 114) notes, "God and only God can be the apex of the graduated pyramid of the realm of that which is worthy of love, at once the source and the goal of the whole." The good or happy life is learning to love God and the parts of creation, including sports, in the right way in the right amount in coherence to one another. It is love for God that gives all these other elements of creation meaning.

This should not eliminate our love for sports and our love for sporting achievement but reveals the need to love sports according to its real value as God values it. One of the great unrecognized glories of the Christian faith "is that it does not call upon us to eliminate our love for things on earth out of our love for God in heaven. It's not either God or the world, but both God and the world in a proper relationship" (Naugle 2008: 21). When our loves are ordered rightly, even our love for sports, we love it no longer as an idol, but as part of creation in a reordered, redeemed way. A proper love for Jesus Christ should bring about a reordering of human affections for God, others, self, and things (including sports):

> This will allow us to worship God in all of life and to serve Him in relatively mundane or in playful activities. Until God is preeminently attractive to us and all things in life are loved in right relation to him, we will seek to satisfy our desires and find our happiness in a creation emptied of its Creator. (Naugle 2008: 12)

Conclusion

James 4:1 asks, "What is the source of quarrels and conflicts among you? Is not the source your pleasures that wage war in your members?" What do they wage war over? They war for primacy over our affections. Wisdom is when our head and heart cooperate in making us virtuous in our relationship to the objects of our affection, including sports. It is thinking rightly and appropriately lining up our affections based on the value of these objects as God has evaluated and determined. Idolatry occurs whenever anything is placed above God in the human heart, and frequently sports maintain this position in the priorities of love. It is actually a rather common occurrence. In the nineteenth century, Soren Kierkegaard spoke of purity of heart as willing one thing, to will one thing appropriate to its true value or rather because of its true value. Here Kierkegaard is referencing God as the primary desire of a pure heart. Humans allow many other objects of affection to interpose themselves ahead of God in life, and one of the most subtle and distinct corrupting objects of affection is sports. But to make anything an object of love above God is to make an idol of that object. Sports cannot fulfill this function, and it is blasphemous when it is given such power. It is not wrong to love sports; it is wrong to love them more than their value and more than they can provide. Psalm 115:8 explains that all who make idols become like their idols or the objects of worship: "Those who make them will become like them." What kind of beings are we becoming when we make sports our God, when we worship our success or status instead of the Creator?

In contrast, in *The Fruitful Life*, Jerry Bridges (2006: 11) says, "A life that grows in loving God becomes like God." The appropriate desire of humans should be to glorify God by becoming more God-like. The Puritan John Owen affirms this by stating that, "Love begets a likeness between the mind loving and the object beloved ... A mind filled with the love of Christ as crucified ... will be changed into his image and likeness" (cited in Bridges 2006: 11). Additionally, the apostle Paul declares, "But we all, with unveiled face, beholding as in a mirror the glory of the Lord, are being transformed into the same image from glory to glory, just as from the Lord, the Spirit" (2 Corinthians 3:18). This is certainly the better image. Earlier it was stated that loving sports like we sometimes do is "killing" us. This is not because of sport itself but because we love it and attach our affections to it in ways that it cannot deliver. It is a temporal love, and when we love it as if it has eternal value, we do lasting harm to our souls. Anything—occupation, recreation, education, or sports—that occupies a higher love than our love for God becomes an idol or false God. However, if God is our first love, love for family, country, or sports will not be in conflict, but will allow us to glorify God to a greater extent.

Study Guide

For people deeply involved in sport, this chapter raises several questions. At times it is obvious that sport can ruin people's lives, but in some situations it isn't as evident nor is it easy to determine a way forward. Reflect on the questions below to clarify the Augustinian framework that the chapter establishes; next, weigh specific sporting situations that challenge people's involvement in sport and in comparison with other loves in their lives.

Study Questions

1. What do Augustine and Scheler mean by "*ordo amoris*"? Discuss this concept. Explain how love has a hierarchy and what this hierarchy is based upon.
2. In this chapter, I have argued that sport is "killing us." What does this statement mean and do you agree or disagree with it?
3. It is stated that, "We should love things as they are viewed by God and as they are meant to be loved." What is meant by this? Do you believe that God created sport, and if so, where and how should sport be loved?
4. Explain what happens to a person when things are not loved in the right order?
5. Is sport a natural good or a natural evil? Explain your response.

Further Reading

Naugle, D. (2008), *Reordered Love, Reordered Lives*. Grand Rapids, MI: Eerdmans Publishing, Co.

Scheler, M. (1973), "Ordo Amoris," in *Selected Philosophical Essays Max Scheler*, ed. by John Wild et al., 98–135, Evanston, IL: Northwestern University Press.

Chapter 13

SPORTS IN THE SERVICE OF SELF-KNOWLEDGE

Ed Hastings

Introduction

People often overlook how sports can offer athletes a greater understanding of themselves, or even a deeper spiritual or religious meaning about life. By offering opportunities to gain self-knowledge, sports can assist athletes to even find their purpose in this world. When athletes understand their feelings and their reactions to circumstances, they can grow in their ability to live according to deeper values and beliefs instead of being led by instinctual responses that can result in decreased sporting performance and a lower quality of life (Peters 2011). The Christian tradition, drawing on sources like Scripture and the past lives of saints, affirms the importance of self-knowledge: the more we come to understand ourselves, even in a sporting context, the more we can come to know who God is. Ultimately, it is through athletes' lives in the created world that God the Creator becomes known.

In this chapter, I ask the question: how can sports help us learn about ourselves as a means to personal and spiritual growth? If we use sports well and we have mentors, teachers, and coaches with whom we can have honest discussions, sports are ripe to teach us about ourselves: our light and dark sides, our strengths and weaknesses. In this chapter, I review three major spiritual writers from the Christian tradition and highlight things that they say about the importance of self-knowledge for spiritual growth. In turn, I apply their insights on self-knowledge to the realm of sports. I also draw from my own experiences as a former varsity athlete, basketball coach, and course instructor on the topic of sport and spirituality over the past several decades to highlight practices that may help athletes understand themselves and God better.

There are two words of caution before beginning. First, the contexts of the writers below are different, time-wise and culture-wise. Consequently, there is a danger that their thoughts and feelings might be misconstrued. It is my belief that if readers can be aware of these differences, they can still benefit from the wisdom offered. The second point of caution has to do with how people might reflect upon their experiences. There is a difference between reflecting upon an experience and dwelling on it. In reflecting upon an experience, we attempt to learn about God's goodness through this event. In dwelling upon it, we keep going over it and can't get beyond it. One author makes a helpful distinction between what he calls introspection and transcendent self-presence (van Kaam 1975: 172). In brief, introspection entails a dwelling on the past where one repeats, in a cyclical manner, thoughts on a particular matter. This dwelling can be obsession and detrimental to the person. This kind of introspection has been called "paralysis by analysis" by some (Outward Bound 2007). If we spend too much time reflecting or trying to figure things, we run the risk of becoming immobilized; we analyze it to death; we think too much. On the other hand, transcendent self-presence involves a gentler approach moving beyond self to a greater awareness of God's love and mercy at work in our lives. In this chapter, we take the example of saints as a means to look deeper into our experiences so that we can become more aware of God's presence. Arguably, there is a gentleness within ourselves, not a harshness, that finds God in the quiet of life like Elijah did on Mount Horeb (1 Kings 19:12).

Self-knowledge in the Christian tradition

It is perhaps not surprising to note that past Christians learned about themselves through reflection upon their life experiences. Learning about self has been a way of learning about God within the Christian tradition down the centuries. In self-discovery, we find out not only who we are but also who God is and our relationship to God. The time spent in honest reflection upon our experiences helps us find God. Looking back at significant moments in our lives reveals something of who we really are. These moments can help us find our "true selves," as opposed to our ego-driven "false selves," as the spiritual contemplative Thomas Merton suggested in the early 1960s. Many great Christian writers have utilized self-knowledge as a way to find God and their true selves in friendship with the Creator. Here I use the works of three major writers from the Christian tradition and from distinctly different times and cultures: St. Augustine of Hippo, St. Teresa of Avila, and Thomas Merton. All three wrote autobiographies where they reflected deeply on their own lives to understand themselves and God more fully. In so doing, they utilize their own experience to reflect more richly upon who they are and their connection to God.

St. Augustine

St. Augustine of Hippo is one of the intellectual giants, not only in the history of Christianity, but also of Western civilization. Augustine was born in 354 AD in Northern Africa in a town named Carthage, which is in the eastern part of what is now known as Algeria. He wrote some of the most influential works in early Christianity, but his most well-known work is his autobiography, *Confessions* (1997).

Augustine uses his experiences and life story to illustrate how he came to know himself and, in knowing himself, how he came to know God. Boulding (1997: 11) comments in her Introduction to her translation of Augustine's *Confessions*, "His own way to God had been the way of deep and searing self-knowledge." Augustine uses his day-to-day life experiences as a means by which to learn about himself. He literally "confesses" many of his past mistakes and admits he was more concerned with how he looked on the outside as opposed to being more familiar with his interior self. When he released *Confessions*, Augustine was a church bishop and openly revealed his sinful past as a way to show his own imperfections, growth, and God's ability to heal.

Let us consider two moments in Augustine's life. In the first moment, he analyzes an incident where he, with the help of friends, stole some fruit:

> I was under no compulsion of need, unless a lack of moral sense can count as need, and a loathing for justice, and a greedy, full-fed love of sin. Yet I wanted to steal, and steal I did. I already had plenty of what I stole, and of much better quality too, and I had no desire to enjoy it when I resolved to steal it. I simply wanted to enjoy the theft for its own sake, and the sin. (1997: 67)

Augustine admits that he did not need these pears; he just wanted to experience the thrill of stealing. Here Augustine is honest about his behavior, and this honesty helps him learn more about himself. He understands that there is something seductive about evil and that it could draw him to do things he would later recognize as harmful or reckless.

The second moment is his major conversion experience. Up to this point, Augustine felt that his life was driven by all kinds of cravings: academics, reputation, sexual cravings, etc. These desires led him to do things that he later saw as destructive to his very self. These passions often controlled his life, and the more he tried to get rid of them, the more powerful they would become. He realized that he could not handle these desires on his own, no matter how he tried.

It happened that he was by himself at one point, lamenting that he did not have enough self-control to overcome these cravings. It was at this time that some young girls were playing a game using everyday language that repeated the phrase, "*Tolle lege*," "Pick up and read." He heard those words and believed that they were literally a message from God meant for him. He picked up his Bible and flipped it open and read where he randomly put his finger. It was at Paul's Letter to the Romans Chapter 13, verses 13–14: "It is not in dissipation and drunkenness, nor in debauchery and lewdness, nor in arguing and jealousy; but put on the Lord Jesus Christ, and make no provisions for the flesh for the gratification of your desires." Augustine believed that it was God speaking mercifully to him through the voices of these young girls; he thought it was God answering his prayers and leading him in the right direction. It was through his attentiveness toward himself and seeking a better path that he had the opportunity to know God. His self-knowledge led to a new awareness of God's goodness, care, love, and mercy for him.

Augustine's *Confessions* reveals how this saintly person contemplated his own experiences, especially those at significant moments in his life, to envision his life with new eyes. Growing in self-knowledge, he considered his life experiences in light of God's active role in them, as did medieval mystic St. Teresa of Avila during the fifteenth century, to whom we now turn.

St. Teresa of Avila

St. Teresa of Avila was born on March 28, 1515, in the small town of Avila in Spain. She was a member of the Carmelite community, a Roman Catholic group of sisters. Teresa was beautiful, a reformer, and a prolific writer who continues to inspire many even today. In her work *Interior Castle*, Teresa uses the metaphor of a castle for her image of the soul. She posits that there are seven mansions (or stages) to the soul and the first of which is primarily entered through self-knowledge or what she refers to as humility. Although she does mention that deeper self-knowledge is needed to navigate all the remaining six stages of the soul, it is through humbly recognizing who one is—warts and all—that one can begin to know God.

Teresa understood how important self-knowledge, or seeing ourselves correctly, is to the transformation of the soul and for a deeper relationship with God. The more we come to know who we are, the good and the bad, the more we are able to come to know God. She comments in *Interior Castle* (1989: 29) how bereft one is if one does not come to a true knowledge of oneself:

> It is no small pity, and should cause us no little shame, that through our own fault, we do not understand ourselves, or know who we are. Would it not be a sign of great ignorance ... if a person were asked who he was, and could not say, and had no idea who his father or his mother was, or from what country he came?

In her *Life*, Teresa (1904: 38) comments on how she became fond of books on chivalry and loved to be among those who admired this kind of lifestyle. She became overly attached to fine dresses, her own appearance, and the importance of social status and who she was seen with. She admits to a preoccupation with looking good, upward mobility, and what she called her "honor." She was aware that she wanted to be around the "right people." It is not that Teresa thought these tendencies were evil in and of themselves, but she realized the more she was willing to be attached to these kinds of values, the more they took her away from connection with God.

Like Augustine before her, Teresa considers the importance of self-knowledge because it was through humbly seeing herself that she was able to acknowledge attachments that took her away from higher virtues. Growing in deeper awareness was a first step toward greater love of God. Such contemplations are something that also permeates the writings of the Trappist monk and modern spiritual writer, Thomas Merton.

Thomas Merton

Thomas Merton was born on January 31, 1915, in Prades, France. He made his way to America at the age of 20 to attend Columbia University. Merton became a Catholic priest and a Trappist monk, eventually living in the monastery of Gethsemani in Kentucky. He is considered by many to be the greatest spiritual master the American Catholic Church produced in the twentieth century (Cunningham 1992: 15). He was a poet and essayist, social critic and autobiographer, satirist and spiritual writer, biographer and literary analyst (5). Merton was accidentally electrocuted while attending an interreligious monastic meeting in Bangkok and died in 1968. Throughout his writings, Merton displayed a deep concern for self-knowledge. He plumbed the depths of his experiences to understand more deeply who he was so that he could come to know who God was. Not many people realize that Thomas Merton was athletic and that he, at times, would incorporate sports into his writings and conferences. He was on the rowing team at Clare College, Cambridge, and later at Columbia University. He also was on the cross-country team at Columbia University. In his time as novice director at his monastery Gethsemani and during conferences that he would give, he frequently used sporting analogies to make his point. He would compare the trials faced by an athlete to the spiritual struggles encountered by a monk (Rembert 2017), just as St. Paul did in several biblical letters (e.g., 1 Cor 9:24–27 and 2 Tim 4:7–8) (Friedrichsen 2002).

A particular experience that is not related to sports, but reveals a moment of self-discovery for Merton, is what has become known as his "epiphany at the corner of 4th and Walnut." Here, Merton came to understand that he was trying to be different from, and even holier than, others by entering the monastery. In this experience, he reflects upon how he had been wrong and now sees that he is like all other people and then feels consoled by it. He recognizes the goodness in others and probably was becoming more aware of the goodness in himself. Merton (1966: 156) describes this famous scene below:

> In Louisville, at the corner of Fourth and Walnut, in the center of the shopping district, I was suddenly overwhelmed with the realization that I loved all those people, that they were mine and I theirs, that we could not be alien to one another even though we were total strangers. It was like waking from a dream of separateness, of spurious self-isolation in a special world, the world of renunciation and supposed holiness. The whole illusion of a separate holy existence is a dream … This sense of liberation from an illusory difference was such a relief and such a joy to me that I almost laughed out loud. And I suppose my happiness could have taken form in the words: "Thank God, thank God that I am like other men, that I am only a man among others." … I have the immense joy of being *man*, a member of a race in which God Himself became incarnate. As if the sorrows and stupidities of the human condition could overwhelm me, now I realize what we all are. And if only everybody could realize this! But it cannot be explained. "There is no way of telling people that they are all walking around shining like the sun."

Merton's experience here helps him see himself in new ways. When he first entered the monastery, it was to flee the evil world and to believe he was better, holier than the ordinary person. In this passage he realizes, even if he is a monk, that he is just like everyone else—and this becomes consoling for him. This insight is new self-knowledge for him and changed how he saw and treated those around him.

These three devoted followers of the Christian tradition reveal to us that deeper self-knowledge can bring us closer to God and to others through humbly accepting our faults and trying to see things as Jesus does. Let us now look to sports for opportunities to understand ourselves more. We tend not to consider sports an acceptable place to learn about ourselves, but there are plenty of examples to counter this assumption.

Examples of self-knowledge through sports

In this section, I consider how the insights of St. Augustine, St. Teresa, and Thomas Merton might be applied to three experiences taken from my own sporting life and which contributed to my own self-knowledge and helped me, in part, become the person God has called me to be.

I played college-level basketball at Villanova University in Philadelphia. Villanova is a Catholic school of an Augustinian tradition with its own strong tradition in basketball. The first experience was when I tore my ACL in my sophomore year at Villanova in 1971. I was 20 years old at the time. I was on the verge of moving into a starting position for the team and I injured my knee. I needed surgery, and when the doctor saw me after the procedure he said, "Your knee is worse than we thought, you have a 50/50 chance of ever playing again." My world was rocked. "Who was I if not a basketball player?" I was forced to begin to think: "What would I do if I cannot play basketball again? Who was I if I was not a basketball player?" I was challenged to confront my own self-identity. I was forced to entertain the thought that I might not play basketball again. And even if I did, would I be as good as I once was before the injury? These questions compelled me to a new self-knowledge. I had always thought that basketball would be a major part of my life, and now I realized this might not be the case. Little did I know that my identity was entirely wrapped up in being a basketball player. I have heard it said, "If I am what I do, what happens when I can't?" I was forced to entertain the idea that I might have to look at myself in a new way just like Augustine, Teresa, and Merton.

The second experience involved my Villanova University basketball team from 1971. (I did not play that year because I was recovering from surgery on my torn ACL.) Although our team placed second in the country, losing to the famed John Wooden and his UCLA team in the National Championship game, we always thought we were the best team in Villanova men's basketball history. This notion was a source of great pride for me and our team. Then along came 1985 with Villanova playing Georgetown for the National Championship. I was at the game in Lexington, Kentucky. I happened to be the only one from our team at the game so I was being interviewed by a host of people before the game with questions such as: Who did I think was going to win? How did our team of 1971 compare to the 1985 team? Which team was better? I found myself in a quandary. Because of my pride and my desire to be part of the enduring legacy of the 1971 team, I was rooting for Georgetown to defeat Villanova—but how could I say this to the media. I felt extremely guilty and disloyal about this, especially because I was a member of Rollie Massimino's first coaching staff at Villanova. (Massimino was the head coach of the 1985 Villanova team.) This dilemma challenged my sense of self-worth. Who was I if not determined by this measurement? Was the team of '71 less valuable because the '85 team won the National Championship? Was the measure of my self-worth determined by who believes the better team was? These questions forced me to a deeper knowledge of who I was and challenged my own attachments in a way similar to St. Teresa described above.

My third experience happened during my senior year at Villanova in 1973. We were used to being a very successful basketball program during my time at Villanova; however, my final year did not follow that script. I was a co-captain on the team, and we started out well that season, but encountered many difficulties and several successive losses after our early success. During all the losing, I could feel fingers being pointed at me—as if I was responsible for those losses. As people lost confidence in me, I found it difficult to maintain belief in myself. It was here that I had to rely on my knowledge of myself despite what people were saying about me. At that time, I found great solace in a poem by Rudyard Kipling (1994: 605) who wrote the below piece for his son.

> If you can keep your head when all about you
> Are losing theirs and blaming it on you;
> If you can trust yourself when all men doubt you,
> But make allowance for their doubting too;
> If you can wait and not be tired of waiting,
> Or being lied about, don't deal in lies,
> Or being hated, don't give way to hating,
> And yet don't look too good, not talk too wise.
>
> If you can dream—and not make dreams your master,
> If you can think—and not make thoughts your aim,
> If you can meet with triumph and disaster,
> And treat those two impostors just the same;
> If you can bear to hear the truth you've spoken
> Twisted by knaves to make a trap for fools,
> Or watch the things you gave your life to broken,
> And stoop and build 'em up with worn out tools.
>
> If you can make one heap of all your winnings
> And risk it on one turn of pitch-and-toss,
> And lose, and start at your beginnings

And never breathe a word about your loss;
If you can force your heart and nerve and sinew
To serve your turn long after they are gone,
And so hold on when there is nothing in you
Except the will, which says to them "Hold On!"

If you can talk with crowds and keep your virtue,
Or walk with kings—not lose the common touch,
If neither foes nor loving friends can hurt you,
If all men count with you, but none too much;
If you can fill the unforgiving minute,
With sixty seconds worth of distance run,
Yours is the earth and everything that's in it,
And—which is more—you'll be a man, my son!

This poem reminded me to keep believing in myself no matter how bad things got and not to blame others. The experience strengthened my sense of self and forced me to rely on my own gifts and talents. This experience contributed to my own belief in myself with the knowledge that the situation need not dictate who I became.

These three stories from my own experience exemplify ways in which I have grown in self-knowledge from playing sports. These were not pleasant moments for me, but they offered opportunities for my growth nonetheless. They remind me of an experience of note as told by Michael Lewis, the author of *The Blindside, Money Game* and several other bestsellers. In his book *Coach: Lessons on the Game of Life* (2005: 25), he recalls a particular moment when his Little League coach helped him come to a deeper awareness of his self-worth. At the time of this incident, Michael did not have much confidence in himself. His coach called on him in a championship game to come in to retire the last two batters and win the game for his team. Michael did not believe he could do it, but he sensed that this great coach believed he could—and do it he did. In a difficult situation, he got the last two outs to win the game. Here is his comment on the experience: "Now this fantastically persuasive man insisting, however improbably, that I might be some other kind of person. A hero." It is because the coach believed in him that he came to a new belief and awareness of himself.

My three experiences and the above story from Lewis illustrate how sports can offer opportunities for greater self-knowledge and awareness if we take sports seriously and take the time to reflect. While not obsessively dwelling on them, moments such as the above can bring us wisdom and new insights about ourselves and open ourselves to contemplate our relationship to God.

Practical implications for gaining self-knowledge through sports

How then can athletes grow in knowledge of themselves, others, and God through self-reflection, listening to others, and using different forms of prayer?

First, many athletes avoid discussing how to handle intra-team competition. Should players root for teammates who are playing when they themselves are not? All players are part of the same team and yet the success of others can prevent some from playing? How does one handle rooting for the team, but not necessarily wanting a particular player who is ahead of me on the team's depth chart? This leads to a conflict situation for athletes. It can be particularly confusing for athletes who find themselves conflicted over issues that implicate their teammates who are also their friends. I found myself in a situation like this in college: my teammate and I were roommates and were competing for the only position that happened to be open at the time. This situation led us to many uncomfortable, awkward dinners, competitions, and practices. In situations like this, it would be helpful to have someone close to the team who could speak with the athletes about this type of experience: perhaps a team chaplain or mentor. There is usually some embarrassment in revealing this internal conflict, but talking about it can bring such relief. It is important to remember that our secrets often lead to sickness (Bradshaw 1988) as people's emotions impact their physical health. What we hide inside ourselves can make us sick. It can be very helpful to speak with a trusted friend about issues like this.

Second, I know of coaches who use affirmations or positive statements about teammates to solidify team unity. One example of the use of these is to have the coach assign each player anonymously to watch another player in a particular practice. The assignment requires one to identify one thing that a teammate did well in practice. At the end of practice, each player goes around and mentions who they had and explains to the whole group the "good" that they saw in the other. This can be done each week or several times in a season. My sense is that it allows individual players to be aware of how their teammates see them; it helps the team to be more bound together, increases the intensity of the practice, and allows the team to be more connected with one another.

Third, sharing who or what you find inspiring is helpful to a team. I have seen the positive impact of teammates sharing their favorite, inspirational quotations. The root of the word inspire comes from the word spirit. Members can share the quote they like and explain what it has meant to them. This does not have to be done at one setting; it can be done throughout the season. The coaches, managers, and anyone else on the team (e.g., chaplains) could do the same; intentionally bringing inspiration builds team spirit.

Fourth, I have in mind what might be called a consciousness examen for athletes or coaches. The consciousness examen is a method or discipline taken from the spirituality of St. Ignatius of Loyola, the founder of the Roman Catholic religious community called the Society of Jesus or the Jesuits. According to this method, a person reflects back on their day and asks a series of questions about their experiences. The questions are meant to help the person notice where the Spirit worked in their experiences, thoughts, feelings, and actions that particular day. Where did I find the Spirit working today with my team? Where did I experience love with my team today? What caused me pain or separated me from my teammates today? These kinds of questions asked on a regular basis can very much contribute to greater self-knowledge and the humility to place ourselves in right relationship with God.

Fifth, a friend of mine, Fran Dunphy, coaches men's basketball at Temple University in Philadelphia. He incorporates a special exercise each Thanksgiving Day in November as a kind of team-bonding. He has the team (coaches, players, and managers) stand at center court and take turns saying what they are thankful for. This practice allows the team to hear what each is grateful for, and this creates a greater sense of team for them. It allows them to get to know themselves and one another better. Coach Dunphy says this exercise sets a real positive tone for the team. Identifying what we are thankful for can be tremendously uplifting. An awareness of thankfulness can bring a sense of gratitude and hope to a unit. In a long season, full of ups and downs, it is helpful to notice and articulate what blessings are on a team.

Sixth, practicing quiet reflection can be beneficial for a team. It can help athletes steer away from self-absorption and instead focus on what is important in and what they want from life. This notion of silence and quiet can open the door for greater spiritual exploration and self-knowledge. Here are some questions for focused meditation that I have found useful for teams and for my students:

a. Imagine yourself at the end of your playing career: What are you thankful for?
b. Imagine that you are injured: What do you miss the most about being on the team? Playing with your team, the camaraderie in the locker room, etc.?
c. Imagine yourself as a coach: What values do you emphasize with your team? What is the most important value for your team to recognize?
d. Who do you need to ask for forgiveness from or forgive?
e. Consider your best friends: How many friends did you meet playing your sport or on one of your teams?

Seventh, members of a team share painful experiences in sports or in life. This kind of sharing can be monitored by the coaches or perhaps even a team chaplain. This sharing allows the players to get to know one another better, be vulnerable with one another, and helps them to be aware that their teammates have their backs. It can strengthen bonds among teammates and develop even love among the players, which is so vitally important. Phil Jackson, the former championship coach of the Chicago Bulls and Los Angeles Lakers, speaks about the significance of these kinds of experiences in his book *11 Rings*. He says, "It takes a number of critical factors to win an NBA championship, including the right mix of talent, creativity, intelligence, toughness, and, of course luck. But if a team doesn't have the most essential ingredient—love—none of those other factors matter" (2013: 4).

Conclusion

The spiritual writer John Shea (2008: 109) offers an example of an encounter between a father and son, where the father does not know how to speak to his son about a life issue in sports. This happens frequently to us all:

You never know what questions kids are going to ask, especially when you are putting them down for the night. That is when there is enough of a slowdown for them to review the day and pursue what is really on their minds.

As Tom tucked in little Tommy, he felt that tonight his eight-year-old son might want to relive the happy events of the day. Tommy's team had won the Little League Championship that morning. Tommy had three hits and his friend Phil had hit the game-winning home run.

"Pretty good day," Tom said to Tommy as he sat on the side of his son's bed. But Tommy did not respond. The boy looked pensive.

"Dad, you know when Phil hit the homer and everyone ran out onto the field and we jumped up and down?"

"Yeah," said the father, not knowing where this was going.

"I was happy, but inside I felt so bad when Phil got the winning hit?"

Tom wished that his son had asked him about sex. It would have been easier.

Just as St. Augustine, St. Teresa of Avila, and Thomas Merton demonstrated opportunities for a deeper awareness of self, we find these instances are ever present in sporting experiences when we take the time to look. Sports can be used as a tool for self-discovery for athletes, provided that athletes have the opportunity for guidance from a trusted mentor or guide. This could include parents, chaplains, and possibly even coaches. There is much about the athletic experience that can provide chances for growth for the athlete, no matter the age. If we believe God is present to us at all moments of our lives, should we not include experiences of sports as moments for recognizing God's hand at work in our lives? My hope is that in highlighting some of these experiences from my life and the experiences of others, we can use these moments as growth promoters for our athletes. I believe that.

Study Guide

It is wise for athletes to utilize insights of some great spiritual writers of the Christian tradition to guide their spiritual journey. This is especially true with the concept of self-knowledge. When athletes reflect upon their own experiences from sports, they can grow spiritually and come to know themselves and God better.

Study Questions

1. Name a powerful sports experience in your life. Explain how it impacted you.
2. In your own words, state the difference between in-depth introspection ("navel-gazing") and transcendent self-presence.
3. Review the stories told about St. Augustine, St. Teresa, and Thomas Merton. Can you connect these to your own sporting experiences?
4. Turn back to the number of practical implications for gaining self-knowledge through sports. Choose one and discuss with a classmate.
5. Overall, why and how is self-knowledge necessary in order to love others and God?

Further Reading

DiPaul, L., E. Hastings and S. Fuqua Retif. (2006), *More than a Game: Stories, Prayers, and Reflections for the Student Athlete*, Winona: St. Mary's Press.
Jackson, P. (2013), *Eleven Rings: The Soul of Success*, New York: Penguin.
Kelly, P. (2015), *Youth Sport and Spirituality: Catholic Perspectives on Sports: From Medieval to Modern Times*, Notre Dame, IN: University of Notre Dame Press.

CONCLUSION

Matt Hoven, Andrew Parker, and Nick J. Watson

When we canvassed opinion on this volume, we were pleased with the positive response from colleagues in the field about our interest toward Christian practices in sport, and this encouraged us with regard to the need for a book of this nature. We believe that the resulting chapters serve to challenge how we think, feel, and act in sport, while, at the same time, raising a series of further questions about the complex nuances of the sport–Christianity relationship.

One of the most prominent aspects of the book is the largesse of play—as the foundation of sport, as an element of worship, and as a primal human need. More than simply relief from the work-a-day world, play connects people to the Creator and to their humanity and can lift the human spirit beyond the mundane toward greatness and joy. It is this spirit of play that makes possible the spiritual practices that many athletes draw upon and which breathes life into their sporting practices.

A central challenge throughout the book is that sport does not always assist in human flourishing, or transformation; rather, it can be hurtful and destructive. The potential blessings available through sport also raise moral conundrums that require weighing the "loves" in one's life through careful prayer and reflection. For instance, the very nature of competition and its frequent friend envy require a fuller understanding of God's creation and one's own heart. Christian voices throughout history have both supported and rejected sport. But contextualizing these situations and thinking about the eternal value of play make possible the affirmation of sport while recognizing its personal enticements of status, dominance, and wealth along with social-political issues arising from various injustices such as corrupt governance or unethical performance.

Passion for transforming sporting practice calls for more than talk and reflection, requiring of us an intentional mind-set around actions and behaviors. As we have seen, the promotion of servant leadership by coaches can reshape sporting communities and individuals, and the use of faith-informed sport psychology can give life to Christian discipleship in sport. Affective moments of prayer, thanksgiving, wonder, scriptural reflection, and service are able to embody and integrate Christian life in sporting actions, much like the simplicity of water, bread, and oil give sacramental moments to communities dedicated to Jesus.

Stories about saints, those living on earth and those living eternally, draw upon established traditions within Christian and sporting communities to renew the intrinsic goodness of particular practices. Working across Christian traditions can enhance sporting experiences and cultivate renewed relationships with others and with God.

Notwithstanding all of the above, this book's ultimate success relies on you the reader. Consider the practices named or suggested. How do these change your viewpoints on sport? More importantly, how might these practices be lived out in ways that reshape the sporting experiences of individuals and communities on a local, regional, national, and global level? As a player, coach, official, fan, or helping professional, we must ask ourselves to what extent practices focused on the love of others and God—with one's mind, heart, and soul—have the potential to renew the face of sport (cf. Psalm 104:30)?

This kind of reshaping and renewal is more easily said than done. Nonetheless, let us be encouraged in our endeavors by the thoughts of Pope Francis (Dicastery for Laity, Family, and Life 2018: 52) who, in endorsing the power of the sport–Christianity dyad, points us firmly toward the legacy of our labors:

And as sportsmen [and women], I invite you not only to play, like you already do, but there is something more: *challenge yourself* in the game of life like you are in the game of sports. Challenge yourself in the quest for good, in both Church and society, without fear, with courage and enthusiasm. Get involved with others and with God; don't settle for a mediocre "tie," *give it your best*, spend your life on what really matters and lasts forever.

REFERENCES

Introduction

Adogame, A., Watson, N. J., & Parker, A. (eds.) (2018), *Global Perspectives on Sports and Christianity* (Preface, Robert Ellis), London: Routledge.

Ellis, R. (2014), *The Games People Play: Theology, Religion and Sport*, Eugene, OR: Wipf & Stock.

Ellis, R. (2017), *Conference Report: Sport at the Service of Humanity*, Pontifical Council for the Culture, Vatican, Italy, October 5–7, 2016.

Evans, C. H., & Herzog, W. R. (eds.) (2002), *The Faith of 50 Million: Baseball, Religion and American Culture* (Foreword by Stanley Hauerwas), London: Westminster John Knox Press.

Harvey, L. (2014), *A Brief Theology of Sport*, London: SCM Press.

Hoffman, S. J. (2010), *Good Game: Christians and the Culture of Sport*, Waco, TX: Baylor University Press.

Kelly, P. (2012), *Catholic Perspectives on Sports: From Medieval to Modern Times*, Mahwah, NJ: Paulist Press.

Lixey, K., Hübenthal, C., Mieth, D., & Müller, N. (eds.) (2012), *Sport and Christianity: A Sign of the Times in the Light of Faith*, Washington, DC: Catholic University of America Press.

McIntyre, A. (1981), *After Virtue: A Study in Moral Theory*, Notre Dame, IN: University of Notre Dame Press.

Parker, A., Watson, N. J., & White, J. (eds.) (2016), *Sports Chaplaincy: Trends, Issues and Debates* (Preface, John Swinton), London: Routledge.

Sports and Christianity Group (2014), *The Declaration on Sport and Christian Life*. Available online: https://sportandchristianity.com/declaration/ (accessed June 15, 2018).

Swinton, J., & Mowat, H. (2006), *Practical Theology and Qualitative Research*, London: SCM Press.

Watson, N. J. (2018), "New Directions in Theology, Church and Sports: A Brief Overview and Position Statement," *Theology*, 121 (4): 243–251.

Watson, N. J., Hargaden, K., & Brock, B. (eds.) (2018), *Theology, Disability and Sport: Social Justice Perspectives*, London: Routledge.

Watson, N. J., & Parker, A. (eds.) (2015), *Sports, Religion and Disability* (Preface, Joni Tada Eareckson), New York: Routledge.

Chapter 1

Babcock, M. (1901), *Thoughts for Everyday Living*, New York: C. Scribner's sons.

Berger, P. L. (1970), *A Rumor of Angels: Modern Society and the Rediscovery of the Supernatural*, Garden City, NJ: Doubleday, Anchor Books.

Bonhoeffer, D. (1971), *Letters and Papers from Prison*, enl. ed., ed. by Eberhard Bethge, New York: Macmillan (letter dated January 23, 1944).

Crouch, A. (2016), "The Myth of 'Engaging the Culture,'" *Christianity Today*, July/August: 33–34.

Drane, J. (2004), "Contemporary Culture and the Reinvention of Sacramental Spirituality," in *The Gestures of God: Explorations in Sacramentality*, ed. by Geoffrey Rowell, & Christine Hall, 37–55, New York: Continuum.

Ellis, R. (2014), *The Games People Play*, Eugene, OR: Wipf & Stock.

Harvey, L. (2014), *A Brief Theology of Sport*, Eugene, OR: Wipf & Stock, Cascade Books.

Hoffman, S. (2010), *Good Game: Christianity and the Culture of Sports*, Waco, TX: Baylor University Press.

Huizinga, J. (1955), *Homo Ludens*, Boston: Beacon Press.

"*I Am Yup'ik*" (2016), [Film] Dirs. Daniele Anastasion and Nathan Golon, United States: ESPN films.

Johnston, R. K. (1983), *The Christian at Play*, Grand Rapids: Eerdmans.

Johnston, R. K. (2014), *God's Wider Presence: Reconsidering General Revelation*, Grand Rapids: Baker Academic.

Leithart, P. (2014), "Sporting Theologically," *First Things*, June 10.

Lewis, C. S. (1955), *Surprised by Joy*, New York: Harcourt, Brace & World, Harvest Books.

Novak, M. (1976), *The Joy of Sports*, New York: Basic Books.

Peterson, Eugene H. (2002), *The Message: The Bible in Contemporary Language*, Colorado Springs: NavPress.

Preece, G. (2009), "'When I Run I Feel God's Pleasure': Towards a Protestant Play Ethic," in *Sport and Spirituality: An Exercise in Everyday Theology*, ed. by Gordon Preece, & Rob Hess, Adelaide: ATF.

Tillich, P. (1966), *On the Boundary: An Autobiographical Sketch*, New York: Charles Scribner's Sons.

Tillich, P. (1987), "Human Nature and Art," in Paul Tillich, *On Art and Architecture*, ed. by John Dillenberger, & Jane Dillenberger, New York: Crossroad.

Updike, J. (1960), *Rabbit, Run*, Greenwich, CN: Fawcett, Crest Books.

Updike, J. (1972), "Is There Life after Golf," *New Yorker*, July 29: 76–78.

Watson, N. J., & Parker, A. (2015), "The Mystical and Sublime in Extreme Sports: Experiences of 'Psychological Well-Being' or 'Christian Revelation'?" *Studies in World Christianity*, 21 (3): 260–281.

Chapter 2

Ackerman, D. (1999), *Deep Play*, New York: Vintage Books.

Brohm, J. M. (1978), *Sport: A Prison of Measured Time*, London: Pluto Press.

Buber, M. (1958), *I and Thou*, trans. R. Smith (2nd ed.), New York: Charles Scribner's Sons.

Chesterton, G. K. (1908), *Orthodoxy*, San Francisco: Ignatius Press/John Lane.

Chesterton, G. K. (1908/2016), "Oxford from Without," *All Things Considered*, Create Space Independent Publishing Platform (no address given).

Guttmann, A. (1978/2004), *From Ritual to Record: The Nature of Modern Sports*, New York: Columbia University Press.

Huizinga, J. (1950), *Homo Ludens: A Study of the Play Element in Culture*, Boston: Beacon press.

Johnston, R. K. (1983), *The Christian at Play*, Grand Rapids, MI: William B. Eerdmans Publishing Company.

Kretchmar, R. S. (2011), "Why Dichotomies Make It Difficult to See Games as Gifts of God," in *Theology, Ethics and Transcendence in Sports*, ed. by S. J. Parry., M. S. Nesti, & N. J. Watson, 185–200, London, UK: Routledge.

Macdonald, M. H., & Tadie (eds.) (1989), *The Riddle of Joy: G.K. Chesterton and C.S. Lewis*, Grand Rapids, MI: William B. Eerdmans Publishing Company.

Mathisen, J. (2005), "Sport," in *Handbook of Religion and Social Institutions*, ed. by H. R. Abaugh, 279–299, New York: Springer.

Miller, D. L. (1969), *Gods and Games: Towards a Theology of Play*, Cleveland, OH: The World Publishing Co.

Miller, D. L. (1971), "Theology and Play Studies: An Overview," *Journal of the American Academy of Religion*, 39 (1): 349–354.

Moltmann, J. (1972), *Theology of Play*, New York: Harper.

Neale, R. E. (1969), *In Praise of Play: Toward a Psychology of Religion*, New York: Harper and Row.

Novak, M. (1976/1994), *The Joy of Sports: End Zones, Bases, Baskets, Ball, and the Consecration of the American Spirit*, Lanham, MD: Madison Books.

Overman, S. J. (2011), *The Protestant Work Ethic and the Spirit of Sport: How Calvinism and Capitalism Shaped American Games*, Macon, GA: Mercer University Press.

Rahner, H. (1972), *Man at Play*, trans. B. Battershaw, New York: Herder and Herder.

Rigauer, B. (1981), *Sport and Work*, trans. Allen Guttman, New York: Columbia University Press.

Wilson, M. V. (1989), *Our Father Abraham: Jewish Roots of the Christian Faith*, Grand Rapids, MI: William Eerdmans Publishers.

Chapter 3

Berger, P. L. (1971), *A Rumour of Angels*, Harmondsworth: Pelican.

Hoffman, S. J. (2010), *Good Game: Christianity and the Culture of Sports*, Waco, TX: Baylor University.

Karkkainen, V-M. (2004), *One with God: Salvation as Deification and Justification*, Collegeville, MN: Liturgical.

Macquarrie, J. (1977), *Principles of Christian Theology*, (2nd ed.) New York: Scribner.

Moltmann, J. (1973), *Theology and Joy*, trans. Reinhard Ulrich, London: SCM.

Peacocke, A. R. (1979), *Creation and the World of Science*, The Bampton Lectures 1978. Oxford: Clarendon.

Rahner, K. (2010), *Foundations of Christian Faith*, New York: Crossroad.

Stubbes, P. (1972), *The Anatomie of Abuses*, Facsimile of the Bodleian Library manuscript, no page numbers, Amsterdam: Da Capo Press.

Theophilus of Antioch (1970), *Ad Autolycum*, Text and translation by Robert M. Grant, Oxford: Clarendon.

Tillich, P. (1968), *Systematic Theology*. Vols I, II, and III Combined, Welwyn: Nisbet.

Weir, J. S. (2008), "Competition as Relationship: Sport as Mutual Quest towards Excellence," in *The Image of God in the Human Body: Essays on Christianity and Sports*, ed. by Donald Deardorff II, & John White, 101–122, Lewiston, NY: Edward Mellen.

Chapter 4

Bruteau, B. (2004), *Radical Optimism: Practical Spirituality in an Uncertain World*, Boulder, CO: Sentient Publications.
Csikszentmihalyi, M. (1975a), "Play and Intrinsic Rewards," *The Journal of Humanistic Psychology*, 15(3): 41–63.
Csikszentmihalyi, M. (1975b), *Beyond Boredom and Anxiety: The Experience of Play in Work and Games*, San Francisco: Jossey Bass Publishers.
Csikszentmihalyi, M. (1990), *FLOW: The Psychology of Optimal Experience*, New York: Harper and Row.
Csikszentmihalyi, M., & Csikszentmihalyi, I. (eds.) (1988), *Optimal Experience: Psychological Studies of Flow in Consciousness*, Cambridge: Cambridge University Press.
Ganss, G. (ed) (1991), *Ignatius of Loyola: The Spiritual Exercises and Selected Works*, New York: Paulist Press.
Jackson, P., & Delehanty, H. (1995), *Sacred Hoops: Spiritual Lessons of a Hardwood Warrior*, Hyperion: New York.
Kelly, P. (2012), *Catholic Perspectives on Sports: From Medieval to Modern Times*, Mahwah, NJ: Paulist Press.
Merton, T. (1965), *The Way of Chuang Tzu*, Bardstown, KY: Abbey of Gethsemane.
Murphy, M., & White, R. (1995), *In the Zone: Transcendent Experience in Sports*, New York: Penguin Books.
Slingerland, E. (2003), *Effortless Action: Wu-Wei as Conceptual Metaphor and Spiritual Ideal in Early China*, New York: Oxford University Press.
Slingerland, E. (2014), *Trying Not to Try: The Art and Science of Spontaneity*, New York: Crown Publishers.
Yuaso Y. (1987), *The Body: Toward an Eastern Mind-Body Theory*, ed. by T. P. Kasulis, trans. Nagatamo Shigenori, & T. P. Kasulis, Albany, NY: State University of New York Press.

Chapter 5

Aslan, R. (2013), *Zealot: The Life and Times of Jesus of Nazareth*, New York: Random House.
Baker, W. (1994), "To Pray or to Play? The YMCA Question in the United Kingdom and the United States, 1850–1900," *The International Journal of the History of Sport*, 11 (1): 42–62.
Brändl, M. (2006), *Der Agon bei Paulus: Herkunft und Profil paulinischer Agon-metaphorik*, Tübingen: Mohr Siebeck.
Freeman, W. H. (1997), *Physical Education and Sport in a Changing Society*, (5th ed.), Boston: Allyn and Bacon.
Guttmann, A. (1978), *From Ritual to Record: The Nature of Modern Sports*, New York: Columbia University Press.
Hamilton, D. (1998), *Golf, Scotland's Game*, Kilmalcolm: The Partick Press.
Hughes, T. (1861), *Tom Brown at Oxford*, London: Macmillan.
Huizinga, J. (1924), *The Waning of the Middle Ages: A Study of the Forms of Life, Thought and Art in France and the Netherlands in the XIVth and XVth Centuries*, London: Edward Arnold & Co.
Kingsley, C. (1855), *Westward Ho!*, Cambridge: Macmillan.

Lee, A. D. (2000), *Pagans and Christians in Late Antiquity: A Sourcebook*, London: Routledge.

Lixey, K. (2013), "The Vatican's Game Plan for Maximizing Sport's Educational Potential," ed. by N. Watson, & A. Parker, *Sport and Christianity: Historical and Contemporary Perspectives*, 250–268, London: Routledge.

Lundskow, G. (2008), *The Sociology of Religion: A Substantive and Transdisciplinary Approach*, Thousand Oaks, CA: Pine Forge Press.

McClelland, J. "Introduction: 'Sport' in Early Modern Europe," ed. by J. McClelland & B. Merrilees, *Sport and Culture in Early Modern Europe*, 23–40, Toronto: Centre for Reformation and Renaissance Studies.

McCluney E. B. (1974), "Lacrosse: The Combat of the Spirits," *American Indian Quarterly*, 1 (1): 34–42.

Mechikoff, R. A., & S. G. Estes. (2006), *A History and Philosophy of Sport and Physical Education: From Ancient Civilizations to the Modern World*, Boston, MA: McGraw Hill.

Meyer, A. R. (2012), "Muscular Christian Themes in Contemporary American Sport: A Case Study," *The Journal of the Christian Society for Kinesiology and Leisure Studies*, 2 (1): 15–32.

Pfitzner, V. C. (2014), "Was St. Paul a Sport Enthusiast? Realism and Rhetoric in Pauline Athletic Metaphors," ed. by N. Watson & A. Parker, *Sport and Christianity: Historical and Contemporary Perspectives*, 89–111, London: Routledge.

Putney, C. (2003), *Muscular Christianity: Manhood and Sports in Protestant America, 1880–1920*, Cambridge, MA: Harvard University Press.

Rizzi, A. (2009), "Regulated Play at the End of the Middle Ages: The Work of Mendicant Preachers in Communal Italy," ed. by J. McClelland, & B. Merrilees, *Sport and Culture in Early Modern Europe*, 41–69, Toronto: Centre for Reformation and Renaissance Studies.

Sansone, D. (1988), *Greek Athletics and the Genesis of Sport*, Los Angeles: University of California Press.

Tozer, M. (2016), *The Ideals of Manliness: The Legacy of Thring's Uppingham*, Truro, UK: Sunnyrest Books.

Watson, Nick, J., & A. Parker (eds.) (2013), *Sports and Christianity: Historical and Contemporary Perspectives*, London: Routledge.

Whittington, M. E. (ed) (2001), *The Sport of Life and Death: The Mesoamerican Ballgame*, London: Thames and Hudson.

YMCA Blue Book: World YMCA Movement in Review (2012), Geneva, SUI: World Alliance of YMCAs. http://www.ymca.int/uploads/media/The_YMCA_Blue_Book_02.pdf

Chapter 6

Ammerman, N. (2014), *Sacred Stories, Spiritual Tribes*, New York: Oxford University.

Ammerman, N. (2016), "Lived Religion as an Emerging Field: An Assessment of Its Contours and Frontiers," *Nordic Journal of Religion & Society*, 29 (2): 83–99.

Bain-Selbo, E., & D. G. Sapp. (2016), *Understanding Sport as a Religious Phenomenon: An Introduction*, London: Bloomsbury.

Bregman, L. (2014), *The Ecology of Spirituality: Meanings, Virtues, and Practices in a Post-Religious Age*, Waco, TX: Baylor University Press.

Bron, T. (2007), "Surfing into Spirituality and a New, Aquatic Nature Religion," *Journal of the American Academy of Religion*, 75 (4): 923–951.

Cipriani, R. (2012), "Sport as (Spi)rituality," *Implicit Religion*, 15 (2): 139–151.

Coakley, J. (2001), *Sports in Society: Issues and Controversies*, (7th ed.), New York: McGraw Hill.

Cox, D. (2016), "Rio 2016: Usain Bolt Out to Prove There Is God-Given Talent in Bid to Become an Olympic Legend." *Independent*, August 9. Available online: http://www. independent.co.uk/sport/olympics/rio-2016-usain-bolt-interview-god-given-talent-olympic-legend-100m-final-a7181401.html (accessed August 10, 2017).

Czech, D. R., & Bullet, E. (2007), "An Exploratory Description of Christian Athletes' Perceptions of Prayer in Sport: A Mixed Methodological Pilot Study," *International Journal of Sports Science & Coaching*, 2 (1): 49–56.

Czech, D. R., Wrisberg, C. A., Fisher, L. A., Thompson, C. L., & Hayes, G. (2004), "The Experience of Christian Prayer in Sport: An Existential Phenomenological Investigation," *Journal of Psychology & Christianity*, 23 (1): 3–11.

Dömötör, Z., Ruíz-Barquín, R., & Szabo, A. (2016), "Superstitious Behavior in Sport: A Literature Review," *Scandinavian Journal of Psychology*, 57 (4): 368–382.

Drehs, W. (2006), "No Ordinary Background," *ESPN*, June 8. Available online: http://www. espnfc.com/columns/story?id=370300 (accessed August 21, 2017).

Egli, T., Czech, D., Todd, S., Shaver, G., Gentner, N., & Biber, D. (2014), "The Experience of Christian Prayer in Coaching: A Qualitative Investigation," *Journal of Psychology & Christianity*, 33 (1): 45–57.

Farley, H. (2015), "The Faith of Usain Bolt in 5 Tweets," *Christianity Today*, August 27. Available online: https://www.christiantoday.com/article/the.faith.of.usain.bolt. in.5.tweets/63092.htm (accessed August 7, 2017).

Gleeson, S. (2015), "York's Loretta Claiborne Talks Faith at Special Olympics World Games," *USA Today*, July 30. Available online: https://www.usatoday.com/story/ sports/2015/07/30/special-olympics-has-message-bigger-than-sports/72142650/ (accessed August 23, 2017).

Hamilton, B. (n.d.), "Soul Surfer," *Bethany Hamilton*. Available online: http:// bethanyhamilton.com/soul-surfer-2/ (accessed August 9, 2017).

Hillman, C. (2016), *American Sports in an Age of Consumption*, Jefferson, NC: McFarland.

Hoven M. (2016), "Faith Informing Competitive Youth Athletes in Christian Schooling," *Journal of Research on Christian Education*, 25 (3): 273–289.

Hoven, M. (2019), "Re-Characterizing Confidence Because of Religious and Personal Rituals in Sport: Findings from a Qualitative Study of 15 Year Old Student-Athletes," *Sport in Society*, 22 (2): 296–311.

Hoven, M., & Kuchera, S. (2016), "Beyond Tebowing and Superstitions: Religious Practices of 15-Year-Old Competitive Athletes," *International Journal of Children's Spirituality*, 21 (1): 52–65.

Kelly, P. (2011), "Flow, Sport and the Spiritual Life," in *Theology, Ethics and Transcendence in Sports*, ed. by S. J. Parry, M. Nesti, & N. Watson, 163–177, New York: Routledge.

King, P. (2013), "Colin Kaepernick Does Not Care What You Think about His Tattoos," *Sports Illustrated*, July 23. Available online: https://www.si.com/2013/07/23/colin-kaepernick-49ers (accessed September 7, 2017).

Marthaler, B. (1993), *The Creed: The Apostolic Faith in Contemporary Theology*, Rev. ed., Mystic, CT: Twenty-Third Publications.

Nesti, M. (2010), *Psychology in Football: Working with Elite and Professional Players*, London: Routledge.

Newkirk, V. R. (2017), "No Country for Colin Kaepernick," *The Atlantic*, August 11. Available online: https://www.theatlantic.com/entertainment/archive/2017/08/no-country-for-colin-kaepernick/536340/ (accessed September 7, 2017).

Orsi, R. (1997), "Everyday Miracles: The Study of Lived Religion," in *Lived Religion in America*, ed. by D. Hall, 3–21. Princeton, NJ: Princeton University Press.

Percy, L. (2016), "Olympians Are Chosen by the Gods—Billy Mills," *On Being*, May 20. Available online: https://onbeing.org/blog/olympians-are-chosen-by-the-gods-billy-mills/ (accessed August 23, 2017).

Premier Christianity. (2016), "Team GB's Christine Ohuruogu on Faith, Disappointment and Rio," *Premier Christianity*, August 5. Available online: https://www.premierchristianity.com/Blog/Team-GB-s-Christine-Ohuruogu-on-faith-disappointment-and-Rio (accessed August 7, 2017).

Scholes, J., & Sassower, R. (2014), *Religion and Sports in American Culture*, New York: Routledge.

Seigneur, C. B. (2012), "Why Gabby Douglas Almost Quit before the Olympics," *Christianity Today*, December 12. Available online: http://www.christianitytoday.com/ct/2012/december-web-only/why-gabby-douglas-thanks-god-even-when-she-falls.html (accessed August 7, 2017).

Taylor, B. (2007), "Surfing into Spirituality and a New, Aquatic Nature Religion," *Journal of the American Academy of Religion*, 75 (4): 923–951.

Taylor, C. (2007), *A Secular Age*, Cambridge, MA: Belknap Press of Harvard University Press.

Watson, N. J., & Parker, A. (2015), "The Mystical and Sublime in Extreme Sports: Experiences of Psychological Well-Being or Christian Revelation?" *Studies in World Christianity*, 21 (3): 260–281.

Wilson, P. (2017), "The MH Interview: Lewis Hamilton," *Men's Health*, March 24. Available online: http://www.menshealth.co.uk/building-muscle/the-mh-interview-lewis-hamilton (accessed August 24, 2017).

Chapter 7

Artress, L. (2006), *Walking a Sacred Path: Rediscovering the Labyrinth as a Spiritual Practice*, New York: Riverhead Books.

Bogard, P. (2017), *The Ground Beneath Us: From the Oldest Cities to the Last Wilderness, What Dirt Tells Us about Who We Are*, New York: Little, Brown and Company.

Foster, R. (1992), *Prayer: Finding the Heart's True Home*, San Francisco, CA: Harper Collins.

Gardner, T. (2014), *Poverty Creek Journal*, North Adams, MA: Tupelo Press.

Hanc, J. (February 1, 2005), Speak Easy: How Do You Know if You're Running at the Right Intensity? Start Talking. Available online: http://www.runnersworld.com/running-tips/speak-easy (accessed May 8, 2018).

Lewis, C.S. (1952), *Mere Christianity*, New York: Macmillan Publishing.

Lysaught, T. (2008), Ten Decades to a More Christ-Like You: Liturgy as God's Workout Plan for the Church, *Liturgy*, 24 (1): 3–15.

MacIntyre, A. (1984), *After Virtue*. Notre Dame, IN: University of Notre Dame Press.

Martin, C. (2015), *To See One Another Broken*. Available online: https://onbeing.org/blog/to-see-one-another-broken/ (accessed May 8, 2018).

Martin, C. (2016), *The New Better Off: Reinventing the American Dream*, Boston, MA: De Capo Press.

Norris, K. (1996), *The Cloister Walk*, New York: Riverhead Books.

Oliver, M. (2004), *Why I Wake Early*, Boston, MA: Beacon Press.

Paintner, C. (2015), The Monk Manifesto: Seven Principles for Living with Deep Intention. Available online: https://onbeing.org/blog/the-monk-manifesto-seven-principles-for-living-with-deep-intention/ (accessed May 8, 2018).

Palmer, P. (2016), Notes from a Week in the Winter Woods. Available online: https://onbeing.org/blog/notes-from-a-week-in-the-winter-woods/ (accessed May 8, 2018).

Ross, D. (2015), Ritual Is Poetry in Action. Available online: https://onbeing.org/blog/ritual-is-poetry-in-action/ (accessed May 8, 2018).

Thoreau, H. (2012), *The Portable Thoreau*, New York: Penguin Books.

Torres, C. (2016), *Running Is Moving Meditation*. Available online: https://onbeing.org/blog/running-is-moving-meditation/ (accessed May 8, 2018).

Chapter 8

Berger, P. (1970), *A Rumor of Angels: Modern Society and the Rediscovery of the Supernatural*, Garden City, NY: Anchor Books, Doubleday & Co.

Bouyer, L. (1963), *History of Christian Spirituality*, New York: Crossroads, 1963.

Brown, W. P. (2012), "Wisdom and Child's Play: Proverbs and Paideia," in *Understanding Children's Spirituality: Theology, Research, and Practice*, ed. by K. E. Lawson, 26–38. Eugene, OR: Cascade Books.

Catechism of the Catholic Church (2002), (2nd ed.), Vatican City: Libreria Editrice Vaticana.

Cardman, F. (1993), "Acts of the Women Martyrs," in *Women in Early Christianity*, ed. by D. Scholer, 98–104. New York: Garland Publishing.

Csikszentmihalyi, M. (1990), *Flow: The Psychology of Optimal Experience*, New York: Harper and Row.

Cunningham, L. S., & Egan, K. J. (1996), *Christian Spirituality: Themes from the Tradition*, New York: Paulist Press.

Dulles, A. (1980), "The Symbolic Structure of Revelation," *Journal of Theological Studies*, 1: 51–73.

Giamatti, A. B. (1989), *Take Time for Paradise*, New York: Summit Books.

Guardini, R. (1997), *The Spirit of the Liturgy*, New York: Crossroad.

Huizinga, J. (1955), *Homo Ludens: A Study of the Play-Element in Culture*, Boston: Beacon.

Ignatius of Antioch (1885), "Letter to the Romans," in *The Ante-Nicene Fathers: The Writings of the Fathers Down to A.D. 325*, ed. by A. Roberts, & J. Donaldson, Buffalo, NY: Scribner's.

Jackson, S. A., & Csikszentmihalyi, M. (1999), *Flow in Sports: The Keys to Optimal Experiences and Performances*, Champaign, IL: Human Kinetics.

John Paul II (October 28, 2000), "During the Time of the Jubilee: The Face and Soul of Sports," Available online: http://www.vatican.va.holy_father/john_paul_ii/speeches/documents/hf_jp (accessed April 10, 2016).

Keenan, J. F. (1994), "Christian Perspectives on the Human Body," *Theological Studies*, 55: 330–346.

Kelly, P. (2012), *Catholic Perspectives on Sports: From Medieval to Modern Times*, New York: Paulist Press.

Kinnard, I. (2006), "Imitatio Christi in Christian Martyrdom and Asceticism: A Critical Dialogue," in *Asceticism and Its Critics: Historical Accounts and Comparative Perspectives*, ed. by O. Freiberger, 131–152. New York: Oxford University Press.

Macquarrie, J. (1983), *In Search of Humanity*, New York: The Crossroad Publishing Company.

McBrien, R. (1994), *Catholicism*, San Francisco: Harper San Francisco.

Mitchell, N. (2006), *Meeting Mystery*, New York: Orbis Books.

Novak, M. (1994), *The Joy of Sports: Endzones, Bases, Baskets, Balls, and the Consecration of the American Spirit*, Lanham, MD: Madison Books.

Rahner, H. (1972), *Man at Play*, New York: Herder and Herder.

Rahner, K. (1977), "Festival of the Future of the World," *Theological Investigations VII*, New York: Seabury Press.

Chapter 9

Association for Applied Sport Psychology (2017), "About AASP. *About Applied Sport & Exercise Psychology*," AASP, January 1. Available online: http://www.appliedsportpsych.org/about/about-applied-sport-and-exercise-psychology/ (accessed October 1, 2017)

Balague, G. (1999), "Understanding Identity, Value, and Meaning When Working with Elite Athletes," *The Sport Psychologist*, 26: 89–98.

Bennett, G., Sagas, M., Fleming, D., & Von Roenn, S. (2005), "On Being a Living Contradiction: The Struggle of an Elite Intercollegiate Christian Coach," *Journal of Beliefs and Values*, 26: 289–300.

Carter, J. D., & Narramore, B. (1979), *The Integration of Psychology and Theology: An Introduction*, Grand Rapids, MI: The Zondervan Corporation.

Clinton, T., & Ohlschlager, G. (2002), *Competent Christian Counseling, Volume One*, Colorado Springs, CO: Waterbrook Press.

Czech, D. R., Wrisberg, C. A., Fisher, L. A., Thompson C. L. & Hayes, G. (2004), "The Experience of Christian Prayer in Sport—An Existential Phenomenological Investigation," *Journal of Psychology and Christianity*, 2: 1–19, 1:19.

Egli, T. J., Czech, D. R., Shaver, G., Todd, S. Y., Gentner, N., & Biber, D. D. (2014a), "The Experience of Christian Prayer in Coaching: A Qualitative Investigation," *Journal of Psychology and Christianity*, 33: 45–57.

Egli, T. J., & Fisher, L. A. (2016), "Moving toward a Faithful Relationship: Sport Psychology Consultants Speak about the Potential of Engaging with Spirituality in Consultation," in *Sport Chaplaincy: Trends, Issues and Debates*, ed. by A. Parker, N. J. Watson, & J. B. White, 170–181, London: Ashgate Publishing.

Egli, T. J., & Fisher, L. A. (2017), "Christianity and Sport Psychology: One Aspect of Cultural Competence," *Journal of the Christian Society for Kinesiology, Leisure, & Sports Studies*, 4: 19–27.

Egli, T. J., Fisher, L. A., & Gentner, N. (2014b), "AASP-Certified Consultants' Experiences of Spirituality within Sport Psychology Consultation," *The Sport Psychologist*, 4: 394–405.

Hochstetler, D. R. (2009), "Striving towards Maturity: On the Relationship between Prayer and Sport," *Christian Education Journal*, 6: 325–336.

Hoven, M. (2019), "Re-Characterizing Confidence Because of Religious and Personal Rituals in Sport: Findings from a Qualitative Study of 15 Year Old Student-Athletes." *Sport in Society*, 22 (2): 296–311, doi:10.1080/17430437.2017.1360582.

Lawrence, B. (1724/2013), *The Practice of the Presence of God: In Modern English*, trans. M. Davis. (n.p.): editor.

Lipe, R. (2015), *The Competitor's Book of Prayer*, Omaha, NE: Cross Training Publishing.

Meier, P. D., Minirth, F. B., Wichern, F. B., & Ratcliff, D. E. (2010), *Introduction to Psychology and Counselling: Christian Perspectives and Applications*, Grand Rapids, MI: Baker Academic.

Mosley, M. J., Frierson, D. J., Cheng, Y., & Aoyagi, M. W. (2015), "Spirituality & Sport: Consulting the Christian Athlete," *The Sport Psychologist*, 29: 371–386.

Nesti, M. (2004), *Existential Psychology and Sport: Implications for Research and Practice*, London: Routledge.

Park, J.-K. (2000), "Coping Strategies Used by Korean National Athletes," *The Sport Psychologist*, 14: 63–80.

Peña, D. dl. (2004), *Scripture and Sport Psychology: Mental-Game Techniques for the Christian Athlete*, New York: iUniverse, Inc.

Smith, J. K. A. (2009), *Desiring the Kingdom Worship, World View, and Cultural Formation*, Grand Repels, MI: Baker Academic.

Stevenson, C. L. (1991), "The Christian Athlete: An Interactionist-Developmental Perspective," *Sociology of Sport Journal*, 8: 362–379.

Stevenson, C. L. (1997), "Christian Athletes and the Culture of Elite Sport," *Sociology of Sport Journal*, 14: 241–262.

Vernacchia, R. A., McGuire, R. T., Reardon, J. P., & Templin, D. P. (2000), "Psychosocial Characteristics of Olympic Track and Field Athletes," *International Journal of Sport Psychology*, 31: 5–23.

Watson, N. J., & Czech, D. C. (2005), "The Use of Prayer in Sport: Implications for Sport Psychology Consulting," *Athletic Insight*, 7: 26–35.

Watson, N. J., & Nesti, M. (2005), "The Role of Spirituality in Sport Psychology Consulting: An Analysis and Integrative Review of Literature," *Journal of Applied Sport Psychology*, 17: 228–239.

Weinberg, R. S., & Gould, D. (2015), *Foundations of Sport and Exercise Psychology* (6th ed.), Champaign, IL: Human Kinetics.

Willard, D. (1988), *The Spirit of the Disciplines: Understanding How God Changes Lives*, New York: HarperCollins Publishers.

Chapter 10

Arthur, C. A., Woodman, T., Ong, C. W., Hardy, L., & Ntoumanis, N. (2011), "The Role of Athlete Narcissism in Moderating the Relationship between Coaches' Transformational Leader Behaviors and Athlete Motivation," *Journal of Sport and Exercise Psychology*, 33 (1): 3–19.

Azadfada, S., Besmi, M., & Doroudian, A. A. (2014), "The Relationship between Servant Leadership and Athlete Satisfaction," *International Journal of Basic Sciences and Applied Research*, 3 (8): 528–537.

Barbuto Jr., J. E., & Wheeler, D. W. (2006), "Scale Development and Construct Clarification of Servant Leadership," *Group & Organization Management*, 31 (3): 300–326.

Bass, B. M., & Riggio, R. E. (2006), *Transformational Leadership* (2nd ed.), Mahwah, NJ: L. Erlbaum Associates.

Burton, L., & Welty-Peachey, J. (2013), "The Call for Servant Leadership in Intercollegiate Athletics," *Quest*, 65 (3): 354–371.

Charbonneau, D., Barling, J., & Kelloway, E. K. (2001), "Transformational Leadership and Sports Performance: The Mediating Role of Intrinsic Motivation," *Journal of Applied Social Psychology*, 31 (7): 1521–1534.

Charmaz, K. (2002). Qualitative Interviewing and Grounded Theory Analysis. in *Handbook of Interview Research: Context and Method*, ed. by J. F. Gubrium, & J. A. Holstein, 675–694, Thousand Oaks, CA: Sage.

Charmaz, K. (2014), *Constructing Grounded Theory* (2nd ed.), Thousand Oaks, CA: Sage.

Chelladurai, P. (1990), "Leadership in Sports: A Review," *International Journal of Sport Psychology*, 21 (4): 328–354.

Chelladurai, P. (2007), "Leadership in Sports," in *Handbook of Sport Psychology*, ed. by G. Tenenbaum, & R. C. Eklund, 113–135 (3rd ed.), Hoboken, New Jersey: John Wiley and Sons.

Chelladurai, P. (2013), "A Personal Journey in Theorizing in Sport Management," *Sport Management Review*, 16 (1): 22–28.

Chelladurai, P., & Riemer, H. (1998), "Measurement of Leadership in Sports," in *Advances in Sport and Exercise Psychology Measurement*, ed. by J. L. Duda, 227–253, Morgantown, WV: Fitness Information Technology.

Chelladurai, P., & Saleh, S. (1980), "Dimensions of Leader Behavior in Sports: Development of a Leadership Scale," *Journal of Sport Psychology*, 2 (1): 34–45.

Dennis, R. S., & Bocarnea, M. (2005), "Development of the Servant Leadership Assessment Instrument," *Leadership & Organization Development Journal*, 26 (8): 600–615.

Evangelical Alliance. (2014), "Basis of Faith." Available online: http://www.eauk.org/connect/about-us/basis-of-faith.cfm (accessed August 9, 2017).

Field, A. (2013), *Discovering Statistics Using SPSS: (And Sex Drugs and Rock and Roll)* (4th ed.), London: Sage.

Gauby, S. F. (2007), *The Effect of Fasting upon the Development of Servant Leaders at Saint Joseph United Methodist Church, Fort Wayne, Indiana* (Doctor of Ministry). Wilmore, KY: Asbury Theological Seminary.

Gillham, A., Gillham, E., & Hansen, K. (2015), "Relationships among Coaching Success, Servant Leadership, Cohesion, Resilience and Social Behaviors," *International Sport Coaching Journal*, 2 (3): 233–247.

Greenleaf, R. K. (1977), *Servant Leadership: A Journey into the Nature of Legitimate Power and Greatness*, Mahwah, New Jersey: Paulist Press.

Grudem, W. (1994), *Systematic Theology: An Introduction to Biblical Doctrine*, Nottingham, UK: Inter-Varsity Press.

Hammermeister, J., Chase, M., Burton, D., Westre, K., Pickering, M., & Baldwin, N. (2008), "Servant Leadership in Sport: A Concept Whose Time Has Arrived," *International Journal of Servant Leadership*, 4 (1): 185–215.

Hunt, K. (1999), "Pressure to Win? But I'm a Christian Coach in a Christian College," in *Physical Education, Sports and Wellness: Looking to God as We Look at Ourselves*, ed. by J. Byl, & T. Visker, 235–247, Sioux Center, Iowa: Dordt Press.

Jenkins, S. (2014a), "John R. Wooden, Stephen R. Covey and Servant Leadership," *International Journal of Sports Science and Coaching*, 9 (1): 1–24.

Jenkins, S. (2014b), "John R. Wooden, Stephen R. Covey and Servant Leadership: A Response to Commentaries," *International Journal of Sports Science & Coaching*, 9 (1): 73–83.

Kim, M., Kim, Y., & Wells, J. E. (2017), "Being a Servant-Leader in Sport: Servant Leadership as the Key to the Coach-Athlete Relationship," *International Journal of Sport Management*, 18 (1): 19–43.

Page, D., & Wong, P. T. P. (2000), "A Conceptual Framework for Measuring Servant Leadership," in *The Human Factor in Shaping the Course of History and Development*, ed by S. Adjiboloos, 69–110, Lanham, MD: American University Press.

Patterson, K. A. (2003), *Servant Leadership: A Theoretical Model* (PhD thesis). Virginia Beach, VA: Regent University.

Price, M. S., & Weiss, M. R. (2013), "Relationships among Coach Leadership, Peer Leadership, and Adolescent Athletes' Psychosocial and Team Outcomes: A Test of Transformational Leadership Theory," *Journal of Applied Sport Psychology*, 25 (2): 265–279.

Rieke, M., Hammermeister, J., & Chase, M. (2008), "Servant Leadership in Sport: A New Paradigm for Effective Coach Behavior," *International Journal of Sports Science and Coaching*, 3 (2): 227–239.

Rowold, J. (2006), "Transformational and Transactional Leadership in Martial Arts," *Journal of Applied Sport Psychology*, 18 (4): 312–325.

Rude, W. (2004), *The Connection between Servant Leadership and Job Burnout* (Master of Arts thesis), Langley, BC, Canada: Trinity Western University.

Russell, R. F., & Stone, A. G. (2002), "A Review of Servant Leadership Attributes: Developing a Practical Model," *Leadership and Organization Development Journal*, 23 (3): 145–157.

Sendjaya, S., Sarros, J. C., & Santora, J. C. (2008), "Defining and Measuring Servant Leadership Behaviour in Organizations," *Journal of Management Studies*, 45 (2): 402–424.

Smith, B. N., Montagno, R. V., & Kuzmenko, T. N. (2004), "Transformational and Servant Leadership: Content and Contextual Comparisons," *Journal of Leadership & Organizational Studies*, 10 (4): 80–91.

Spears, L. C. (1995), *Reflections on Leadership: How Robert K. Greenleaf's Theory of Servant-Leadership Influenced Today's Top Management Thinkers*, New York: Wiley.

Stenling, A., & Tafvelin, S. (2014), "Transformational Leadership and Well-Being in Sports: The Mediating Role of Need Satisfaction," *Journal of Applied Sport Psychology*, 26 (2): 182–196.

van Dierendonck, D. (2011), "Servant Leadership: A Review and Synthesis," *Journal of Management*, 37 (4): 1228–1261.

van Dierendonck, D., & Nuijten, I. (2011), "The Servant Leadership Survey: Development and Validation of a Multidimensional Measure," *Journal of Business and Psychology*, 26 (3): 249–267, doi:10.1007/s10869-010-9194-1.

van Dierendonck, D., & Patterson, K. (2010), *Servant Leadership: Developments in Theory and Research*, London: Palgrave Macmillan.

Vella, S. A., Oades, L. G., & Crowe, T. P. (2013), "A Pilot Test of Transformational Leadership Training for Sports Coaches: Impact on the Developmental Experiences of Adolescent Athletes," *International Journal of Sports Science and Coaching*, 8 (3): 513–530.

Walker, S. P. (2010), *The Undefended Leader*, Carlisle, UK: Piquant Editions Ltd.

Watson, N. J., & White, J. (2007), "'Winning at All Costs' in Modern Sport: Reflections on Pride and Humility in the Writings of C.S." Lewis," in *Sport and Spirituality: An Introduction*, ed. by J. Parry, S. Robinson, N. J. Watson, & M. Nesti, 61–79, London: Routledge.

Wong, P. T. P. (2004), "The Paradox of Servant Leadership," *Leadership Link*, Spring, 3–5.

Wong, P. T. P., & Page, D. (2003), *Servant Leadership: An Opponent-Process Model and the Revised Servant Leadership Profile*, Servant Leadership Research Roundtable, Virginia Beach, VA. http://www.drpaulwong.com/wp-content/uploads/2013/09/Wong-Servant-Leadership-An-Opponent-Process-Model.pdf

Chapter 11

Annoni, V., Bertini, S., Perini, M., Pistone, A., & Zucchi, S. (2017), "Containing Workplace Envy: A Provisional Map of the Ways to Prevent or Channel Envy, and Reduce Its Damage," in *Envy at Work and in Organizations*, ed. by R. H. Smith, U. Merlone, & M. K. Duffy, 475–504, New York: Oxford University Press.

Celse, J. (2011), "Damaging the Perfect Image of Athletes: How Sport Practice Promotes Envy," 10th Tilburg Symposium for Economics and Psychology, August 19, 2011, Tilburg, The Netherlands.

Cohen-Charash, Y., & Larson, E. (2017), "What Is Envy?" in *Envy at Work and in Organizations*, ed. by R. H. Smith, U. Merlone, & M. K. Duffy, 1–38. New York: Oxford University Press.

Campolo, A. (1987), *Seven Deadly Sins*, Wheaton, IL: Victor Books.

Epstein, J. (2003), *Envy: The Seven Deadly Sins*, New York: Oxford University Press.

Girard, R. (1996), *The Girard Reader*, ed. by J. G. Williams, New York: Crossroad Herder.

Konyndyk DeYoung, R. (2009), *Glittering Vices: A New Look at the Seven Deadly Sins and Their Remedies*, Grand Rapids, MI: Brazos Press.

Kretchmar, R. S. (1995), "From Test to Contest: An Analysis of Two Kinds of Counterpoint in Sport," in *Philosophic Inquiry in Sport*, ed. by W. J. Morgan, & K. V. Meier, 36–41. Champaign, IL: Human Kinetics.

McNamee, M. (2010), "Schadenfreude in Sports: Envy, Justice and Self-Esteem," in *The Ethics of Sports: A Reader*, ed. by M. J. McNamee, 327–339, New York: Routledge.

Oliveira, A. (2017), "Everything You Need to Know about Tonya Harding's Epic Feud with Nancy Kerrigan," *Marie Claire*, March. Available online: http://www.marieclaire.com/celebrity/a25649/tonya-harding-nancy-kerrigan-feud/ (accessed May 8, 2018).

Rowling, J. K. (2003), *Harry Potter and the Order of the Phoenix*, London: Bloomsbury.

Simon, R. L. (2010), *Fair Play: The Ethics of Sport*, Boulder, CO: Westview Press.

Zaentz, S. (Producer), & Forman, M. (Director). (1984), *Amadeus* [Motion Picture], United States: Warner Bros. Pictures.

Chapter 12

Augustine (1996), *Teaching Christianity (De Doctrina Christiana), The Works of Saint Augustine for the 21st Century*, intro., trans., notes Edmund Hill, ed. by John E. Rotelle, Part 1, vol. 11, p. 118 (1.27, 28), Hyde Park, NY: New City Press.

Bridges, J. (2006), *The Fruitful Life*. Colorado Springs, CO: Navpress.

Chalmers, T. (1971) "The Expulsive Power of a New Affection," in *20 Centuries of Great Preaching: An Encyclopedia of Preaching*, ed. by Clyde E. Fant Jr., & William M. Pinson Jr., vol. 3, Wesley to Finney, 300–314, Waco, Tex.: Word Books, 1971. Available online: http://www.newble.co.uk/chalmers/comm9.html (accessed July 22, 2017).

Edwards, J. (1997), *Religious Affections*. Edinburgh: The Banner of Truth Trust.

Lewis, C. S. (1970), *God in the Dock*, ed. by Walter Hooper. Grand Rapids, MI: Eerdmans Publishing, Co.

Naugle, D. (2008), *Reordered Love, Reordered Lives*. Grand Rapids, MI: Eerdmans Publishing Co.

Pascal, B. (1995), *Pensees and Other Writings*. New York: Oxford University Press, The World's Classics.

Scheler, M. (1973), "Ordo Amoris," in *Selected Philosophical Essays Max Scheler*, ed. by John Wild et al., 98–135, Evanston, IL: Northwestern University Press.

Chapter 13

Bradshaw, J. (1988), *Healing the Shame that Binds Us*, Deerfield Beach, Florida: Health Communications.
Cunningham, L. (1992), *Thomas Merton: Spiritual Master*, Mahwah, NJ: Paulist.
Friedrichsen, T. (2002), "Disciple as Athlete," *The Living Light*, Winter 39 (2): 13–20.
Jackson, P. (2013), *Eleven Rings: The Soul of Success*, New York: Penguin.
Kipling, R. (1994), *Collected Poems by Rudyard Kipling*, London: Wordsworth.
Lewis, M. (2005), *Coach: Lessons on the Game of Life*, New York: Norton.
Merton, T. (1966), *Conjectures of a Guilty Bystander*, Garden City, NJ: Doubleday.
Outward Bound. (2007), *Leadership the Outward Bound Way*, Seattle, WA: The Mountain Books.
Peters, S. (2011), *The Chimp Paradox*, New York: Penguin.
Rembert, R. (2017), "Merton on Sports and Spirituality," *The Merton Seasonal*, 42 (1): 18–25.
Shea, J. (2008), *Stories*, Skokie, Il: Acta.
St. Augustine. (1997), *The Confessions of St. Augustine*, trans. Maria Boulding, New York: New City Press.
St. Teresa of Avila. (1904), *The Life of St. Teresa of Avila*, trans. David Lewis, New York: Benzinger Brothers.
St. Teresa of Avila. (1989), *Interior Castle*, trans. E. Allison Peers, New York: Doubleday.
Van Kaam, A. (1975), *In Search of Spiritual Identity*, Denville, NJ: Dimension.

Conclusion

Dicastery for Laity, Family, and Life (2018), *Giving the Best of Yourself: A Document about the Christian Perspective on Sport and the Human Person*, June 1. Available online: http://www.laityfamilylife.va/content/laityfamilylife/en/documenti/dare-il-meglio-di-se.html (accessed July 16, 2018).

SCRIPTURE INDEX

SUBJECT INDEX

Printed in the USA
CPSIA information can be obtained
at www.ICGtesting.com
LVHW011308281223
767614LV00004B/256